Women in American History

Series Editors

Mari Jo Buhle
Jacquelyn D. Hall
Anne Firor Scott

Better Than Second Best

Better
Than Second Best

Love and Work in the Life of
Helen Magill

GLENN C. ALTSCHULER

UNIVERSITY OF ILLINOIS PRESS
Urbana and Chicago

Library of Congress Cataloging-in-Publication Data

Altschuler, Glenn C.
    Better than second best : love and work in the life of Helen
Magill / Glenn C. Altschuler.
    P. cm. —(Women in American history)
    Bibliography: p.
    Includes index.
    ISBN 0-252-01669-6 (alk. paper)
    1. White, Helen Magill, 1853–1944. 2. Women educators—United
States—Biography. 3. Women—Education (Higher)—United States—
History—19th century. 4. Women—Education (Higher)—United
States—History—20th century. I. Title. II. Series.
LA2317.W42A57   1990
370′.92—dc20
[B]   89-5041
                                                                              CIP

For May Altschuler

Contents

Illustrations follow pages 48 and 128.

Acknowledgments

I am most grateful to Judith Totman, who discovered, preserved, and organized Helen Magill's letters and diaries. She has generously donated many of these papers to the Cornell University Library and allowed others to be microfilmed. Mrs. Totman invited me into her home, gave me several of the photographs reprinted in this book, and shared her memories of Aunt Helen and other relatives.

Several colleagues and friends read part or all of the manuscript, provided encouragement, pointed to sources, quibbled with style and interpretation. Lynne Abel, Miriam Brody, Scott Elledge, Howard Feinstein, Jim Hijiya, Hilmar Jensen, Isaac Kramnick, and Larry Moore made this a better book. Every day they make me a happier, more fulfilled person. Abraham S. Eisenstadt taught me how to teach, research, write, and be a friend. In conspiring to grant me an administrative leave, two deans, Alain Seznec and Geffrey Chester, made it possible for me to turn note cards into text. I am also grateful for the careful assessments of this biography provided by Anne Firor Scott, Mari Jo Buhle, and an anonymous reader for the University of Illinois Press. Carole S. Appel, senior editor at the Press, has been patient and perceptive. Theresa L. Sears, associate editor, brought a pencil and considerable intelligence to my prose.

The staff of Manuscripts and Archives, Olin Library at Cornell, has been unfailingly helpful. In fact, I'm beginning to think that Tom Hickerson, Nancy Dean, and Elaine Engst like to be pestered. Certainly, they are the answers to a historian's dream. The staff of the Frost Library at Swarthmore College was also indispensable, especially in tracking down Helen Magill's grades.

My research assistants, superb Cornell undergraduates Adam Gale, Alice Shragowitz, and Roberta Tulman, provided insights as well as note cards. They deserve credit along with the credits they've already earned.

Marilyn Hine processed my words, revised and re-revised, inserted, repaginated, retyped the entire manuscript when we switched computers—and convinced me that she enjoyed doing it. May her fingers be enshrined in the Typists' Hall of Fame.

This book is dedicated to a gutsy, gracious, occasionally irascible lady whom I love more every minute.

A Note on Primary Sources

The Helen Magill White Papers, housed in the Department of Manuscripts and Archives, Cornell University Library, contain Magill family correspondence, letters to and from Eva Channing (Helen's lifelong friend), material related to Helen's work as principal of the Howard Collegiate Institute, and correspondence with Andrew White and other members of the White family. Helen kept a diary intermittently; microfilms of nineteen diaries, covering a sixty-six year period (1867–1933), are part of this collection (originals are held by Judith Totman). The Karin White Papers contain microfilms of Karin's diaries, kept rather faithfully for much of her life (originals are held by Judith Totman). Her preoccupation with her mother is readily apparent in these diaries. The Andrew Dickson White Papers include useful material on the Magill-White courtship. I am grateful to the Department of Manuscripts and Archives, Cornell University Library, for permission to quote from these sources.

The following abbreviations are used throughout the chapter notes: HM = Helen Magill; HMW = Helen Magill White; ADW = Andrew D. White; KW = Karin White; EHM = Edward H. Magill; SWM = Sarah Warner Magill; EC = Eva Channing. Unless otherwise indicated, all references to correspondence, diaries, and so forth, are in the Helen Magill White Papers.

Introduction

For those who recognize her name, Helen Magill exists as a disembodied "first." Included in *Notable American Women* because she was the first female awarded a Ph.D. in the United States (1877), Magill was also the first and only female to attend the prestigious Boston Public Latin School in the nineteenth century, a member (and salutatorian) of the first class of Swarthmore College, and the first American woman to receive an honors degree from Cambridge University. Because a successful public career did not follow her academic achievements, Magill has been perceived as a Crispus Attucks of the women's movement, a brave casualty, just a name in a pantheon of pioneers. In a 1984 text on women's history, she is blinked at as a "rare exception," a woman "ahead of her time in higher education."[1]

Magill, it turns out, is as fascinating in failure as she was singular in success. In an era when women were barred from virtually all the professions, she pressed against the doors shutting out female faculty, published articles, ran a school, and tilted against a board of trustees. As she struggled, she explored the border between two American ideologies—individualism and the "cult of true womanhood"—and experienced the contradictions of an encouragement of aspiration encased in an endorsement of domesticity. Self-reliance and subordination, ambition and familial responsibility, desire and duty, all existed in explosive and sometimes enervating tension in her education, career, and marriage. Magill never found the path to reconciliation, nor did she feel as free to make choices as did some of her successors in the Progressive Era. She had few guideposts and fewer role models. But if she doubted that a woman should exist for herself, neither did she accept all the pieties about her "proper place." Like many of her contemporaries, she did not view "true womanhood" as a static concept, nor did she feel compelled to accept all of its axioms. As we shall see, she rejected the notion that men were logical and women emotional, relied on the rhetoric of service to camouflage her ambition, launched a career while waiting for an "ideal mate." Ultimately, Magill drew back from the implications of her critique of the woman's sphere, exchanging a career for marriage and motherhood. By no means docile in domesticity, she remained acutely conscious of and articulate about gender, work, and love, in search of an identity that would allow her to discover how far her talent could take her.[2]

Born in 1853, Magill approached adulthood in a period of transition for advocates of woman's rights. During the first half of the century, the women's movement burst on the national scene with a convention in Seneca Falls, New York, and agitation for the vote, the right to hold property, to sue in court, and to initiate divorce proceedings. As women found their public voice, they demanded equal opportunity and unfettered choice, daring to hope that the same forces that made the United States the land of self-reliant men—free land, economic mobility, no fixed social classes, Protestantism, democracy—might work for them as well. Contemporary observers confirmed that American females were less inhibited, more free. In Europe, women "almost think it a privilege to appear futile, weak and timid," Alexis de Tocqueville wrote wistfully, while American girls, frequently left to look after themselves, "never lay claim to rights of that sort." Margaret Fuller, although well aware of the obstacles to equality, believed that individualism was taking root in American soil: women "have time to think, and no traditions chain them. . . . "[3]

Paternalistic practices and assumptions did, of course, bind women by defining them as weak, submissive, emotional, nurturant, pious. With the rise of industrial capitalism, some historians argue, the woman's sphere may have become more narrow as the home became "a haven in a heartless world," free from predatory competition and "productive" labor. In many ways the freedom of males was made possible by the dependence and domestic service of women. Tocqueville, for whom individualism was a masculine noun, thought mature women should be submissive "as security for the order and prosperity of the household." Even when women worked, they usually contributed to a family income they did not control. Expected to marry, women could exercise influence but not power; excluded from the professions, denied the right to vote, they were considered to have been designed by God to assist men. By mid-century the cult of domesticity had become a powerful ideology, an American tradition, malleable and occasionally ambiguous, but a palpable constraint on instincts of individual achievement.[4]

The Civil War applied the brakes to the women's movement by diverting attention to slavery and the preservation of the Union. From 1861 through 1866, reformers canceled woman's rights conventions, and by 1870 it was clear that in the Reconstruction amendments to the Constitution, women had not been guaranteed equal protection under the law or the right to vote. Critics of woman's rights seemed bolder and more outspoken than they had been for decades. In *Women's Suffrage: The*

Reform against Nature, for example, theologian Horace Bushnell beseeched women to recognize "what superior grades of beauty and power they fill, and how far above equality with men they rise, when they keep their own pure atmosphere of silence and their field of peace...." When women worked outside the home or involved themselves in politics, their voices became "wiry and shrill," their faces thin and hungry-looking, "bearing a sharper look of talent, yet somehow touched with blight and fallen out of luster." Such sentiments spurred some women to greater activity but put others on the defensive; in both cases, they played a role in the debate over means and ends.[5]

While the National Woman Suffrage Association and the American Woman Suffrage Association, two rival organizations, continued to agitate in the 1870s for reform, many women sought to bring feminine virtues to a dissolute masculine world through temperance, evangelicalism, and moral purity. Still others turned to higher education to provide greater opportunity for women. The performance of those females who scrambled into college classrooms emptied by the Civil War, women argued, demonstrated that they were the intellectual equals of men. To be sure, most graduates would use their education to be better mothers and wives, but while women were single, they needed the tools of economic independence. Practical and adaptable to individual circumstance, higher education seemed to its proponents a reform vital to the women's movement and more important, perhaps, than the vote.[6]

Throughout the nineteenth century, education was a popular panacea because it appealed to champions of change and supporters of the status quo. Advocates of higher education for women did not always agree about its benefits. A few welcomed its radical implications: the creation of a society where merit, not birth or sex, constituted the only legitimate claim to power and authority; where women, given free use of their faculties and full access to occupations, could become fulfilled, productive citizens. We will never know how many others agreed with this view but chose, for strategic reasons, to join those who chained college to the cult of true womanhood, an opportunity to study the fine arts and domestic sciences and—since women raised sons to be citizens—history, economics, and civics. Only a relatively small number of women would want to go to college, they asserted, and the vast majority of them would happily relinquish self-reliance when they took vows to love, honor, and obey. By the 1870s, however, the subversive potential of higher education was more and more a reality: enrollments surged and female graduates, in alarming numbers, did not marry. Few were prepared to face the consequences; that is, having tasted freedom, the genie might refuse to jump back into the bottle.[7]

A precocious girl, Helen Magill was in many ways the embodiment of her parents' faith in higher education for women, a cause to which Edward Magill dedicated his career as professor and president at Swarthmore College. She inherited as well the Magills' mixed message about aspiration: more than most parents, they encouraged ambition, competitiveness, pride, cultivation of talent; at the same time they stressed Christian duty, familial responsibility, sacrifice. Equal opportunity for women did not yet exist, they knew, but it could be seized by someone with wit and willpower. If the gates around Harvard remained shut, Helen had history on her side and might well become prophet and professor in the promised land. Although the Magills hoped their daughter's career would be temporary, they never said it should be, and they applauded her resolution to vindicate the honor of womanhood as a coeducational pioneer and distinguished scholar of classical languages.

Pioneers frequently travel alone, and Helen Magill's life constitutes a negative test case of the importance of female networks in nineteenth-century America. Following the lead of Carroll Smith-Rosenberg, scholars have recently excavated "the female world of love and ritual." Unlike men, who often endorse a hierarchical order and images of winning and losing, women value responsibility within a web of relationships. From infancy to old age, during courtship and childbirth, women have given and gotten emotional and material support. Intimacy, moreover, has often found institutional and organizational outlets. In colleges, clubs, and churches, women have exchanged information, trained leaders, agitated for reform. For some, separation has become a conscious strategy, whereby women learn that when they try "to assimilate into male dominated institutions without securing feminist social, economic, or political bases, they [lose] the momentum and the networks. . . . " Although the bonds of womanhood can constrain, by tacitly accepting a separate sphere, women have found strength in unity and the potential for change through collective action.[8]

Many women never find themselves inside a female circle, and for Magill the gospel of individualism was an invitation to isolation. In her zeal to prepare for the professoriate, to establish her own persona, she did not often look outward. If she sometimes expressed the desire and need for a female network, she did little to secure one. The eldest of five sisters, she thought of herself as an advisor, even a surrogate parent, but rarely an equal. She held back even with her lifelong friend and correspondent Eva Channing, adopting poses of self-deprecation, confidence, and contentment. Nancy F. Cott has captured perfectly this conflict between individualism and the creation of a woman's world: "As much as feminism asserts the female individual by challenging delimitation by sex and by opposing the self-abnegation on behalf of others historically expected of women—pure individualism negates feminism because it removes the basis of women's collective self-understanding or action." Magill's early successes seemed to confirm that she could accomplish more by going it alone.[9]

Although the impact of coeducation has not been studied with the care recently devoted to women's colleges, the "mixed system" in its early years probably did not enhance opportunities to forge friendships with either men or women. Until the twentieth century, Rosalind Rosenberg has suggested, male students "pointedly shunned" coeds, who in turn adopted "a self-consciously stiff manner," perhaps to prove their academic seriousness, certainly to protect themselves against charges of inappropriate behavior. In traditionally male institutions, women were ostracized and mocked even after they ceased to be a token presence, while in fledgling colleges like Swarthmore, with a dearth of well-qualified men, women condescended to "farm boys" who were neither their social nor their academic equals.[10]

Relationships between women in coeducational colleges could also be problematic. Many women, it is important to remember, had consciously rejected single-sex colleges as shallow and unnatural and thus may have been disinclined to rely too much on female company. Some institutions, like Swarthmore (six students graduated in 1873), lacked a critical mass of women; others, as Helen Lefkowitz Horowitz has pointed out, had no dormitories, no social setting in which to share ideas and experiences. In these early days, moreover, competition for academic distinction often pitted women against one another. Magill experienced all of this and more: at Boston Latin her classmates were male; at Swarthmore her classmates may have been wary of President Magill's daughter, and she lived at home for part of her freshman year to help care for her sisters; the only female doctoral student at Boston University, she lived in an apartment, accustomed to a "rather unsocial existence."[11]

Like many women Magill sought professional status through super-performance rather than separatism. With its excessive faith in rewards based on merit, the strategy was fateful, almost apocalyptic: "I shall either conquer gloriously or fail ignominiously, in this battle for life." Ironically, even success did not necessarily vindicate the honor of womanhood because men greeted these transformed Cinderellas "not only willingly, but with Triumph," as Margaret Fuller acidly observed: " 'Can this be you? . . . We will tell everyone that you have surpassed your sex.' " For many women, of course, talent and hard work were not enough, and it is easy to identify the obstacles in Magill's way: a cycle of academic pressure, overwork, physical illness, and nervous tension, compounded by charges

that women were constitutionally incapable of doing "brain work" without damaging their health; a degree in classics, a field depleted by the rise
of modern languages and electives; a refusal to hire women in men's
colleges and a reluctance to do so in coeducational institutions; an
inclination in women's colleges, where the jobs were, to hire their own;
an assertive personality and a blunt manner of speech deemed inappropriate
in a woman.[12]

Magill blamed neither Providence nor paternalistic prejudices for her
self-described failures. Without really knowing why she had not succeeded,
she took stock of her shortcomings: lack of discipline, lack of stamina,
and a slow, mediocre intelligence. Raised to believe that explanations
were excuses, she was imprisoned as well by the achievements of exceptional women, who seemed to prove that any truly talented woman could
succeed. Nor could Magill be content with anything less than transcen-
dent success. A teacher, principal at a collegiate institute, professor at
Evelyn College (the female "annex" to Princeton University), she thought
of herself as an also-ran who was not "man enough" to make it.[13]

Many Victorian women saw a career, no matter how successful, as a
consolation prize for the unattractive and unwed. Magill's life suggests
that the relationship between work and love is more subtle and complex.
To be sure, Magill always claimed that marriage and motherhood were
her primary goals, that women *were* more nurturant, intuitive, and spiritual.
She also rejoiced that she could "plan like a man," making the most of an
ideology that ceded to women some control over education and employment while they played the waiting game of courtship. In refusing to
settle for anyone but an ideal mate—whom, Magill claimed, she did not
deserve and could not attract—a woman could combine ambition and
convention; being an old maid could be honorable, provided the old
maid was never happy with her position. Unrequited love thus allowed
Magill to "cheerfully take up the next best thing and make the most of it."
She was most receptive to love in moments of professional uncertainty or
stress and was attracted only to academics, who she hoped might encourage her to teach and write. When she did step into marriage, and the
shadow cast by an illustrious husband, it was something of a second
choice, made when her career was going nowhere.

For Helen Magill, marriage did not provide a happily-ever-after ending
to her life story, in part because the fires of aspiration and independence
still smoldered and sometimes burned within her, as they probably did
(and still do) for countless other women who cut short careers to become
wives and mothers. She thought however, that she could fuse Romantic
aspirations with Victorian assumptions; and, despite a stormy courtship,
she generated great expectations for marriage. She wanted more than a

proper union, where the couple, brought close together at first, eventually draws a dignified distance apart. Indeed, she believed that the cult of true womanhood, which called for subordination to a husband's wishes and needs through self-forgetting and self-sacrificing, might free her limited self by fusing her identity with that of her spouse. This view, a conjoining of Christian doctrine and transcendental idealism, was risky because it relied on reciprocity, as Leon Chai makes clear in a brilliant analysis of Romantic subjectivity: "The loss of self without compensation occurs when an individual surrenders himself or herself without eliciting a corresponding self-surrender from the other." Magill married to love and be loved; she discovered instead that she had been possessed, her self appropriated as the object of her husband's desires.[14]

Like Elizabeth Barrett Browning's "Every Man," Andrew D. White went to his "knees before ladies carrying lint." He wanted a wife who would support and not criticize, who did not place so high a value on her rational power, who accepted in marriage a sphere of influence and not a balance of power, who had the grace to acquiesce. In his professional life, as president of Cornell University, ambassador to Germany, and minister to Russia, he had to cajole, compromise, and keep silent; at home he wanted no challenges to his sovereignty. Dependency, psychologists claim and experience confirms, frequently finds an outlet in chronic explosions of anger. With a husband who controlled the purse-strings and was capable of suggesting the impossible to salve his conscience (that she "pursue her chosen studies" if they separated), Magill knew how dependent she was. And how alone. In her despair she could not settle on an explanation or a satisfactory response. She blamed herself. She settled into a domestic routine. She surrendered. But in the end she lashed out. She could be caged but not tamed. She simmered when her husband chose to travel with male companions and suffered when he forgot their anniversary yet honored his first wife. She resented his dismissal of her ideas. Some slights she imagined; some she exaggerated. Because she would not risk the shame and scandal of confiding in her parents, a diary and letters not sent remained her best friends, the silent ears for sentiments about sex and suicide. Magill held her husband to a Platonic ideal of perfection, I suspect, to justify her choice and her life: she looked for absolute devotion as proof of and reward for her sacrifices and was shocked that selflessness could be seen as self-indulgence.[15]

Ambivalence about independence also shaped Magill's relationship with her daughter. Perhaps because she knew the long odds against a fulfilling career, she was more reluctant than her parents had been to encourage her own daughter to cultivate professional aspirations. At the same time, she did not hide her conviction that marriage was a "lottery."

Her advice, therefore, came in fits and starts, complicated further by her own need to make motherhood the crown of her second career and her daughter her legacy to the world. Without close friends who might have helped displace mother-daughter hostility, and craving a companion and confidante, Magill reared a rebel who preferred a distant father to a smothering mother, the principal obstacle to independence. It is not insignificant that Karin White chose a women's college and a profession over her mother's objections; or that she, too, cut short her career to respond to "the family claim." In essence, Karin was her mother's daughter, a rebel but not a revolutionary, whose insights did not add up to a clear vision of the woman's path to happiness.

Biography, Oscar Wilde once said, "adds to death a new terror." Helen Magill might well recoil at her life re-viewed, yet I suspect she would be pleased to be remembered and proud to be part of the story of the struggle of women for equality in the domestic sphere and the public arena. With a double consciousness, lurching from a self indulged to a self ignored in a quest for an identity, she is a teacher still, shedding light on a world of constraint and possibility, a world not yet lost, one that even now resists as it gives way.

NOTES

1. Catharine Clinton, *The Other Civil War: American Women in the Nineteenth Century* (New York, 1984), p. 138. Clinton devotes one sentence to Magill.

2. Biographers should take a lesson from social historians and recognize the value of the lives of the less than transcendently successful. Jean Strouse has lead the way in her biography of that conspicuous failure *Alice James* (Boston, 1980), who made invalidism her career. Carolyn G. Heilbrun's *Writing a Woman's Life* (New York, 1988) is full of insights about how to do just that. Revisionist women's history cannot ignore an analysis of the "average" woman's experience, cautions Carroll Smith-Rosenberg in "Politics and Culture in Women's History: A Symposium," *Feminist Studies,* 6, no. 1 (1980): 26–64. See also Joyce Antler, "Culture, Service and Work: Changing Ideals of Higher Education for Women," in *The Undergraduate Woman: Issues in Educational Equity,* ed. Pamela J. Perun (Lexington, Mass., 1982), pp. 15–41. For an illuminating analysis of the dual potential of the ideology of separate spheres, see Linda Kerber, "Separate Spheres, Female Worlds, Woman's Place: The Rhetoric of Women's History," *Journal of American History,* 75, no. 1 (June 1988): 9–39.

3. Alexis de Tocqueville, *Democracy in America,* ed. J. P. Mayer (1835; reprint: New York, 1969), p. 602; Margaret Fuller, "Women in the Nineteenth Century," in *The Writings of Margaret Fuller,* ed. Mason Wade (New York, 1941), p. 172. See also Joyce Warren, *The American Narcissus: Individualism and Women in Nineteenth-Century American Fiction* (New Brunswick, N.J., 1984), pp. 1–19;

Norma Basch, *In the Eyes of the Law: Women, Marriage, and Property in Nineteenth-Century New York* (Ithaca, N.Y., 1982).

4. Christopher Lasch, *Haven in a Heartless World: The Family Besieged* (New York, 1977); Tocqueville, p. 602. See also Nancy F. Cott, *The Bonds of Womanhood: "Women's Sphere" in New England, 1780–1835* (New Haven, Conn., 1977); Ann Douglas, *The Feminization of American Culture* (New York, 1977); Barbara Welter, "The Cult of True Womanhood: 1820–1860," in *American Sisterhood: Writings of the Feminist Movement from Colonial Times to the Present,* ed. Wendy Martin (New York, 1972), pp. 243–56.

5. Horace Bushnell, *Women's Suffrage: The Reform against Nature* (New York, 1869), pp. 62–63, 135–36.

6. Barbara Epstein, *The Politics of Domesticity: Women, Evangelicalism and Temperance in Nineteenth-Century America* (Middletown, Conn., 1981); Steven M. Buechler, *The Transformation of the Woman Suffrage Movement: The Case of Illinois, 1850–1920* (New Brunswick, N.J., 1986).

7. Some historians, citing the popularity of Edward Clarke's *Sex in Education: A Fair Chance for the Girls* (Boston, 1873), which argued that higher education damaged a woman's health and reproductive capacity, believe that women's colleges became defensive during this period and began to stress genteel domesticity. See, e.g., Sheila Rothman, *Woman's Proper Place: A History of Changing Ideals and Practices* (New York, 1978).

8. Carroll Smith-Rosenberg, "The Female World of Love and Ritual: Relations between Women in Nineteenth-Century America," *Signs,* 1, no. 1 (1975): 1–29; Estelle Freedman, "Separation as Strategy: Female Institution Building and American Feminism, 1870–1930," *Feminist Studies,* 5, no. 3 (Fall 1979): 512–29. See also Carol Gilligan, *In a Different Voice: Psychological Theory and Women's Development* (Cambridge, Mass., 1982), pp. 159–61; Blanche Wiesen Cook, "Female Support Networks and Political Activism: Lillian Wald, Crystal Eastman, Emma Goldman," *Chrysalis,* 1, no. 3 (1977): 43–61; Cott, *The Bonds of Womanhood.*

9. Nancy F. Cott, *The Grounding of American Feminism* (New Haven, Conn., 1987), p. 6.

10. Rosalind Rosenberg, *Beyond Separate Spheres: The Intellectual Roots of Modern Feminism* (New Haven, Conn., 1982), p. 189. By 1900, college women and men appear to have mixed together rather freely. See Louise Sheffield Brownell Saunders, "Government of Women Students in Colleges and Universities," *Educational Review,* 20 (Dec. 1900): 491, 498; Paula Fass, *The Damned and the Beautiful: American Youth in the 1920s* (New York, 1978). For the experience of women in single-sex colleges, see Helen Lefkowitz Horowitz, *Alma Mater: Design and Experience in Women's Colleges from Their Nineteenth-Century Beginnings to the 1930s* (New York, 1984).

11. Helen Lefkowitz Horowitz, in *Campus Life: Undergraduate Cultures from the End of the Eighteenth Century to the Present* (New York, 1987), suggests that until the 1890s there was no "female equivalent of the college man" (p. 201). The best treatment of women in coeducational institutions is Barbara Miller Solomon, *In the Company of Educated Women: A History of Women and Higher Education in*

America (New Haven, Conn., 1985). Solomon believes women joined together either "as a defense against the hostilities of their male classmates or as a natural preference for segregated bonding" (p. 103); her evidence, however, is drawn from a somewhat later period. See also Lori D. Ginzberg, "The 'Joint Education of the Sexes': Oberlin's Original Vision," in *Educating Men and Women Together: Coeducation in a Changing World,* ed. Carol Lasser (Urbana, Ill., 1987), pp. 67–80; Barbara Miller Solomon, "The Oberlin Model and Its Impact on Other Colleges," in ibid., pp. 81–90.

12. For definitions of superperformance and separatism as career strategies, see Penina Migdal Glazer and Miriam Slater, *Unequal Colleagues: The Entrance of Women into the Professions, 1890–1940* (New Brunswick, N.J., 1987), pp. 210–13, 219–27. Fuller is quoted in Pauline Nestor, *Female Friendships and Communities: Charlotte Bronte, George Eliot, Elizabeth Gaskell* (Oxford, 1985), p. 106. See also Thomas Woody, *A History of Women's Higher Education in the United States* (New York, 1929); Roberta Frankfort, *Collegiate Women: Domesticity and Career in Turn-of-the-Century America* (New York, 1977); Susan Carter, "Academic Women Revisited: An Empirical Study of Changing Patterns in Women's Employment as College and University Faculty, 1890–1963," *Journal of Social History,* 14, no. 4 (Summer 1981): 615–97. Although the proportion of women faculty jumped from 12 to 32 percent between 1870 and 1880, the increase was probably a statistical anomaly due to small numbers and a lack of precision in the terms "faculty member" and "institution of higher education." See Patricia Albjerg Graham, "Expansion and Exclusion: A History of Women in Higher Education," *Signs,* 3, no. 4 (Summer 1978): 764–66.

13. For an examination of how exceptional women constrain other women, see Heilbrun, p. 81.

14. Leon Chai, *The Romantic Foundations of the American Renaissance* (Ithaca, N.Y., 1987), pp. 352–57. The extent to which wives in the late nineteenth century used these ideas to legitimize a demand for reciprocity in marriage is a subject well worth further study.

15. The subject of marriage is explored in Phyllis Rose, *Parallel Lives: Five Victorian Marriages* (New York, 1983); Francesca M. Cancian, *Love in America: Gender and Self-Development* (Cambridge, U.K., 1987), p. 95; John Bayley, *The Characters of Love* (New York, 1960).

CHAPTER ONE

"I owe it to the honor of womanhood to try my best"

U nlike many of their contemporaries, Edward and Sarah Magill were not disappointed when their first child, born on November 28, 1853, was a female. Both Magills had been raised as Quakers in Bucks County, Pennsylvania, where they learned that the Inner Light was granted to women as often as men. Involvement in antislavery, abolitionism, temperance, and, most important, coeducation, deepened the Magills' commitment to equal opportunity for women. Almost from birth, their precocious daughter became a veritable test case of the efficacy of education and the intellectual ability of females.

Helen's birth coincided with the end of her father's long and arduous preparation for a career in teaching. Born to a prosperous farm family in 1825, Edward Magill was educated at home by private tutors until his mother reluctantly allowed her twelve-year-old out of her sight. Two years later he attended Westtown, a Friends school in Chester County, where he demonstrated great aptitude in mathematics. When he returned home in 1841, the board of managers of the township hired him as a teacher. Edward worked on the family farm in the summer, then taught children of all ages in the late fall and winter. The conscientious young man quickly won a reputation as a fine instructor, firm but kind in discipline, clear in class presentations. He moved on to larger schools at more substantial salaries and might have been a productive, if anonymous, country schoolteacher but for two significant events, in both of which he detected the hand of Providence.

The Friends School in Abington, Montgomery County, was one of the finest in the region, but Edward's tenure there was brief. He balked when required to attend a weekly Quaker meeting with his charges, his antislavery convictions being too radical for most of the Abington Friends. Edward resigned in 1844 and embarked on an odyssey that took him to several boarding schools near Philadelphia. In 1848 he accepted a position in an excellent school in Alexandria, Virginia. The principal, Benjamin Hollowell, a superior mathematician, took a fatherly interest in Edward, whose education he thought inadequate. To an ambitious young man Hollowell's advice seemed sound: if teaching was really his vocation, he must be able to give instruction at any grade level.

To learn Latin and Greek, Edward attended Williston Seminary in Easthampton, Massachusetts, in 1848. Supporting himself by splitting wood, subsisting on bread and molasses, he worked with an impatient determination that was rewarded in 1850 by admission to Yale University. Success followed him to New Haven, where he won first prize in mathematics in his freshman year. But at age twenty-six he did not want to spend four years working for his degree. When Francis Wayland, president of Brown University, offered an A.B. in 1852, Edward moved to Providence. Soon after graduation he became principal of the classical department of Providence High School and married Sarah Warner Beans. Hard work and educational opportunity, the nineteenth-century recipe for success, became his credo, a catechism chanted to his children and to generations of students. If they reached out to grasp the hand of Providence, as he had, they could not fail.[1]

Not surprisingly, much less is known about Sarah Magill than about her husband. Along with Rebecca Magill, Edward's sister, Sarah attended Williston Seminary, an indication that her family, like the Magills, placed a high value on education for women. She was engaged to Edward for five years and did not go on to college. An ideal spouse, Sarah shared her husband's abhorrence of slavery and frequently served as host to itinerant abolitionist lecturers. She retained as well a lifelong interest in woman's rights, especially coeducation, but restricted herself to the domestic sphere, where her "wise counsel and broad intellectual outlook" influenced her husband, five daughters, and son.[2]

The governing principle of the Magill household was that God was best served through assisting others. Helen accompanied her parents, who were Liberal Christians, to church every Sunday. The Magills attended the services of several denominations, but they were no less devout for being latitudinarian, no less intent on teaching their children to try to divine God's will and to do it. Yet alongside Christian submissiveness—a concept compatible with a restricted woman's sphere—the Magills instilled in Helen ambition, pride, and a conviction that her talent could carry her far.

Helen was a fine reader at age five, solemnly absorbed in secular and religious lessons. With a parent's pride, Edward found ways to put his daughter's talents on display. She entertained guests at the piano and, on one occasion, stood on a stack of hay in the front yard in response to the invitation of Edward's students that she declaim. "Not at all abashed," she "spread out her little hands and began the repetition in Greek of the oration which one of them had been trained to speak at commencement."

As he tutored his daughter, Edward could already compare "his little gem" with his advanced students at Providence High School.[3]

Of course, some time remained for fun, especially in summers spent on Grandfather Beans's farm in Bucks County, surrounded by aunts, uncles, and cousins. But Helen never forgot that she had been called to academic excellence. From an early age she was more comfortable with adults than children, more eager to work than play. She was born an eighty-year-old, her mother recalled. Little wonder that as a sober teenager she pitied children: the girls in particular had "nothing to do but go around and look at things, put little pieces of wood together or play with dolls." Leisure squandered precious time and energy; without productive labor, existence was "a tiresome thing."[4]

In 1859 Edward Magill was hired as submaster and teacher of languages at the prestigious Boston Public Latin School. He quickly won the respect and friendship of the headmaster, Dr. Francis Gardner, and persuaded him to allow Helen to attend classes in the all-male institution. Thus, from 1863 until 1867 Helen accompanied her father to Boston Latin, in a sense trading her childhood for education. Deprived of access to girls her age during these formative years, she was "rather solitary and unsocial." Her only friend, Eva Channing, was at school elsewhere. Helen said little about her experiences at Boston Latin, but we can imagine her discomfort, all eyes upon her, the object, perhaps, of boyish pranks, listening intently to her instructors. She knew she did not belong there, that she would deliver no commencement oration, but she must have delighted in beating the boys to an answer. Felled by scarlet fever the first year, she braved the taunts of her former classmates and began the next "at the beginning." Her academic progress persuaded the Magills that the experiment had been a success, and her robust health during her last three years at the school refuted the claims of doctors and educators that the female constitution was too frail for intense study. Years of "severe application," Sarah Magill concluded, had sharpened Helen's intellect, "and certainly they never injured her health or impaired her constitution." Helen's performance at Boston Latin proved that coeducation was practical and ultimately would be beneficial to females and males.[5]

At the end of the academic year in 1867, Edward Magill resigned from Boston Latin, for the trustees of the newly founded Swarthmore College had appointed him principal of its "preparatory" department. Hard work, good advice, and God's grace was transforming a country schoolmaster into a leader in higher education. By now an accomplished teacher of Latin and French, Edward decided to spend a year in Europe, mastering languages "through eye, ear, tongue and hand," while carpenters and masons constructed classrooms at Swarthmore. The Magills left four of their children, Eudora, Beatrice, Gertrude, and Francis Gardner (Marian was born soon after their return), with relatives in Bucks County, but they brought fourteen-year-old Helen along to introduce her to European culture and to provide companionship for themselves.[6]

During the two-week trip across the Atlantic, Edward tutored his daughter in French and marveled at her facility with the language. Both parents noted as well, with a mixture of admiration and anxiety, Helen's growing independence, so uncharacteristic of her sex. On the first night at sea, while Edward and Sarah were reading French, Helen had slipped away. When she did not return in a few minutes, they searched for her, finally climbing to the upper deck as a last resort, "little supposing that she would venture up there alone." They spied their daughter at the side of the ship, gazing over the railing into the water, which glistened in the moonlight. "Our relief was so great," Edward remembered, "that we did not even scold her," although a lurch of the vessel might easily have sent her under the rail into the Atlantic. For the rest of the voyage, however, Sarah kept her daughter within her sight.[7]

In France, the Magills placed Helen in a pension school for young girls just outside Paris at Nevilly-sur-Seine. The only American at the school, she was once again an outsider, proficient but not fluent in French, unable to penetrate the closed circles of friends. Accustomed to her father's firm but gentle guidance, Helen chafed at the discipline of the school, where mail was censored and bad marks were given for tardiness in dressing. She bristled when Madame Charbonnier mistook meticulousness for laziness: "It is not true. I have been slow but not idle." Throughout her stay at Nevilly-sur-Seine, Helen complained of colds and pain in her throat. More and more she sought refuge in her diary, as she worked and waited for Saturday evening, when her father fetched her for the weekend. Her physical symptoms disappeared when the Magills journeyed to Italy in the spring of 1868. "She climbed Vesuvius alone and almost unaided the other day," Sarah reported, "a thing the guide told us no females ever did." The Magills remained in Europe through much of 1868, and Helen's progress in French, German, Italian, and music seemed just as rapid outside of the classroom as in it.[8]

An enormous task awaited Edward Magill when he returned to Swarthmore. The college was founded in 1864 when the Friends Educational Association, made up of members of the Philadelphia, New York, and Baltimore Yearly Meetings, purchased ninety-four acres of land in West Dale, Pennsylvania, then only a station stop on the West Chester and Philadelphia Railroad line. Swarthmore's first building was not completed for five years, however, because of a shortage of capital and the trustees' decision not to encumber the institution with a mortgage.

Qualified applicants, moreover, proved difficult to find. To make an educational virtue of economic necessity, Swarthmore, like most colleges founded in the nineteenth century, established a preparatory division for students not yet ready to do college-level work. This decision seemed inspired when, in 1869, exams were given to the 130 students who arrived at Swarthmore and more than three-quarters of them were placed in various grades of the preparatory department. For a time Swarthmore would have to be a high school, but that did not obscure the larger goal: to create a first-rate institution of higher learning. With his students, Edward hoped someday soon to enter the collegiate ranks.[9]

Typical in so many ways of fledgling colleges founded just after the Civil War, Swarthmore was exceptional in the insistence of the Quaker board of managers that it be fully coeducational. A few institutions, virtually all in the Midwest, had accepted young men and women after Oberlin led the way in 1833, but the experiment continued to be viewed with a mixture of scorn, alarm, and abhorrence among presidents and faculty of the more prestigious colleges in the East. The delicate female constitution, they argued, could not withstand the rigors of intricate analysis, late-night study, or examinations. If women needed a college education at all, they should learn skills appropriate to the female sphere, with an emphasis on music, art, and domestic economy, a curriculum that reminded them that the role of wife and mother was far superior to any other. Coeducation robbed women of good health and femininity; it also distracted young men from their studies by presenting more beautiful objects for contemplation. However well intentioned, many educators concluded, coeducation was a dangerous doctrine.

The Hicksite Quakers who founded Swarthmore, among them woman's rights advocate Lucretia Mott and her daughter, Anna Hooper, acknowledged the separate spheres of the sexes but insisted that women should learn to support themselves so they would not feel pressured into making bad marriages. Educated women were more likely to enter into unions based on love and common interest—and if the right man did not come along, they could contribute to society instead of depending upon it. The founders dismissed notions that females were ill suited to reason and analysis. At Swarthmore, there would be neither a separate curriculum nor separate classes for women. If possible, the college would enroll equal numbers of men and women, although the board of managers recognized that at first the former might disdain such a radical institution. Designed as a family community, with responsibilities shared equally by each student, Swarthmore also provided protection and privacy for the young women: although all students dined together, dormitories were segregated by sex and females were accompanied by chaperons on all social occasions, including any visits to the west (male) end of the campus. The founders sought to demonstrate, even to the most skeptical, that co-education actually enhanced the character, manners, and scholarship of both sexes.[10]

Coeducation became the personal and professional passion of Edward Magill. At age thirty-six, with a wife and family to support when the Civil War began, he had decided not to enlist in the great crusade of his generation. Thus, coeducation afforded an attractive arena for zealotry, all the more so for a man with five daughters. Edward stumped Pennsylvania in the 1860s and 1870s, campaigning for the reform that would emancipate more than half the nation. At Providence High School, he told his audiences, males occupied one side of the building and females the other, except for the graduation exercises when they sat together. At commencement, young men delivered orations from the platform while young women read essays from the lowest of the three steps leading to the platform. Swarthmore, Magill hoped, would demon-strate that such practices were as unnecessary and unproductive as they were degrading. Not only did principles of economy and simplicity of organization demand coeducation, he argued, but the practice of more than three decades offered conclusive testimony in behalf of the "mixed system." Coeducation was natural, an approximation of the family, where brothers and sisters "exercise a mutually refining and elevating effect upon each other." Mingling of the sexes in the classroom and competi-tion in study was not distracting; if anything, coeducation helped "rub off the halo of young romance" and enabled young people to "see each other as they really are." Edward did not doubt nor lament that acquaintanceship in college often ripened into marriage, and he was certain that the resulting alliances would be based on knowledge, shared values, and common interests.[11]

If coeducation improved the moral and social condition of young people, it also had a beneficial effect upon scholarship. Edward saw no evidence that the capacity to acquire knowledge, even in advanced work, had any "settled relation to distinction of sex." Indeed, given the obstacles young women had to overcome, their academic achievements were remarkable. Even if one could demonstrate, moreover, that women gener-ally were not intellectually equal to men, or were more emotional than reasoning by nature, one should not bar all women from college. Admis-sions examinations could identify the well qualified, as they did "for boys and men of varying capacity." Coeducation, he assured its critics, would fashion no social revolution because most women would never seek a college education; rather, they would shrink from study, or hasten to enter society, or give their attention to dress and fashion. Indeed, Edward never doubted that women were made to marry. He simply asserted that higher education was desirable for wives and mothers, and often necessary for single women. In a democratic society, no one, regardless of sex, who had the ability and desire should be barred from any college.

Edward Magill took great pains as well to address the argument that higher education ruined women's health. He insisted that the evidence from coeducational institutions indicated the contrary, that collegiate studies were more favorable than injurious to health. Absent from class less frequently than men, female collegians were less prone to illness than women who had not gone to college. Did anyone, he asked, really think that disciplined study would affect health more adversely than the "frivolous excitements and irregular hours indulged in by the devotees of society"? Evolution and progress, two idols of the late nineteenth century, were on the side of coeducation, he believed. In fact, the time was not far off when posterity would read "with amazement and incredulity" that supposedly enlightened educators of the nineteenth century actually debated "whether women were intellectually equal to men, and whether the sexes should be educated together in our higher institutions of learning."

An earnest advocate of woman's rights through coeducation, Helen Magill had a sober sense of the historic importance of Swarthmore's mixed system and of her own role in the experiment. She was, after all, the living embodiment of her father's system of beliefs; and, as one of the few students admitted into the college course of study, she was destined to be a member of Swarthmore's first graduating class. By distinguishing herself scholastically, she would further the cause and please her father. Yet she must somehow do so without betraying her femininity or her Quaker rearing by calling attention to herself.

Not surprisingly, Helen drove herself relentlessly and found herself inadequate. As "stern a self-denial in physical pleasures as the flesh will bear without dangerous revolt," she thought, "is probably always good in its influence." She lavished an envious praise on her father's prodigious capacity for work, as if to call attention to her own shortcomings. The strain and sacrifice of Edward's educational odyssey had become the stuff of family legend, and when he became president of Swarthmore in 1871, he worked so hard that his wife thought his health might break. Whenever Helen thought of her father, however, she felt "reproached for not working more earnestly." It was almost as if she took good health as evidence of indolence. She recognized that she was "dreadfully ambitious" but feared that her perseverance and talents did not equal her desire. Although most people thought her a very hard worker, she was too often deterred by "light reading" (i.e., contemporary novels): "I often wish I had enough strength of purpose to study myself to death. It is a *very* safe wish." Yet when one of her instructors asked if she did not sometimes feel that she should take a break, Helen responded with a wish that "there were forty-eight hours in every day and fourteen days in every week and that I had twice as much brains so I could do work fast and thoroughly." Young women, she admitted, were often not as strong as men, but her constitution was "pretty good," and, after all, she studied much less than fifteen hours a day.[12]

A typical week during Helen's first year, 1869–70, underscores the commitment of Swarthmore's founders and faculty to close supervision in and outside the classroom. Students rose early, usually at dawn, had breakfast at 7:00 A.M. (Sundays at 8:00), made their beds, and attended devotional exercises. Each school day was divided into periods announced by the ringing of a bell. On Mondays and Thursdays, the first-year students had no recitation between 8:30 and 9:15 A.M. During the second period, students recited Greek and Roman history with Miss Sandford. At 10:00 they had a half-hour to promenade in the fresh air, returning to a study period, followed at 11:15 by a laboratory class in which President Edward Parrish lectured on natural science and botany. From noon until 1:45, all students had lunch, then the first-year students had a study period until 2:30. Edward Magill was the instructor of the sixth-period Latin class; and Professor Smith taught German during the seventh. Classes ended at 4:00 P.M. First-year students were required to attend an evening study hour, and the whole school assembled in the Collecting Room for another hour of study or quiet contemplation before all students were dismissed to their dormitories. On Tuesday morning, first-year students had classes in English literature and mathematics (algebra and geometry). Helen also took Greek, her only elective; the only girl in the course, she found it "terribly hard" but was first in the class. In the afternoon she rejoined her classmates in French and Latin. On Tuesday evenings students attended lyceum, where one or more of them participated in a debate or gave a lecture. First-year students attended classes in elocution, ethics, and botany on Wednesday mornings; Wednesday afternoons were school holidays. Helen made no note of her Friday schedule, but on Saturday mornings she had classes in mathematics and botany. On Sunday, President Parrish hosted an "hour for reading" in his large, beautifully furnished parlor. At one of these sessions the students decided to set up a Sunday school for the younger children. Helen volunteered to teach, with the hope that she would be assigned "little ones and mostly girls." From the president's house Helen went to Quaker meeting. In the evening, after dinner, some of the female students attended a reading society where they discussed books like *The Last Days of Pompeii*. At 9:00 P.M. the women returned to study in a room separate from the men, until 10:30 P.M., when all first-year students were required to go to bed.[13]

Swarthmore noses were not always buried in books, of course, yet Helen engaged in only a small share of the horseplay and failed to forge the friendships that were so vitally important to the college experience of young women and men. With a small collegiate division (only five others graduated with Helen), the Swarthmore circle of acquaintanceship was necessarily limited for everyone. Helen, however, frequently found herself outside the circle. Solitary and unsocial before her first year, she spent her first semester at home, helping her mother with housework and child care. When she finally moved into the dormitory she remained reserved, an ambitious and competitive student who was suspicious of play and conscious, no doubt, that the daughter of Professor, then President, Magill must maintain a proper decorum. Helen seemed to prefer the controlled intimacy of correspondence with her lifelong friend Eva Channing to the risks of new relationships. She occasionally antagonized others with a frankness that could be brutal, and some Swarthmore women, we can guess, kept their distance from a classmate who was uncomfortably close to power and authority.

On rare occasions Helen let go, almost always in the safety of her dormitory room, where she was free of parental supervision and family responsibility. With roommate Lizzie Miller she often talked late into the night, long after the nine o'clock bell had hushed them to silence. Once or twice they had a pillow fight, each trying somehow to subdue the other without awakening the teacher next door. Lizzie would, at times, aim her little perfume sprinkler (filled not with cologne but water) at her roommate, and when things didn't work just right, she would tip the cup and give Helen a bath. Helen, for her part, was capable of revenge. When she divined that the mischievous Lizzie had placed torn paper at the foot of her bed, perhaps to give the impression that the furnishing committee had substituted miserable corn-husk mattresses for the hair mattresses they had promised to buy, Helen made Lizzie's bed "pie-fashion" and placed several starchy articles at the foot. With a giggle, Lizzie offered to show her innocent friend how mischief was really done. "And the way she made that bed, dancing all the time to the tune of Captain Jenks, was most comical." Helen sat, laughed, and plotted.[14]

Although the dormitories were segregated by sex, the Swarthmore trustees encouraged contact between the young men and women. They studied together and recited together; at the tables in the dining room, each with a teacher or one of the older scholars at the head, students chattered away, paying little attention to their food, anticipating the announcement of rules about dressing (females were forbidden to wear unnecessary or expensive jewelry or clothing with much trimming) or worrying about an imminent exam. Yet the only students Helen ever mentioned by name were Lizzie Miller and Maria Pierce, her friendly competitors. Male students remained a collective category, a group to be outperformed scholastically.

Whether in study or in play, Helen viewed Swarthmore through the prism of gender. Coeducation seemed to remind her that the sexes were different and to underscore that the burden was on women to prove that they deserved equal treatment. When the female students organized a baseball game, for instance, the males climbed a high tree and watched the spectacle below with derisive amusement, suggesting that if the competitors used a football and large aprons they might be able to catch the ball. Helen wished the women were more enthusiastic about baseball, but she knew they were not. Instruction in sports began "one might almost say from the cradle" for boys, and she had to admit that they seemed to have an aptitude born of instinct. More ominously, the advantages of males were scarcely confined to sports. Helen believed that men had an intuitive knowledge of business, while women were "as ignorant of these things as men are of mantua-making." However, she vehemently resisted her Aunt Susan's assertion that boys spoke better than girls, dismissing the older woman as "fearfully anti-woman's rights," though she felt forced to admit that "some things we can do better than they, but very few."[15]

Upon what basis, then, could women relate to men if both association and separation were reminders of inferiority? Helen seemed unsure. She liked a young man to skate with, she confessed to Eva Channing, but was irked that all the males at Swarthmore were better skaters than the females: "I should not like to skate all the time with them as some girls do, for I think it best for one who wishes to learn much to go a great deal alone." Her ambivalence about parties, dancing, and other rituals of courtship, moreover, set her apart from most of the Swarthmore coeds. When she formed a reading group, she did not invite anyone from the set to which she had once, perhaps, aspired. Excluded by them, she would retaliate, even if that meant isolating herself still more. These young women did not seem studious enough, had made fun of Helen's reluctance to "flirt or cut-up," and resented a too freely expressed "opinion when what they do does not exactly suit me." She would not promenade down the hall with a boy, she announced to Eva and others, yet her attempts at self-deprecation "(good reason why some of the boys say)" did not lighten the harshness of her implied judgment. "You never go to parties or dancing school," Eva remarked sometime later, "so you can't realize the misery and mortification of being a wall-flower or of dancing with a small specimen of the feminine gender."[16]

Eva was wrong. Helen longed for male companionship but feared that her looks, her ambition, her sharp tongue, even her intelligence made her unattractive to men. Uncomfortable with her own desires, she thought them evidence that she was undeserving. Self-denial and humility were Christian, ladylike, and practical, and she asked why she should expose herself to embarrassment and ridicule by wanting what she could not have. Helen did, however, express great interest in Eva's accounts of her own "little dissipations," and her admission that she could hardly tell whether she would enjoy parties "or be blue after them, never having had much opportunity to make the experiment," sounds more like a call for sympathy than a statement of principle. In congratulating Eva on turning sixteen, she supposed, with tongue only partly in cheek, that "in two years you expect to give up studying, consider yourself a young lady, go into society and think of nothing but music, the weather, French, dancing, your dress and your hair." Only in the privacy of her diary did Helen give voice to the emotions that knew no resolution: "I am a strange girl, for a young girl, I think—I hope. Surely there cannot be many such. Often I watch other girls, especially a certain class of whom I do not exactly approve . . . yet I fear I almost envy them."[17]

Uncomfortable in social situations, Helen excelled in academic work at Swarthmore. She was ranked fourth among the first-year students and relished the fact that the top seven places in the class were occupied by women. Ever the rationalist, she acknowledged that Swarthmore attracted only males from rural areas with inadequate secondary schools, while many of the females had had superior opportunities for study. Until she competed with well-trained young men, Helen could not be sure of her own academic ability. Still, the year had been a success, and she could not wait to begin again.

The rigors of the Swarthmore curriculum had discouraged several young scholars, and Helen's sophomore class was alarmingly small, numbering only six girls and two boys. The absence of familiar faces made Helen "very blue," and she "wandered about like a ghost" as the new term began, although the arrival of Lizzie Miller and Maria Pierce lifted her spirits. Helen took Latin, French, German, Greek, algebra, composition, declamation, and shorthand, a heavy schedule but lamentably one that obliged her to leave out some subjects in which she was interested. She decided to concentrate on the study of languages, a perfect choice in many ways: she could win the respect of her father, whose French and Latin textbooks were widely used, and attain scholarly distinction while remaining in a field deemed appropriate for women. She could, perhaps, strike a blow for woman's rights while somehow residing within a slowly widening female sphere. Helen's enjoyment of languages was in marked contrast to her frustration with mathematics, especially galling because the latter was supposedly difficult for girls to master and also Edward Magill's great strength. She studied algebra "furiously," abandoning for a time more feminine pursuits: "I am afraid I shall forget how to thread a needle I do so little sewing." Mathematics, however, remained a millstone around her neck. With some reluctance she dropped advanced mathematics in her sophomore year and took more algebra, with a younger class. Even so, her difficulties persisted. Hard work, she was learning, could not always subdue a stubborn mind.[18]

Helen's grades (except in mathematics) belied her assertion that examinations and essays disagreed with her. In fact, she seemed to thrive on them. Eva Channing was half inclined to attribute her friend's tribulation to a "little innocent feint to cover your radiant satisfaction concerning some production which is to make the name of Helen Magill famous forever." Hadn't Helen written and delivered a spirited address on capital punishment, to universal acclaim? Could one take seriously Helen's complaints about not having any original ideas, as if she were "the only unhappy mortal thus afflicted?"[19]

Eva's suspicions were no doubt on the mark, although Helen's self-doubt was genuine, a product of the Quaker doctrine of self-abnegation and a cultural consensus (albeit under siege) that self-development for its own sake was inappropriate behavior for women. Her parents had challenged that consensus, but their advice abounded in contradictions: she should aspire and submit, prepare for a career and expect to marry, compete with and outdo the men but never forget that she was a woman. They had come to expect excellence. How, then, could she tell them— or anyone—how little she knew, how much time she needed to master a subject? "I lose all self-confidence," she wrote in her diary, "from the knowledge that the lesson is imperfectly prepared; from this results confusion." She knew that her impressive achievements raised the stakes of aspiration and expectation, but if she was to be the first woman to attend Harvard—as she hoped—very good was not nearly good enough. For better and worse she was a marked woman, alone in the spotlight. Although some thought higher education made women masculine, Helen feared at times that she was not "man enough" to represent her sex.[20]

In the spring of her sophomore year, Helen prepared to deliver a declamation to the students and faculty at Swarthmore. But unlike the little girl on the haystack, she was no longer unabashed. Writing and rewriting until the last minute, when she mounted the platform she was not sure she had fully committed the speech to memory. All of a sudden, she later wrote, "something made me think my white skirt was coming down, a thing which I do not remember happening to me before in my life. Well there I stood and spoke on, I looked down at my dress but could see nothing. I looked around at the audience and fancied they too were looking in the same direction." Helen stumbled through the address, skipping paragraphs, but somehow kept her composure. Her greatest fear, that she would be revealed as an inadequate, vulnerable female, had almost come to pass. The audience apparently applauded her talk, scarcely aware of the inner turmoil of this coeducational pioneer.[21]

Harvard's siren call had aroused, seduced, and angered Helen ever since she sat in the Boston Public Latin School listening to her father tell his students that each of them could enter the venerable college "without conditions." Indeed, all Boston Latin graduates ranked in the first division went to Harvard without having to take an examination or additional course work, while those in the second division were only occasionally rejected. Women, of course, could not expect admission under any conditions, but Helen was determined "to give the old stubborn doors a knock. It may be feeble but, even if it does not succeed, may be one of the little waves which, you know, in time near smooth the hard rock. If I do not get in, the first or among the first, I owe it to the honor of womanhood to try my best to succeed well."[22]

The Harvard gates shook a bit in the late 1860s and 1870s as spouses and children of alumni and faculty, joined by reformers Wendell Phillips and Thomas Wentworth Higginson, demanded equal education for women. Charles W. Eliot, the president of Harvard, proved a formidable adversary. He traveled to coeducational institutions in the west and found the women in attendance "warm, frail and bloodless." In his inaugural address in 1869, he announced his opposition to the mixed system: Harvard "did not wish to face" the problems attendant upon providing common residence for young men and women of "immature character and marriageable age." Consequently, women would not be accepted into any part of the university.[23]

Eliot relented somewhat. In 1869–70, Harvard offered two courses of instruction open to "graduates, teachers and other competent persons." These lectures, which satisfied no degree requirements but might "edify" men and women at "the advanced level," had a total enrollment of nine (three women and six men). By 1872 Eliot faced renewed agitation for more thoroughgoing reform, this time initiated by the Women's Educational Association (WEA) of Boston. When the association's members discovered that Cambridge University in England administered examinations and granted diplomas to women, it pressed Harvard to do the same. After some debate the Harvard Corporation agreed, with the stipulation that the WEA bear all incidental expenses. Women seventeen or older could pay fifteen dollars and take a preliminary examination, roughly equal to the test for prospective Harvard freshmen, which measured "variety rather than depth of knowledge" in French and English literature, German, Latin or Greek, mathematics, history, physics, and botany. Those who passed could take an advanced exam (ten-dollar fee) in languages, natural sciences, mathematics, and history or philosophy. Examinations were held throughout the country, and the diploma equivalent, though clearly not to be equated with a Harvard degree, supposedly might raise the standard of scholarship in girls' schools and "prove of great service to ladies" who were preparing themselves for careers in teaching. The corporation, which had invited women to study horticulture, entomology, and agricultural chemistry in the Bussey Institution, also promised to set up a graduate department, open to women, for doctorates in nonprofessional areas, but these programs did not get off the ground. Harvard, in short, was willing to lend its name to the certification of educated women but wished to reserve its resources exclusively for men.[24]

While Eliot fiddled, Helen burned. When one sarcastic Harvardian wrote that women were more concerned with looks than learning, she shot back that young ladies who sought admission to Harvard "did not generally make their hair the main object of their lives." However, those whose love "for neatness equalled [their] scholarly zeal" would simply rise a half hour before prayers, "a practice evidently unfamiliar to the disheveled young gentlemen who often presented themselves in the chapel." Neither logic nor sarcasm moved Harvard's Committee on Women in Higher Education, and in 1872 Helen grudgingly acknowledged that her "great hope" had all but vanished. When she learned that the examinations given to women differed from those given to men, requiring less and failing to yield a regular degree, she was ready to denounce Harvard: "Where now is the 'herald of light' to be found? Not in Cambridge, America. I don't care half what I did two or three years ago for a Harvard degree. It seems to me possible that the college will never gain the patronage of women." Still, she predicted that Harvard, Brown, and Yale would not hold out much longer; that as soon as one accepted coeducation, the rest would surely follow, and the daughters of Helen Magill and Eva Channing would be among Harvard's graduates—*if* they ever had daughters and *if* they were suited for "that kind of education." Upon reflection, a third if was in order: *if* Harvard was of any importance compared to the exciting new coeducational institutions contending for preeminence in higher education.[25]

Tragedy in the Magill family interrupted Helen's thoughts of Harvard. Francis Gardner Magill, not ten years old, contracted diphtheria and died ten days later, on October 6, 1872. Helen, who often helped her mother with the children, must have been at home at the time and surely felt herself aging as she glimpsed death up close. Thereafter, she claimed to look at things from a new perspective. Yet Francis had had little impact on her; indeed, her letters, filled with news of her four sisters, make virtually no reference to her brother. If she sensed her father's sorrow, or knew about his hopes for his only son, she did not say so. When the family took Francis's body to New Hope, Pennsylvania, for burial, Helen stayed at home, sick with a fever and sore throat, "a very severe attack of my well-known enemy the tonsillitis." The rapidity of her recovery and the tone of her narrative, however, hint at ambivalence about her brother's removal from the family. Of all the Magill children, of course, only Francis could have attended Harvard. "And now we are all girls, on earth," she wrote, presumably with no unfair advantages in the competition for distinction and affection.[26]

The death of her only brother was certainly not as significant for Helen as it was for eleven-year-old Elizabeth Cady (later Stanton). When Eleazor Cady died in 1826, a few weeks after his graduation from Union College, his father seemed beyond consolation. When Elizabeth tried to comfort him, Judge Cady stroked her hair, heaved a sigh, and wished she were a boy, prompting Elizabeth to resolve to be all that her brother had been, "manly and courageous." But Daniel Cady would not countenance college or career for a female, no matter how bright and determined, and his disapproval was, by all accounts, a decisive stimulus to Elizabeth's life of achievement, teaching her the primacy of gender and drawing her to other women as natural allies. Helen Magill, the favored first-born before and after her own brother's death, did not feel the sting of inferiority in the bosom of her family. Her father's expectations were different, providing another kind of pressure. He did not wish that Helen were a boy because he wanted her to strike a blow for coeducation and the equality of women. For Helen, then, woman's rights was an inherited cause, intimately connected to a desire to satisfy her father, to surpass his academic achievements, to earn his love. To reach her goal she needed neither strategy nor allies, for hers was, by definition, a solitary task, and she had learned that she could go as far as her will, discipline, and intelligence would take her.[27]

The approach of commencement in June 1873, the first in Swarthmore's history, forced the Magills to set aside their sorrows. While President Magill invited guests and wrote speeches, and Sarah Magill planned receptions, Helen studied with a vengeance. Her senior year was her best: Latin, 98; German, 96; Greek, 94; French, 92; elocution, 85; English literature, rhetoric, and composition, 89½. The more she studied, however, the more her health suffered, and as she prepared for finals she was troubled "with the strangest pains, now here and now there and a tiresome cough"; she wanted to read her rhetoric text, but her eyes hurt. Ever conscious of her father's conviction that the health of young women would not be damaged by study, she tried to make light of her ailments. "It is strange," she mused as she studied into the night, "that German seems to affect Lizzie's eyes and Greek, mine." In one sense, illness could be noted with pride as a sign of hard work. But Helen began to accept the argument that illness was the mark of Woman. Perhaps her father was wrong; perhaps study would not hurt only "strong girls [who] are the exception in this age and country."[28]

Second in scholarship in Swarthmore's graduating class of six, Helen prepared a salutatory and poem, choosing "women's influence" as her subject. Taking care not to claim too much for the suffrage movement, she promised that her address would be "woman's rights too a little." Helen completed her speech on commencement day, and this time she did not have a lapse of memory, although some thought she spoke a bit too softly. Then came a torrent of feelings and fears. How could she judge the quality of her scholarship when well-trained young men stayed away from coeducational colleges? Was her resolve strong enough to surmount the obstacles placed in the path of women? The Swarthmore years, she worried, might well be the best of her life, for the past seemed "pleasanter to look at than the future, almost always. I can't build sand castles in the air; they all seem impossible and immediately tumble down before I have begun."[29]

Thoughts of failure were reserved for nighttime reflection and her diary, to be replaced by hope when dawn broke. Helen did not share her apprehensions with her Swarthmore friends, with whom she maintained at best a desultory correspondence after graduation. Even with Eva Channing she was guarded, communicating by joke and enigma, with enough ambiguity to allow her to deny serious interpretations. Privately, Helen set forth her two great ambitions: serving God and a happy marriage, which was her primary goal ("Yes, it is my first because reason as I will, I find it lies nearest my heart and the other [i.e., being a scholar] seems a little cold compared with it"), along with motherhood, "the divinist of all" feminine roles; and being a scholar "more or less great," an earnest student "in the noble field of language." To pursue the first, Helen knew, was to play a waiting game; to pursue the second, she might diminish her chances of marriage. When she bemoaned her "instability of purpose," she meant that she did not know whether she could or should pursue two aims. Like most women, she was not free to choose, yet she had to do something.[30]

Her dilemma was all the more pressing because the man she thought she loved hardly noticed her. Twelve years older than Helen, William

Hyde Appleton had been one of Edward Magill's favorite pupils at Providence High School, had studied at Harvard and then done post-graduate work in Bonn and Berlin. In 1872, Magill brought Appleton to Swarthmore as professor of Greek and German. Helen had undoubtedly met Appleton in Providence, but as she sat in his classes in Swarthmore, respect turned to passion, "strong, unreasoning, overmastering." Appleton represented everything Helen desired in life: a Harvard education, study abroad, a scholarly career in Greek and German, the respect and friend-ship of her father. When "Herr A" joked with her, she yearned to express her feelings for him, but she held back, afraid that he would not return her love because she did not deserve it. At the commencement reception, other faculty members cordially greeted Helen, but Appleton permitted himself only a "short stiff talk." She realized that she knew little about him, almost nothing at all "but the moustache and the smile." She knew very well her own imperfections and the great responsibilities of a wife and mother, but she had a "hard kind of conscience and reason it as I will. . . . I am too selfish to wish that one whom I might love should not love me, even knowing myself . . . as I do." Helen thought she lacked the depth of character and purity of spirit to love anyone "with that high holy feeling which is my ideal"; and she claimed she would have no lover if she fell short of that ideal, although Swarthmore's professor of Greek and German remained the apple of her eye.[31]

In the months following commencement, Helen wrestled to subdue, reason with, or escape her passion. She convinced herself that her attrac-tion for Appleton was not love and would probably pass if she left Swarthmore for a year; if, however, he chose to reciprocate her feelings, "I should cease to consider it in the same dispassionate way." Helen alter-nated between avoiding Appleton and seeking him out; she saw reason to hope, then concluded he did not care for her. She was "most miserable because a certain thing can never be" yet hoped for such misery all her life "rather than forget or give up that one impossible hope." She tried to govern herself, to walk and talk and eat and sleep and laugh and work and study so that no one would ever dream "what a wild heart I carry about and how bitterly I am longing for that rest and resignation which I can never seem to attain."[32]

Helen thought that she might find refuge from such disappointment in ambition, as men did. To be "a scholar, an ornament to her profession," would keep her from having to "pass through this fire again. Gold is tried and purified by the fire. But I am not gold. The black coal turns to ashes." If at times a career seemed to be her second choice, a consolation prize for a lost affair of the heart, we must remember that she thought she would never attain her ideal of love and marriage. To approach Appleton was unladylike; to love from afar allowed her to have it several ways: she could avoid the possibility of rejection, retain sexual purity, practice self-denial, and pursue a professorship while embracing the institution of holy matrimony. If Helen came to terms with unrequited love, she could "cheerfully take up the next best thing and make the most of it." If asked to marry Appleton, she might very well abandon scholarship for home and hearth, "but why think of improbabilities."[33]

Had Helen chosen to become an elementary or high school teacher, an increasingly feminized profession in the nineteenth century, her Swarthmore degree would have been more than sufficient. But she wished to extend the woman's sphere by invading the terrain of the university intellectual. Scholars, of course, were teachers too, and students of all ages needed to be nurtured. A scholarly career, then, was the logical extension of teaching, just as coeducation was the inevitable outcome of higher education being open to women. Helen could be a pioneer without being a revolutionary— but only if her weak will and "frail" feminine nature sustained her noble ambition. The stakes were high: "I shall either conquer gloriously or fail ignominiously, in this battle of life."[34]

The path to a professorship was by no means clearly marked, as the career of Ellen Swallow Richards, one of Helen's most successful contemporaries, suggests. When she graduated from Vassar in 1870, Swallow decided to do advanced research in chemistry, but no university would accept her. Very few institutions at this time had distinct graduate curricula or degree programs, even for men; a stipulated time in residence often sufficed for a master's degree, and the Ph.D. was conferred upon only a handful. Prestigious institutions, as we have seen, disdained to educate women for any degree. Fortunately for Swallow, the new Massachusetts Institute of Technology admitted her as a "special student," charging her no fees so that the president could deny that she was a matriculant. A brilliant student, she was granted a second undergraduate degree, a B.S., in 1873. Vassar awarded her an M.A. in the same year, upon submission of a thesis on the amount of vanadium in iron ore. With more impressive credentials than any woman in the sciences, Swallow's professional prospects were nonetheless uncertain. Then good fortune intervened in the guise of a marriage, shortly after her graduation, to Robert Hallowell Richards, a professor of metallurgical and mining engineering at M.I.T. The two did research together, and Richards no doubt played some role in his wife's long association with M.I.T. Yet even with her extraordinary talent and connections, a regular academic appointment (and then only as instructor in sanitary chemistry) did not come until 1884, a decade after she graduated.[35]

Helen Magill also had difficulty finding an institutional home for her professional aspirations. Staying at Swarthmore for a year or two, she finally decided, had several advantages. It gave Appleton another chance to become a suitor—and if he did not act, she promised herself that she would leave without uncertainty or regret. By living at home, Helen could reduce family expenses, thus making it easier for her sisters to go to college. Moreover, her father needed a secretary to help with office work and correspondence. In essence, then, she could meet the "family claim" that Jane Addams once observed was so often pressed upon women when they graduated from college. The Magills, however, considered the claim temporary, encouraging their daughter to do something of worth in the world and take classes in mathematics in preparation for university entrance examinations. The family bond, as Joyce Antler has argued, could be useful in legitimizing some forms of social behavior; Edward and Sarah Magill, in this case, believed that a teacher, no less than a dutiful daughter, put the good of the whole before that of the self. While they expected and wanted Helen to marry, they supported her education away from home.[36]

Appleton's "utter indifference" no doubt helped precipitate the religious crisis Helen experienced in 1874. While in a state of "dull hopelessness," she read John Tyndall's address to the British Association at Belfast. A professor of natural history at the Royal Institution of Great Britain, Tyndall was the bête noire of the orthodox, the infidel who rejected God and embraced a pure and simple materialism. Science, he argued, demanded "the radical extirpation of caprice and the absolute reliance upon law in nature"; soon, the modern age would "sweep from the field of theory this mob of gods and demons." His lecture presented "in its worst and clearest form" the Darwinian argument that since science could explain neither the origin of life nor the phenomena of human consciousness, "in other words, God and the soul," they do not exist. Helen was attracted to and repelled by this paean to reason rooted in research. She had, after all, subordinated "cold reason" to emotion when she made marriage her first aim. What might Tyndall make of her decision—or of her passion for Appleton, a man she hardly knew?[37]

As she sought to test the limits of Tyndall's thesis, Helen was stunned when Eva Channing ridiculed her opposition to suicide as outdated religious prejudice. Could her friend be right? Her despair was deep, she told Eva, but in a few weeks she regained her balance, little changed. God's existence and human immortality could not be proved to a scientist's satisfaction, she acknowledged, but Tyndall himself admitted that reason and the heart often reached different conclusions and neither faculty "should be repressed" by an excessive regard for the other. Perhaps he wasn't such a thoroughgoing materialist after all. In any event, Helen knew that her passion was no less real because it was invisible to the microscope. She "did *not* expect to fade away 'like a morning cloud into the infinite blue of the past'." Under God's care, Helen's heart told her, there could be "no such mockery as our life here necessarily seems without confidence in a hereafter." Thus, she resolved her crisis, as did many of her contemporaries, by assigning head and heart to separate spheres, each capable of insights hidden to the other. How could God love all things and let them prey upon each other? "A finite mind," she wrote, could not comprehend "such things."[38]

Helen buried her doubts beneath a busy regimen of work and study. On a typical day she arose at 5:30 A.M., tended her plants and reviewed French, straightened her room, studied Greek from 8:15 to 10:15, recited French until 11 and Greek until 11:45, read Latin with the girls until 12:20 (Miss Austin, the regular Latin preceptress, had been called away to care for a sick brother), ate lunch, monitored the reading room from 1 until 2, worked in the president's office until 3:30, and taught a "light" gymnastics class before supper. Whenever possible she took a walk or read with Lizzie Miller. She was always home by 5 P.M., and after supper she helped her sister Marian undress, then put her to bed with a story or a song. From 7:45 until 9 she read Greek by candlelight, fighting off eye strain and blurred vision—like Portia, she told Eva Channing, she preferred cautioning others about their health to taking her own advice. After all, indolence was "the gatekeeper of hell and the squire of Satan." When she could concentrate no more on Greek, she often read fiction until she went to bed at 10. Although she admitted that novels tended "to foster self-consciousness, that weakness of character which renders its victim miserable," she refused to bow to the convention that fiction corrupted the morals of women. George Sand's *Ma Seure Jeanne* might vividly describe sensual passion, but it concluded with praise for the spiritual as the superior passion. Helen occasionally reproached herself for frittering away time with "light reading" (Wednesdays and Saturdays, when she had no official duties, she forced herself to contend with conic sections and to review Homer), but novels in no way deterred her from academic work.[39]

As she got over her initial trepidation about speaking in front of a class, Helen took to teaching, in part because it forced her out of an insular existence. She took her responsibilities seriously, traveling to Vassar to see how gymnastics was taught and to measure the pace of language instruction at an all-girl's school. A hard taskmaster, she even enjoyed grading the papers of the "not too brilliant" sophomore Greek class, smiling as she imagined James Parson's scowl when he received a 33. With grades, a teacher meted out justice, rewarding effort, punishing laziness. If Helen sometimes regretted that she had to steal time from her own work to teach, she was pleased that she had an affinity for what was to be part of her lifework.[40]

Somehow Helen made time to keep abreast of the ongoing debate over woman's rights. On several occasions she listened to Abby Kelley Foster and Lucretia Mott, their voices no longer strong, still demanding equal rights for blacks but also testifying on behalf of their sex. Mott, the gentle Quaker "most worthy of love and admiration," eloquently urged young women to prepare to support themselves. Buoyed by the presence of women on the platform, Helen monitored the progress of woman suffrage in the pages of the *Woman's Journal,* perhaps the most important journal of women's issues published during the 1870s. The *Woman's Journal* also reviewed Edward Clarke's controversial polemic *Sex in Education; or A Fair Chance for the Girls,* an indictment of higher education for women that singled out coeducation as particularly dangerous to health and welfare. Upon examination, Helen found *Sex in Education* all the more dangerous because it had enough truth mixed with "fallacies and absurdities" to make it credible. Worried that women, as a class, might actually be physically weaker than men, she fought off Clarke's theories, confident that coeducation would prove that women were as rational and intelligent as men. Only then, in fact, could the case for suffrage be assured.[41]

Helen disagreed with proponents of dress reform, whose views she read in the pages of the *Woman's Journal,* that tight-laced corsets made bending excruciating or impossible and contributed to the physical problems of women. Concerned about comfortable clothes, she also cared about how she looked and thus saw no alternative to constricting corsets except "waists stiffened with whalebone," which were just as bad. Skirts, too, would no doubt remain fashionable until someone designed a substitute that was "pretty and convenient." At bottom, she was skeptical of the claims made in the name of dress reform and thought that the movement obscured the main issue: why discuss "what I shall wear when the great question of what I shall do in that same unhappy dress is yet so dark and uncertain"?[42]

The *Woman's Journal* provided information about educational opportunities as well, including a summer 1873 article describing the soon-to-be opened Boston University. Helen would be eligible to enter in the fall, she thought, if she brushed up on Virgil and refined her knowledge of Latin prose composition. But given the uncertainty about graduate curricula and degree requirements, she was not at all sure where she would be placed. Since a B.A. from Swarthmore carried little weight, she might need a second undergraduate degree. B.U. ("Blessed Utopia," Helen dubbed it) was particularly attractive because it promised to provide women access to all educational programs. The dogma of education for men only, announced President William Fairfield Warren, "should be retired to the museum for pedagogical paleontology." B.U. practiced what it preached, welcoming women "not merely to the bench of the pupil, but also to the chair of the professor." It boasted seven women and eleven men in the first class of the College of Arts and Sciences and three women on the faculty of the Medical School. Here was a place where a woman might spend a lifetime.[43]

Helen pressed Eva Channing, who began study at B.U. in the fall of 1874, for information about the institution. Excited at the prospect of being reunited with her friend, Eva stressed the cultural advantages of Boston and reported that the institution's religious sectarianism did not constrict the curriculum. Yet she was cautious, urging her friend to judge B.U. on its merits and not "on dit." Many of the courses would be review to Helen, as they were to Eva, but as better students arrived, standards would, no doubt, be elevated and Helen might work out a suitable course of study.[44]

Eva's advice underscored Helen's dilemma. Barred from the very best schools, she excluded all-female institutions for reasons of philosophy and strategy: they segregated women in an unnatural environment and allowed opponents of coeducation to assert that women already had outlets for their educational aspirations. Left with a mere handful of choices, Helen was forced to lower her standards. Despite Eva's caveats, then, she wrote to President Warren, whose replies indicate how fluid graduate degree requirements actually were. If she kept fresh in the classics and mastered analytic geometry, he wrote in 1874, she could enter as a junior and graduate at B.U.'s first commencement. When Helen probed for information on ancient languages, Warren made an offer she could not refuse: if she sent her Swarthmore course of study and certification of her A.B., he would review her record and, in all likelihood, offer her a postgraduate course of two years with a virtually free choice of studies and the Ph.D. degree on completion. To be a "Philosophic Doctor," Helen admitted, would be "quite an honor," and she enthusiastically accepted.[45]

Support for Helen's postgraduate study came at least as much from Sarah as from Edward Magill. Mother and daughter had not always seen eye-to-eye. Sarah was not "a very successful housekeeper," and Helen sympathized with her father's lack of patience with "people's careless, unsystematic ways." The two women squabbled, perhaps in bids for Edward's affection. Sometimes, Helen suspected, her mother disliked "a thing because I like it." Envying those girls whose mothers were their friends, Helen thought Sarah acted toward her "like a flint of steel." She knew her mother was fond of her but wrote that she had an unfortunate "way of showing, or rather concealing it." Nonetheless, Sarah sympathized with her daughter's ambitions and remonstrated with her husband, no doubt in private, to let Helen go to Boston. We do not know what concerns Edward raised with his wife, but with four daughters already in school he probably worried about family finances. If she "had not set [her] face firmly in that direction," Sarah recalled much later, Edward might have pressed the family claim, at least for another year. But he said nothing to Helen, who made ready to return to New England and began to dream of postgraduate study in Greece or Germany.[46]

On September 20, 1875, "after quite a leave taking," Helen departed for Boston. She had not expected to cry, but as she embraced her mother, father, and four sisters she broke down. More than most college graduates, she had remained in the bosom of her family, and now that she was leaving Swarthmore she realized how much they meant to her. Proud of her educational achievements, they had put the resources of the family behind her scholarly aspirations. For the rest of their lives, Edward and Sarah Magill would be her closest confidantes; if Helen shared her thoughts and fears with anyone, it would be with her parents, not Eva Channing, nor her sisters, nor peers or colleagues. She was proud that she had met and exceeded parental expectations—in educational attainment and, perhaps soon, in scholarly achievement. She was living proof that coeducation worked.[47]

William Hyde Appleton did not see his former student off. He was a "trifler," Helen told herself, who sensed her affection for him "and being curious to find out how much, wishes to make me *think* he likes me. . . . " She had tried to meet his flirtations with "a cordial indifference," smiling "with just the faintest tinge of scorn, very very faint or it will be pernicious." She could not, however, "smother the fires which consume[d]" her or shake off "the deadly chill which seemed to benumb" her faculties. When thinking of him, she felt "miserable self scorn and a sense of degradation, a forlorn feeling of hollowness as of something irrevocably lost." Perhaps, she wrote without much conviction, absence would make the heart grow less fond; she would go off to Boston, forget Herr A, "become indifferent and perhaps marry, if I get a chance." Or might indifference become the friend to her ambition and the foe of entangling alliances?[48]

NOTES

1. For further information on the early life of Edward Magill, see E. H. Magill, *Sixty Five Years in the Life of a Teacher* (Boston and New York, 1907), pp. 1–56.

2. *In Memoriam: Sarah Warner Magill* (Privately Published, 1898), n.p., HMW Papers.

3. Magill, *Sixty Five Years,* pp. 74–75.

4. HM to EC, "Monday Morning," ca. 1871. See also HM to ADW, Nov. 7, 1888, ADW Papers; SWM to Aunt Susan, May 21, 1868. Edward Magill evidently administered "severe whippings" to his children. See Gertrude Magill to Father and Sisters, July 27, 1905; HM to ADW, Sept. 14, 1900. Helen's friend Eva thought children happier than "venerable people": "I fear that I do not keep a great *aim* before me all the time, as you do. . . . I enjoy myself simply for the enjoyment and do no good to pay for it, and I am sure I am *not* happiest when I am *working.* Now it is the same with children, only they have no 'pricks of conscience' if they enjoy themselves without doing their share of work." EC to HM, May 28, 1871.

5. HM to Family, Aug. 4, 1904; SWM to Aunt Susan, May 21, 1868. See also Magill, *Sixty Five Years,* pp. 90–91. Helen often dreamed about the Boston Latin when she accompanied her parents to Europe in 1867. See HM to EC, Dec. 8, 1867; HM, *Diary,* Oct. 25, 1867. Boston Latin has no record of Helen's attendance or performance and did not admit another female for a century.

6. Magill, *Sixty Five Years,* pp. 120–21. Edward Magill mistakenly dated the European trip in 1869.

7. Ibid.

8. HM, *Diary,* Feb. 6, 1868; SWM to Aunt Susan, May 21, 1868. See also HM, *Diary,* Dec. 11, 1867; Magill, *Sixty Five Years,* p. 127.

9. See Magill, *Sixty Five Years,* pp. 137–53.

10. Barbara Miller Solomon, *In the Company of Educated Women* (New Haven, Conn., 1985), pp. 50–51, 100–101; Thomas Woody, *A History of Women's Education in the United States* (New York, 1929); Mabel Newcomber, *A Century of Higher Education for Women* (New York, 1959).

11. The summary of Magill's views on coeducation in this and the next two paragraphs relies on Magill, *Sixty Five Years,* pp. 58–59; E. H. Magill, *An Address upon the Co-Education of the Sexes* (Philadelphia, 1873); E. H. Magill, *Co-Education of the Sexes in Swarthmore College* (Philadelphia, 1874). Helen noted that her father believed "the way to begin was with the young folks and if they were rightly brought up they would have the partition down in a generation." HM to EC, Aug. 25, 1874.

12. HM, *Diary,* Oct. 18, 1874, May 3, 1873; HM to EC, Jan. 22, 1872, Feb. ?, 1871, Dec. 10, 1871, Nov. 24, 1871. Helen read with interest Edward Everett Hale's article prescribing nine hours of sleep and suggesting no "brain work" for five hours before going to bed. Allowing two or three hours for meals and an hour or two for dressing, Helen calculated "four left to work in!! . . . I who am a very slow worker seem to leave a hundred necessary things undone every day of my life." HM to EC, Sept. 14, 1872. At times, excessive study caught up with Helen: "I seem to myself to be more tired every morning than the morning before so that I begin to find it even an effort to rise at half past six." HM to EC, Nov. 26, 1871.

13. HM to EC, Apr. 10, 1870.

14. HM to EC, Feb. 11, 1870. See also HM to EC, Apr. 10, 1870.

15. HM to EC, Apr. 23, 1871. See also HM to EC, Apr. 10, 1870, Nov. 14, 1870, Apr. 16, 1871, Nov. 9, 1873; HM to EHM, Aug. 23, 1870.

16. HM to EC, Dec. 17, 1871, Apr. 10, 1870; EC to HM, Feb. 5, 1871.

17. HM to EC, May 4, 1873, May 17, 1870; HM, *Diary,* May 7, 1873.

18. HM to EC, Sept. 10, 1871, Feb. ?, 1871, May 5, 1872. See also HM to EC, Apr. 17, 1870. For languages as "appropriate" areas of study for women, see Roberta Frankfort, *Collegiate Women: Domesticity and Career in Turn-of-the-Century America* (New York, 1977), pp. 80–83.

19. EC to HM, June 2, 1873, Feb. 9, 1873.

20. HM, *Diary,* May 6, 1873.

21. HM to EC, Apr. 29, 1872.

22. Magill, *Sixty Five Years,* pp. 88–89; HM to EC, Oct. 15, 1871.

23. Eliot is quoted in Hugh Hawkins, *Between Harvard and America: The Educational Leadership of Charles W. Eliot* (New York, 1972), pp. 193–94. See also Samuel Eliot Morison, *Three Centuries of Harvard, 1636–1936* (Cambridge, Mass., 1937), p. 391.

24. Hawkins, p. 55; Morison, pp. 334–91. See also "The Revolution at Harvard," *New York Times,* Oct. 18, 1872, 4:6.

25. HM to EC, Dec. 10, 1871, Sept. 8, 1872; HM, *Diary,* July 7, 1873; HM to EC, Dec. 14, 1873. See also HM to EC, June 23, 1872, Apr. 27, 1873.

26. HM to EC, Oct. 14, 1872. Edward Magill wrote of his son's death: "I must not dwell here upon what has been a bright and hopeful period of my life, but can only say that this boy, after the promise of a bright future, passed on to the life beyond." Magill, *Sixty Five Years,* p. 91.

27. See Elisabeth Griffith, *In Her Own Right: The Life of Elizabeth Cady Stanton* (New York, 1984), pp. 13–15. See also Margaret Foster, *Significant Sisters: The Grassroots of Active Feminism* (New York, 1985), pp. 209–11.

28. HM to EC, ca. April 27, 1873; HM, *Diary,* April [*sic*] 20, 1873. The grades of early Swarthmore graduates are housed in the Friends Historical Library, Swarthmore College.

29. HM to EC, Mar. 29, 1873; HM, *Diary,* May 26, 1873. See also Swarthmore College Commencement Day Program, June 13, 1873, HMW Papers; HM to EC, June 10, 1873, June 18, 1873, June 20, 1873. Susan B. Anthony had visited the Magill family a month before commencement, and Helen's address, which has not survived, was no doubt influenced by conversations with her. See HM, *Diary,* May 27, 1873.

30. HM, *Diary,* July 1, 1873, May 26, 1873.

31. HM, *Diary,* Dec. 13, 1873, June 20, 1873, Oct. 12, 1873, May 5, 1873, May 3, 1873. See also Magill, *Sixty Five Years,* pp. 167–69.

32. HM, *Diary,* Nov. 3, 1873, Nov. 2, 1873, Dec. 13, 1873.

33. HM, *Diary,* Dec. 13, 1873, Apr. 17, 1874, Mar. 28, 1874. See also HM, *Diary,* Oct. 12, 1873, Apr. 23, 1874. Helen's humor sometimes stressed the fulfillment of aspiration through influence rather than accomplishment. Her great missionary plan, she told Eva, was "to marry the Chinese emperor (I look so like their court beauties) and so insinuate myself into his good

graces as to get him to assist me in educating the women in China." HM to EC, Aug. 8, 1873.

34. HM, *Diary,* Oct. 12, 1873.

35. *Notable American Women, 1607-1950* (Cambridge, Mass., 1971), 3:143-46 contains a brief biography of Ellen Swallow Richards.

36. Helen thought the quip of a Harvard mathematics professor to a dim-witted undergraduate equally applicable to her: "Sumner, I can't whittle a mathematical idea small enough to get it into your head." HM to EC, Oct. 4, 1874. See Joyce Antler's astute discussion of the "family claim" in "After College, What?: New Graduates and the Family Claim," *American Quarterly,* 32, no. 4 (Fall 1980): 409-34.

37. John Tyndall, *Address Delivered before the British Association at Belfast, 1874* (London, 1874), pp. vii, 2; see also Tyndall, *Six Lectures on Light Delivered in America in 1872-1873* (London, 1873). Tyndall lectured in Philadelphia, and Helen almost certainly read the text of his address. For the connection between Helen's love for Appleton and her religious crisis, see HM, *Diary,* Oct. 8, 1874.

38. HM, *Diary,* October 8, 1874; HM to EC, Sept. 30, 1874; HM, *Diary,* May 3, 1873. See also HM to EC, July 21, 1875. Helen respected Tyndall's mind: the atoms, she thought, had "made a good thing of it when they formed his combination." After this crisis, Helen claimed, "nothing since has ever quite looked so bright to me," but her actions, feelings, and perceptions do not seem any different after the fall of 1874. HM to EC, July 21, 1875. In *The Feminization of American Culture* (New York, 1977), Ann Douglas has brilliantly explored the "softening" of religion by an alliance of women and clergymen. Helen would have attributed the decline of theology in the nineteenth century to the growing dominion of reason, not to its diminution.

39. HM to EC, May 17, 1874; HM, *Diary,* Apr. 23, 1874. See also HM, *Diary,* Mar. 30, 1874, July 1, 1874, Dec. 13, 1874; HM to EC, July 19, 1874, Aug. 30, 1874.

40. HM, *Diary,* Mar. 28, 1874, Jan. 17, 1875, Feb. 26, 1875; HM to EC, Sept. 21, 1873, May 23, 1874, May 30, 1875.

41. HM to EC, Nov. 8, 1873, Dec. 28, 1873, Apr. 18, 1875, May 16, 1875; HM, *Diary,* May 14, 1875. For a useful summary of Clarke's argument and the responses to it, see Rosalind Rosenberg, *Beyond Separate Spheres: Intellectual Roots of Modern Feminism* (New Haven, Conn., 1982), pp. 5-17.

42. HM to EC, July 13, 1873, March 16, 1873. John and Robin Haller discuss the medical implications of dress reform in *The Physician and Sexuality in Victorian America* (Urbana, Ill., 1974), pp. 146-74.

43. HM to EC, Sept. 20, 1874; Warren is quoted in Barbara Miller Solomon, *In the Company of Educated Women* (New Haven, Conn., 1985), p. 51. See also HM, *Diary,* June 30, 1873; Warren O. Ault, *Boston University: The College of Liberal Arts, 1873-1973* (Boston, 1973), p. 7. When the Association of Collegiate Alumnae (an organization of women graduates of college) was organized in 1882, Swarthmore was not included in the list of member institutions.

44. EC to HM, Oct. 25, 1874, Nov. 15, 1874. See also HM to EC, Oct. 21,

We know very little about Helen's two years at B.U. Few letters to her family during that period have survived; and since she was in the same institution as Eva, her erstwhile correspondent, the two seldom wrote. Many women in the nineteenth century experienced college as a "glorious interlude" where independence was the norm, responsibilities relatively few, and marriage and family duties present only as future possibilities. In dormitories and classrooms, groups of intelligent and sensitive young women studied, argued, and played together, sharing aspirations, supporting one another in failure and success, forging friendships that would last a lifetime. For Helen, however, it was never quite that way. At Swarthmore, as we have seen, she could escape neither the family claim nor the onus of being the president's daughter. At B.U. she was even more isolated. The only female graduate student, she had few opportunities to socialize with undergraduates. In poor health and a restless sleeper, Miss Baright turned out to be less than an ideal roommate, and when the rent was increased in January 1876, Helen took a room by herself. Ever conscious of family finances, she tutored students in Latin and Greek to help defray expenses. No doubt, she saw a good deal of Eva, with whom, unfortunately, she shared few classes. But for the most part B.U. was an academic rather than a social experience.[4]

During much of her last year in Boston, Helen worked on her doctoral thesis on the Greek drama. She pushed herself, never satisfied with what she accomplished yet always afraid that she might break down and permanently impair her ability to do scholarly work. If she could some-how be certain, she wrote, that constant study would not result in physical collapse, she would abandon all restraint. Nor did she know for sure that her degree would pry open "the gates of a successful career." Higher learning, it seemed, neither dispelled uncertainty nor definitively disproved the charge that women were endangered by too much "brain work."[5]

Teaching positions for women in higher education were few and far between, especially for someone who was unenthusiastic about all-girls' colleges. When asked by a sympathetic B.U. professor about a place at Swarthmore, Helen replied that "the Latin was all filled and Professor A had all the Greek." Rumors that Appleton might leave were "a dreadful turn" of the wheel of fortune, beyond contemplation. A temporary opening at Wellesley in Greek might be attractive, she told Professor Buck, but she wanted to finish her Ph.D. first. And Wellesley's "obnoxious rules," so typical of women's colleges, gave her pause. Perhaps parental anxiety made the rules necessary, "but it is almost incredible to me that a body of college girls should need such restrictions, as for instance the inspection of correspondence. It makes me think of the days when the

Mlles. [*sic*] Charbonnier would not allow us to mail letters even to our parents which had not been left open upon her desk." Apparently, Wellesley never offered a position to Helen, who continued to work and wonder.[6]

There was another option, one increasingly open to women. Study abroad had become virtually de rigueur for those Americans who contemplated scholarly careers. Helen, who thought herself ill prepared to sit in a professor's chair, could think of no better place for a classicist than Athens or Rome, each of which had faculties "cooperating" with Boston University. A story in the *Woman's Journal* about a woman who had attained the Ph.D. at the University of Leipzig suggested that Helen might be more welcome in Germany, where freedom of learning was apparently extended to women without reservation. "Qu'en penses-tu?" she asked Eva. "But I cannot let anything come between my mind's eye and Athens, the beautiful. If the familiar fairy should pop down the chimney and give me three wishes, I am sure that one of those wishes would be that after our two years at the B.U. we might study together abroad for two more years."[7]

In search of information about European universities, Helen wrote to the B.U. president. Opportunities for advanced study were limited in Italy and Greece, Warren replied. In Germany, women still had difficulty gaining permission to attend either public or private lectures. At Cambridge, he thought, Helen would find "all advantages." Further investigation confirmed his judgment of German universities, where, Helen learned, women had to "make the most of such crumbs as were grudgingly let fall" by the faculty. In England, female students seemed to be gaining access to all university resources, so she prepared to attend lectures at venerable Cambridge in the fall of 1877.[8]

More and more, Helen took "a certain satisfaction in being able to plan ahead like a man and not have to say, if I do not marry." Even if her certainty did not quite carry conviction, if her conclusions seemed calculated to "bring [her] mind a little more contentedly to the idea that there is not the least possibility of marrying," we need not doubt that she enthusiastically embraced the idea of study abroad. B.U. provided a degree; Cambridge promised a first-rate education.[9]

Although B.U. had been a disappointment, commencement in June 1877 was a joyous day for the Magill family. The university graduated "its first representatives," President Warren noted in his annual report—one master of arts, two doctors of philosophy. "Of the latter, one was a young woman—the first English-speaking women that ever received this high academic honor." The Ph.D., in fact, had been awarded to very few men in the United States. At B.U. this *schola scholarum* was designed primarily for those college graduates "who with little or no direct reference to fitting themselves for a professional life, may desire to receive post-graduate instruction"; secondarily it was for professionals in theology, law, and medicine who wished to "supplement their professional culture" by study in related fields. The "crowning and unifying department of the entire University organization," the Ph.D. was to resemble the *Studium Generale* of the Middle Ages, "restored and vitally adjusted to the modern Educational system."[10]

On the rare occasions that she referred to her doctorate, Helen made light of her achievement. Full of pomp, it signified little—not even a first-rate education. She did not wish to be addressed as Dr. Magill and professed embarrassment when the *Woman's Journal* ran a short announce-ment of her degree. Yet in the disclaimers one detects pride and a more focused ambition. "I can not regret my connection with the Boston University," she told her mother, "where I hope to find a permanent position, for which I believe I shall be thoroughly well prepared when I have finished my Cambridge course."[11]

While at B.U., Helen wrote for a public audience for the first time. The ostensible target of her essay "The Poor Little Birds," sent to the editor of the *Boston Advertiser,* was the movement to outlaw the slaughter of birds to obtain feathers to adorn bonnets. But in her "practical" observations on "the plumage agitation," she explored traditional views of gender differences, especially the male monopoly on reason and the female reliance on emotion. While exposing the "extravagant language and sentimentalism" of men, she tested the limits of a pragmatic calculus, unchecked by emotion and ethics.[12]

Sacrificing a bird for a bonnet, Helen began, was certainly no more objectionable than killing it for "the pleasure of a sportsman." Feathers, moreover, were as pretty or prettier and as useful on bonnets as on their natural wearers. They were seen by more people, lasted longer, and did more good so placed than feather-filled vases or stuffed birds in a trophy room. Flowers were not a satisfactory substitute because no woman could look into the "unwinking eye" of a violet, lily, or rose and "*not* be ready to allow the murder of a dozen birds to escape the nightmare." Whether ladies' hats should serve the purpose of exhibition was less a question of morals than of taste. "And for the birds themselves," Helen had no doubt that,

> if they realize the situation, they are as proud as an Ancient Egyptian at the idea of this mummified extension of their corporeal existence. I am quite sure that the more brilliant and showy of them are by nature and character wholly in sympathy with the motives in human breasts which prompt this display, and would willingly give up a year or two of hopping from twig to

twig in their native wilds for as many or more of posthumous ranging the
city thoroughfares and places of amusement, the admired of all beholders.
So for them *personally,* I am not concerned, at least not for those who gain
by a painless death a little longer memory, a little wider admiration.

Having admitted that a woman's desire to be attractive could be
deadly, Helen insisted that men had little justification "for horror at
feminine cruelty." After all, men insisted that women be pretty, and it was
masculine admiration that was the target of every feathered bonnet. As
long as men sought "eternal realities" through the medium of dress, they
should pause before they criticized the female preoccupation with
appearance. It was ironic, she thought, that men, who prevented women
from engaging in intellectual activities, now commanded: "You shall not
read Plato and Newton or Mill, neither have ten birds on your bonnet."

Perhaps, Helen concluded, the use of birds for adornment should
be restricted, but as long as men and women enjoyed "with entire com-
placency" a dinner of fowl, tame or wild, and as long as people forced those
who sang in a pleasing manner to live "the life of wretched prisoners . . .
[hopping] from one bare stick to another in conscious or unconscious
regret for the leafy boughs of their native or ancestral home," then the
moral revulsion they felt "if informed that natural taste and a defective
musical ear have led the cat to appropriate the canary" seemed like so
"much fudge." People liked birds for selfish reasons—their beauty, their
utility in destroying insects—and only secondarily, if at all, out of unity
with them as living creatures. Not for a moment did this affection
withstand "the lightest personal annoyance, inconvenience or advantage."
Thus, rather than yielding to a squeamish sanctimoniousness, reformers
should call attention to "the false economy of the present ruthless
destruction, and the inhumanity of any special processes of torture" by
identifying endangered species and examining the proper use of animals
by men and women. In the meantime, she would rather, "as cruelty goes,
wear a dozen stuffed birds on my bonnet than keep a caged canary."

"The Poor Little Birds" was an ingenious vehicle for Helen's medita-
tions on gender. Her practical approach demonstrated that a woman
could be logical, even cold, willing to accept the destruction of some
birds as part of the "operation of natural causes, good and bad." And since
the essay was ironic, she had the added advantage of not having to believe
everything she asserted. At the same time, she called attention to men's
inconsistencies and their complicity in the social value placed on adornment.
Nor did she shrink from mocking the vacuous sentimentalism of women,
who could weep for a flower while ordering a bird to be butchered. At
bottom, Helen believed that women did have an especially well developed

ethical and aesthetic sense, although too often the desire for admiration became the motive for self-adornment, with cruelty justified in the name of beauty. Best equipped to disentangle "an ideal love of the beautiful" from "vain self-gratification," women could only do so, she implied, apart from men, who encouraged them to please themselves by satisfying their beaus. Men tempted women to betray their true nature by trading an instinct for selflessness for a habit of hedonism. Nor was it surprising, finally, that Helen was more horrified by the traffic in caged birds than by the death of a living creature. Her own imprisonment had been by exclusion, from Harvard and from many European universities, and she knew that most women were less mobile than she. Birds did not belong in cages; and, by implication, her human sisters also should either live free or die.[13]

Unfortunately, Helen had not liberated herself from desiring to be the object of William Hyde Appleton's affections. For two years she had told herself that her regard for him was a passing fancy, but she admitted that when she returned home for the summer she might "be singing quite another song." Without feeling "quite reconciled" to the idea, she also entertained the notion that nieces and nephews could substitute for children of her own. She protested that she had "too good taste to fall in love with a man not worth having and no idea that a man worth having would make such a mistake as to wish for me." Still, she fantasized about keeping a case of choice cigars handy as solace for refused suitors, and when she met a young Bostonian who smiled like Appleton, she rejoiced in "a substitute, a reflection, which is a great satisfaction when I can't see the original."[14]

Most of all, Helen feared that her emotions were stronger than her judgment. She might enter into marriage, she thought, in the same way she purchased apparel: "When I enter a hat store all the discrimination which I seem to myself to have possessed on the street leaves me, a sudden frenzy possesses my mind, and I seldom come home without something which I detest as soon as I get it fairly home." Helen hoped to "die as chaste as Diana" rather than make the wrong marriage, yet did not think she was meant to be a spinster—"perhaps no woman is." Fearing pursuit as much as rejection, unwilling to tell Appleton how she felt, she returned to Swarthmore to prepare for the trip across the Atlantic.[15]

Two encounters with Appleton convinced Helen that he could "never have been especially interested" in her. Although she concluded that he lacked "moral earnestness," she told her diary that she still loved him and would marry him, if asked, but that she would not be stopped from going to Cambridge. Relief seemed mixed with disappointment as she booked passage to England.[16]

In the 1870s the doors of Cambridge University began to open to women. With the founding of Hitchin (later Girton) College in 1869, women had their first residential college, a separate environment where they could study full-time, free from family responsibilities. Girton's residential head, Emily Davies, insisted that women essay a curriculum identical to that of men, including the required test in Greek and the tripos (honors exam) for undergraduates. Girton students tended to concentrate their studies in mathematics and classics. In 1871 Cambridge professor Henry Sidgwick rented a house, arranged for Anne Jemima Clough, a leader of the North England Council for Promoting the Higher Education of Women, to become residential head, and Newnham College was born. Uncomfortable with the "outdated requirements at Cambridge," Sidgwick urged women to take a more modern (though at the time less prestigious) curriculum in political science, history, philosophy, and the natural and physical sciences. He did not insist on absolute equality between men and women, either in standards of admission or courses of study. On these issues and others, Sidgwick and Davies were constantly at odds, united only in the conviction that women could benefit from the intellectual environment at Cambridge.[17]

Two houses near the university grounds (it was considered too daring to bring the young women into town) did not, however, guarantee full access to Cambridge. At first the university agreed only to allow females to take the local examinations (admissions or qualifying tests for young men) under its control; soon a special examination for women over eighteen was designed and administered. The tripos was opened to women, but their papers were informally marked and they were not classed or ranked like the men. Professors could tutor the women, if they chose to do so, or open their lectures to both sexes. By the time Helen arrived, virtually all university lectures were open to women, while the more substantive college lectures were "gradually, but very gradually" being made available. Most important, Cambridge did not officially recognize Girton or Newnham and refused to grant women university membership, voting rights, or degrees. With a toe in the door, three Girton students passed the tripos in 1872, and two Newnham women followed suit in 1874. By then the university had a new category, graduate without degree, "a sort of wingless bird," Helen called it. Progressive dons and determined students predicted that women would soon join the ranks of Cambridge graduates.[18]

If Helen had known about the restrictions at Cambridge, she might have decided against study in England. Cambridge's policies resembled those of Harvard, although permission to study in residence made a great difference. Women could get an education, Sidgwick and other reform-minded dons emphasized; a degree certificate would follow in due course. Helen was not quite so sanguine, but she valued the generosity of the faculty. Harvard professors, she wrote, "wish that institution to hold out as long as possible," while Cambridge dons, more than half of whom opened their lectures to women, "wish just the opposite." She also loved Cambridge for the enemies it made, among them Charles W. Eliot, who must have known that the reform in England would soon spread to more provincial institutions like Harvard.[19]

The enthusiasm and erudition of the Cambridge faculty convinced Helen to stay and, after a year of uncertainty, to take the classical tripos. Although an undergraduate exam, the tripos was an ordeal requiring fourteen three-hour papers: two in prose composition, two in verse, two in ancient philosophy, one in classical philology, one in ancient history, and six in reading at sight. Helen's preparation at Swarthmore and B.U. was comparatively poor, especially in sightreading and prose and verse composition (skills not taught in American universities), and caused her to declare: "It is one thing to write in Greek unconnected sentences, however difficult, about what Cyrus could, would, or should have done if Clearchus had done something else, and it is quite another thing to be set down to a piece of Macaulay, Burke or Carlyle, and be expected to give it in some kind of Greek or Latin." Nonetheless, the tripos seemed "just the thing" to equip her for a scholarly position. The expense of several years of study was formidable, she knew, but teachers took "a more lively interest" in students who were "doing regular work."[20]

An inability to obtain a place at Newnham College, which was full when she applied, probably contributed to Helen's indecision about the tripos. Her choice of Newnham is a bit surprising, given Girton's emphasis on the classics, yet Newnham's support of philosophy was equally attractive. Evidently, Helen also had corresponded with the forceful Professor Sidgwick, perhaps through William Fairfield Warren, before she arrived in England. While she waited for an opening at Newnham, she found a place in Norwich House, one of several buildings that had been an all-male college in the town and now accommodated several Cambridge women. To save money, Helen selected a small room (board and lodging was £18 for the term, or $11.25 per week). The English style of living was quite spartan—no furnace, no bathtub, no closets, and a "pokey" fire that "livens the room and ventilates it, but heating is something rather out of its line." Once furnished, however, the room was cozy and Helen barely noticed the damp chill that invaded every English home.[21]

About seventeen girls lived at Norwich House under the watchful eye of Madame Rasch, a cultured, yet impractical and tactless, woman who was constantly at odds with her charges. Virtually all of Helen's housemates were younger than she, often by four or five years, and far less advanced scholastically; while she studied for the tripos, they prepared for Cambridge's less rigorous "higher local examinations." She found no friends at Norwich, but some of the girls looked to her for guidance and academic assistance, and she responded with an almost maternal affection that came naturally to the eldest of five sisters. Acclaimed "leader of the house," she frequently got into trouble with Madame Rasch by openly challenging the rules. Helen attributed the conflict to her irrepressible independence, but clearly the girls looked to her to undermine her rival's authority. Although she missed the companionship of intellectual equals, she felt herself settling into the position of a "not too discontented old maid—having reached the advanced age of twenty-four and never caused a sigh. At least, I think not." At Norwich House, Helen glimpsed into the future of a spinster-teacher with resigned acceptance.[22]

Newnham College was different, as was Anne Clough, a wise, sympathetic, and maternal woman of "culture and high principle" to whom Helen turned for advice. Unlike the Norwich girls, the Newnham women were comrades in the struggle to demonstrate that intellectual distinction was not monopolized by men. Newnham's neat brick building with white trim and spartan furnishings hinted at its serious purpose, but when the students gathered in unison for dinner, in small groups over cocoa, or in pairs in someone's room, they shared aspirations and fears, the frivolous and the portentous. When two women got firsts in the tripos of 1880, a feat equaled by none of the men who took the exam, the Newnham community rejoiced. The official lists were a blank, a delicious if disturbing irony noted by the Newnhamites, who guessed that Cambridge reactionaries were willing to let "the women go in but . . . hoped they will know their place." For perhaps the first time in her life, Helen experienced the bonds of womanhood. In the sorority of Newnham, she drew strength from the triumphs of brilliant students like Miss Merrifield, who was sure to join the staff of Newnham as a lecturer.[23]

Helen was able to share confidences with her new friends, especially with Alice ("Peggy") Lloyd, an eighteen-year-old orphan. More and more, Helen and Peggy paired off, with the older woman combining the roles of friend, advisor, mother, and lover. Helen tucked Peggy into bed each night with a tender caress; and Peggy often sat on Helen's lap, placing her head gently on her shoulder. All of Helen's emotional energy was poured into the relationship. "I have never loved anyone as deeply as I do Alice," she wrote in her diary, certain that life would lose all value the moment it became clear that "Peggy's friendship would not last forever." She knew that when Peggy married, the relationship would be transformed or even ended, a fate too likely to dismiss but too far in the future to confront.[24]

Helen's relationship with Peggy was stormy. Taking a platonic view that pure love commanded absolute devotion, Helen was demanding and suspicious, quick to brand her young friend's attentions to other women a betrayal. Helen began to feel that Peggy valued affection most when she did not have it, and she was compelled to be cross and cold to rekindle Peggy's passion. Because she "could not bear to see the thing decay gradually," Helen suggested that they "break the connection," hopeful, no doubt, that Peggy would refuse. Again and again they fought and reconciled. Yet even when Helen returned Peggy's letters and "threw the envelopes with the daisies into the fire," her anger could not hide her desperate desire. Early in 1879, when Peggy spurned her advances, Helen thrashed about in bed, dreaming that she saw Miss Crofts putting Alice to bed; rude to her rival, she then imagined that Miss Martin (a Newnham lecturer) "was in my bed and trying to kill me. And I struggled to move but could not, when suddenly it changed to Alice who was weeping bitterly and came and laid her head beside me on the pillow. But when I asked what made her weep so, she said she had hurt her finger." In her dreams, Helen could release rage at her rivals and entice Peggy into her bed; but even her unconscious could not extract an expression of love.[25]

Homoerotic relationships were quite common in women's institutions on both sides of the Atlantic. Because the women who formed such attachments often accepted heterosexual love as normative, "smashing" was rarely seen as deviant. In a recent discussion of relationships between college women, Martha Vicinus observes that lover and loved came together in a communion of sorrow and self-sacrifice, gaining knowledge and fulfillment through a seemingly "endless articulation of each newly aroused feeling, each action, each hope." If not quite love by conversation, these often chaste, but always passionate, couplings allowed women to explore new roles, express feelings, take initiative, solicit and spurn, be cross and cold with their partners. We do not know the nature of Helen's physical relationship with Peggy, but her writing implies that she was confused, even afraid, of the sexual urges she felt. Helen, who dared not approach William Hyde Appleton, could pet and tuck in Peggy, teach and taunt her, travel with her, mother her. Confined to the halls of Newnham and the pages of her diary, the affair was comparatively safe. Helen, an "absurdly cautious" person, had this once risked her feelings but not her reputation. Burned by the fires of love, she resumed her studies. And in time, she even established a correct and occasionally cordial relationship with Peggy, confined to public places or group activities.[26]

Helen regained her equilibrium, but only by withdrawing from female intimacy. She pronounced her capacity to love a casualty of the moral frailty of others and the risks of making herself vulnerable: "I doubt if I could ever again throw my heart so completely and so confidingly into an attachment." She felt herself growing "cooler every day," her ideal of love more and more "a beautiful impossibility." Reconciled to spending much of her time alone, she looked more critically at the three classes of Newnhamites: a small set of church people, "pleasant enough but quiet and indifferent," a bit too pious; a group of good-hearted, fairly clever girls with little culture; and a cultured and interesting, but weak, affected, and conceited, clique who wore "insufficient underclothing" and embraced high art and atheism. Helen was not disliked, but no one really took to her. Yet she was determined to succeed at Cambridge, and as she sat alone with her diary she vowed: "If this does not kill me, I believe it will [make] me stronger and better, more of a woman." To be a woman, presumably, required retreat from the sorority of Newnham. If Helen loved again, she would love a man—and she would be passive in her passions.[27]

Newnham's academic advantages continued to outweigh the discomfort Helen felt at remaining in the house. As soon as she had arrived in England, Henry Sidgwick and Anne Clough had taken an active interest in her. In early October 1877, Mrs. Sidgwick invited Helen to lunch, soon followed by tea with Miss Clough at Newnham. The Sidgwicks introduced Helen to Richard Dacre Archer-Hind, a tutor and lecturer in Greek at Trinity College, who gave instruction to women interested in the classics. Only four years older than Helen, Archer-Hind had received a "first" in the classical tripos at Cambridge and won the first Chancellor's Medal for classical learning. Appointed assistant lecturer in 1877 and assistant tutor a year later, he was to have a long and distinguished career at Cambridge as a fine teacher and specialist in Platonic studies. Small, short, and bashful, with side whiskers that almost met as a beard and a very English voice and manner, he seemed almost comical to Helen: "Has not he a name? It represents an entire hunting scene, pursued and pursuer." When the two retired to the study for a tête-à-tête, Helen took note of his intellect, knowledge, and quiet conviction. He said he regretted that Cambridge was "not yet enlightened enough" to grant her a degree and listened intently as she told him all she had read in Greek and Latin. Within days Archer-Hind sent his pupil printed passages from Plato, Aristotle, and Thucydides, to be translated without reference books. Helen passed this examination, though she "succeeded very badly." He announced that while there was a good deal yet to do ("You must remember that these papers were designed to test to the utmost students who have had many years' practice in translation"), she had the makings of a good Greek professor.[28]

Helen Magill, ca. 1873. Courtesy of Friends Historical Library of Swarthmore College.

The Magill sisters: (*standing, left to right*) Gertrude and Beatrice; (*seated*) Helen, Marian, and Eudora. Author's collection.

Edward H. and Sarah Warner Magill. Courtesy of Friends Historical Library of Swarthmore College.

William Hyde Appleton, professor of Greek and German at Swarthmore College. Courtesy of Friends Historical Library of Swarthmore College.

R. D. Archer-Hind, Cambridge classicist and Helen's coach for the tripos. Courtesy of Trinity College, Cambridge.

With Archer-Hind as her coach and Mr. Verrall, another brilliant Trinity man, as her Latin instructor, Helen set her sights on the tripos. She dropped Sanskrit (which was not part of the exam), joined three students in her coach's Greek class, took Latin with Mr. Verall, and Latin composition ("very, very hard") with Mr. Nixon of King's College. Although she declined Archer-Hind's offer to repeat the lectures for his advanced class in Greek at his home, in order to save her the fee, she thought her mentor "an angel." Indeed, when her parents began to "cogitate" on her enthusiasm for him, she reminded them that he was "short-sighted and far from handsome" and then quoted Madame Rasch's remark "that he was 'very safe,' by which I suppose she means that I am very safe." For the moment, however, she felt "quite as if I had come to Trinity," the college she would have chosen if she were a man: "I wish I were, for three years, almost."[29]

Caught up in the spirit of Cambridge competition, Helen contemplated first class, a distinction not yet won by a woman in the classical tripos. Such a grade, or even a "good second class," would assure her a position in England if one did not open up immediately in the United States. Although she preferred Boston University ("that is far enough from home"), Helen was willing to accept expatriation as the price of a scholarly career. She also began to allow herself moments of confidence. She spent hours on her sight-papers, wrestled with Aristotle and Thucydides, "made something out of Plato, [and] managed almost all of Tacitus, if not of Cicero." Before the first term ended, she was bold enough to correct Archer-Hind on a point of Greek grammar; by the second term, she had moved into the first division of Greek. Archer-Hind was so pleased with her Latin philosophy paper, "he said that if I could do that I could do what no one else had done." Helen told her mother not to mention her tutor's comment about the possibility of a first class, but she began to think that desire just might give birth to the deed.[30]

As in the past, Helen's hopes also bred doubts and fears. The mere thought of a third class, or even a second, gave her a "premonitory chill." If she disgraced herself and her family, she would "disappear into parts unknown." Less well prepared than Cambridge men, who had had the thorough training of the public schools, women were forced to study harder, but Helen suspected they were often unable to withstand "the prolonged strain." She tried to shrug off the trouble with her right eye but could not study, and a consultation with an oculist provided little relief. Might the critics of higher education for women be right? Or might it be that *she* was not smart enough? After a "bad paper" on Agamemmon she described herself as "very stupid in class—had to have the same thing explained seventeen times and then didn't understand very well. Poor Mr. A–H had a hard time but was very politic. Finished the Ag. at last!!! No I can't believe it. Began in October growing stupider and lazier every day. Think two years will be enough to forget all I have ever learned. Poor Tripos!" To be mediocre, "seated in the mean," would be the most miserable of all fortunes, fatal to aspiration but not unlikely for a woman who thought herself slow and uncertain, who tired whenever she worked hard.[31]

The family claim reached across the Atlantic to add to the pressures Helen felt. Although Edward Magill assured his daughter that "no money that I pay out is paid with a better will or less grudgingly," he acknowledged that the family was making substantial sacrifices to support her. Her four sisters could not study abroad until she was established, "as it is about all Papa can do with the whole income derived from the investment of [his] money and his own salary to meet the family expenses and carry his insurance." To catch up with the men, moreover, would take Helen at least three years. She tried to economize, but England was expensive, especially if a woman wanted to be suitably attired to venture into society. Helen wanted to help, but all she could do was worry while her sisters waited.[32]

Because she dreaded that the results of the tripos would neither satisfy parental expectations nor justify the expense, Helen was subject to "low spirits." "How I wish I had your freedom from limitation," she wrote to Eva Channing. She often thought of going home, and in 1878 Edward Magill responded to his daughter's letters, filled with evidence of anxiety, ill health, and overwork, with the news that he had submitted a teaching application for her at the Boston Public Latin School. Helen was stunned. Mr. Healey, her alleged champion in Boston, was, she claimed, "the gentleman who said the only girl ever at the Latin School was 'a complete failure'." Helen agreed to do what her father thought best, but she made it clear that she wanted a university appointment:

> I should prefer, if you think I may, to take the tripos course here, as I hope to do well, and I think it will be of the greatest advantage to me. And then something might grow out of it such as a lectureship here which would keep me longer in Cambridge. I spoke to Miss Clough incidentally of my Latin School possibility and she said it was a pity for me to take such a situation and that if I staid for the tripos something might be done. But she spoke very indefinitely and I can't tell what she meant, but I know they want to have lady lecturers at Newnham as soon as they can. And then I think I ought to have no difficulty in getting a situation in America when I return.[33]

Against such a brief Edward Magill made no rebuttal, though from time to time he asked Helen to consider returning home. Concerned about her health, he no doubt thought a high school position, especially at Boston Latin, an excellent opportunity. On another occasion he advised her to return to Swarthmore to replace William Hyde Appleton, who planned to spend a year in Europe. Sarah Magill proposed a different solution for her daughter's "dyspepsia": marriage. Whatever the inducement, Helen did not waver. She thought of marriage as one of those "remedies worse than the complaint. Not that I do not consider marriage a most excellent institution, theoretically; but at least in taking the dose I should be extremely particular about the person who should administer it." She could be content, she was sure, living with one of any number of people, man or woman; but marriage, which could not be dissolved like friendship, was too risky. "Not that I am led to consider this subject by any applicants. . . . and I'm afraid my opinion of anybody would not be improved by his doing so." As to the tripos, Helen argued against "running away" when she could fight "for the honor of my sex and country." When her father cabled "Helen's decision to stay approved," she disingenuously insisted that she had made no such decision and may even have "inclined toward going home if thee could find me a suitable place." She did not feel that a dutiful daughter should insist on staying; indeed, she wanted her father to be a partner in her aspirations. She had been given her three years and knew that she must prove they had been worth the expense.[34]

By exercising feminine influence—ritualistic and rhetorical submission to male authority combined with assertion in the form of request—Helen got her way. But the experience was distasteful. In commenting on Grandma Magill's paean to the ways of women, Helen asked: " . . . but *how* do they get it? by diplomacy and pretending they are not getting it at all. And let them get it, but that will *never* be my method. I am willing to be submissive, as much as I can, because it is the right thing in certain positions, but *not* to get my way. If anything is to be got in this world by candour and also by propriety of behavior I am willing to try for it, but I prefer to leave diplomacy to people a little more sophisticated, and much good may it do them." Of course, this one time it *had* been her method.[35]

The pillar on whom Helen leaned in these uncertain times was Archer-Hind. In his quiet way he expressed confidence in her academic prowess, and to ease her financial problems he helped engineer a $175 scholarship, sending praise along with congratulations. He wrote that he knew Helen too well "to imagine you capable of returning across the Atlantic . . . allowing the examiners to retain possession of the field and set up a trophy over your pusillanimous flight." He had seen the work of many students and was sure that she was capable of becoming a scholar. That

Helen disparaged her progress did not surprise him, "for everyone whose work is worth a cent is dissatisfied that it is not better—and I don't want you to be satisfied; but discouragement is quite another thing, and in your case I see no cause of it whatsoever."[36]

Careful not to generate unreasonable expectations, Archer-Hind gingerly touched on his student's weaknesses as well. Helen's "persistent thoroughness and intellectual honesty," her refusal to rest content until she understood a subject completely, and her implacable determination to think things out for herself would, he felt, hinder her in the tripos, which rewarded those who amassed "the maximum quantity of facts and opinions in the minimum of time." She must understand that a second in the tripos for a woman was equal to a first for a man, especially in her case, since she would not take the exam in verse. Archer-Hind was convinced that if Helen preserved her health, remained calm, avoided discouragement, and conquered her tendencies toward "discursiveness and want of concentration," she could acquit herself quite well.[37]

The results of Helen's exams in 1880 were encouraging. Her three philosophy papers were better than those of any of the men at Trinity. Among the few students she had not bested were two who were expected to be at the top of the tripos lists in 1881. Mr. Jackson, Helen's lecturer in philosophy ("that married old bachelor with the pipes and cats") expressed surprise at any doubt about a first; she, in turn, cautioned herself that he did "not know about [her] exam capacities." Even Archer-Hind could not contain his enthusiasm. When Helen told her tutor that several of her teachers were "quite hopeful," he responded: "And I suppose you think I am very much discouraged." "I know you are," she replied, and when he smiled, Helen got the point. Only two of the fourteen tripos papers were in philosophy, and she therefore begged her parents not to take any "general encouragement." But with Archer-Hind's blessing she scheduled her exams for early 1881.[38]

By 1880 Helen's respect for Archer-Hind had turned to love. The two seemed well matched in many ways, sharing intellectual interests and a passion for music and gardening. With the end of her affair with Peggy Lloyd, Helen had shivered in loneliness. Now she could contemplate marriage with a man prepared to accept her as an equal—and perhaps work as a lecturer at Newnham as well. Not fully trusting her feelings, and certain that Eva Channing, fellow spinster, would not understand, Helen turned to her mother, asking in a note marked "private" how she had known she was in love. Had it been gradual or sudden? Helen's request for "some remarks on the subject in general" was accompanied by a stern admonition: "But don't draw any unwarranted inferences." Mar-

riage should secure Helen's happiness, Sarah Magill advised, and her
sisters' needs should not get in the way of a suitable match, especially not
at her somewhat advanced age. As for the man in question, he should
have a fine character, suit Helen's taste, fill a prominent station in life, and
not be too young or without experience; after all, her parents had great
hopes for their first-born and did not want to see her "claimed by any
second-rate person." Although Archer-Hind fit the profile, Helen kept
her own counsel, denied the existence of a likely candidate, and extracted
a pledge from her mother to say nothing to Edward Magill. Meanwhile,
her love grew with each tutoring session. Archer-Hind was as attentive as
William Hyde Appleton had been coy and distant—yet every bit as
enigmatic as his American counterpart.[39]

As the tripos approached, Helen learned that Archer-Hind was in love
with Miss Merrifield, the pre-eminent student at Newnham. The young
woman had burst into Helen's room one day with the news that he had
revealed his feelings. The two chatted for a while, but when left alone
Helen "turned cold and trembled violently for some time." Was a judgment of her intellect implied in Archer-Hind's choice? That Miss Merrifield
loved another man and had gently rebuffed Archer-Hind's offer of affection did not ease Helen's pain, but it may have raised the stakes of the
tripos, for Miss Merrifield planned to leave Cambridge after her marriage.
Might Helen take her place as lecturer or as wife? Because Cambridge was
teaching Helen to expect disappointment, she dared not hope that Archer-
Hind could love her—but she hoped nonetheless.[40]

Helen turned to poetry to plumb the depth of passion felt and repressed,
writing in "The Passing of Love":

> Speak not a word breathe not a sigh
> While the sweet spirit of love goes by
> From thence an after-chill may be
> Upon thy heart too heavily.
>
> No word she spoke, no sigh she breathed
> With careless smiles her lip was wreathed
> And in a silence all unbroken
> Love came and went and knew no token.
>
> I wonder if she felt at all
> Deep in her heart one slow tear fall
> One soundless sigh no echo stirred
> A dream of pain that knew no word.
>
> Love came and went: she sat alone
> But in the silence deeper grown.
> The afterchill brought her no moan
> 'Twas breathed upon a heart of stone.

She had always been "inclined to distrust any passionate feeling," she wrote in her diary in the space just below the poem, because she feared it might be instigated by "that skillful counterfeiter the imagination, whose articles are only to be told from the genuine by the wear—when it is too late to retrieve the venture." Passion for Alice Lloyd and now Archer-Hind, however genuine, had not worn well, but Helen knew that to distrust her feelings was not to control them; nor did it seem to matter whether she expressed her love or held it in reserve. Without explaining what had prompted her to write the poem, she sent it to her mother, who asked Helen to explain its meaning. In her response, Helen distanced herself from the protagonist who wished to avoid suffering by now allowing herself to feel and in the process "lost her capacity for feeling . . . [and with it] not only that which she may have gained of joy, but suppose the joy to have failed—the gain which it is even to suffer nobly." In this curious way, then, she flirted with what one might call the cult of Christian spinster-hood, replete with notions of the joy of sacrifice and suffering, of a chaste life ennobled by service and ushered in by unrequited love.[41]

While wrestling with her feelings, Helen entered the final months of study for the tripos. Eyestrain, various aches and pains, and nervousness broke her concentration. Unwilling to confide all the sources of her difficulties to anyone, she turned to her parents. Had Edward Magill really read fourteen hours a day in college? How had he done it, and could a woman hope to match such a pace? Would Sarah Magill get a physician to prescribe medicines "which will make me able to study very hard"? There simply seemed to be too much to learn in too little time. Any passage in Greek or Latin literature might appear on the exam; any English tale, no matter how "musty or crabbed," might have to be translated into one or the other language. Anxiety and physical weakness worked together to sap Helen's willpower and transform her brain into a colander; once in their grip, she could not free herself. The "remarkable memory" she had had as a child was gone; the "hard brain work" required for advanced study seemed beyond her. Inclined to believe the average woman weaker mentally than the average man, she was certain she was weaker physically. Willpower, courage, and determination depended on a sound physical and mental constitution. She could not forget the prediction of Dr. Hermann, the Magill family physician: if she worked too hard she would take the edge off her mind.[42]

In part to escape Archer-Hind, whose efforts to help no doubt increased her agitation, Helen journeyed to Brighton but found little relief in the damp and cold of an unusually severe winter. Her mother's homeopathic remedies, so successful in the past, could not conquer "sleeplessness, mental dullness and indigestion, frontal headache," and the expressions of concern and encouragement from home made her even more distraught. Sarah Magill worried about her daughter's health but sent contradictory messages across the Atlantic, at once prescribing rest and quiet and then asserting that Helen's maladies would not be seriously affected by increased work—"go on fearlessly," she advised. One day, she believed, Helen would write a "remarkable book." Archer-Hind, noting Helen's "tendency to take the most despondent view," urged his pupil to keep up her health rather than bury herself in paperwork. With little stamina she could neither study hard, rest, nor free herself from a sense of impending disaster.[43]

Helen took the tripos during the last week in February 1881—and did as badly as she had feared. The strain of the exams was great, and with a sense of "unfitness for the work," she became "positively frightened," unable to cope with the papers before her. If some "fortunate questions" had not been asked in history, she would have written nothing. As it was, she wrote "great bosh, repeated [herself,] and said queer things." The Greek exam was little better. She left out the "piece of Aristotle and did the rest badly. Theocritus atrociously." As she waited an agonizing three weeks for the results, she could only hope to avoid a "pluck" (failure). Archer-Hind tried to soften the impending blow. As they strolled through Trinity Garden, he remarked that her philosophy paper had been very good and some of her translation papers "very fair"; but rhetoric was not so good, and her compositions had really pulled her down. If Helen got a third, she must take comfort in knowing she did not deserve it. She was not so sure, Helen told him, for she hadn't "much opinion of [herself] lately." "But I have," Archer-Hind replied. "I have enough for two." Unfortunately, Helen observed, he could not give her the superfluous half, for when she learned that she had gotten a third, placed somewhere in the middle of the class, she returned to her room for "a little weep," walked "to and fro, and buried [her] ambitious hopes."[44]

Even her family could not console her. More concerned about her "morbid condition" than the exam results, they were sure Helen would bring honor to her sex and country in a responsible educational position at home. Wouldn't testimonials from her teachers compensate for her place in the tripos? Hadn't she done splendidly in philosophy? And wasn't it better to stand high in one department and do poorly in others than hand in average work in all? After all, Americans understood little about the tripos and could simply be told that she had excelled in ancient philosophy, while ill health hindered her in other areas. The harder her family tried, it seemed, the colder the comfort they provided. "Some greater good" would surely come out of "the toppling ruins of this cherished ambition," Sarah Magill predicted. If Edward had not forgone scholarship for teaching and administration, "He might have edited some wise edition of the ancient philosophies and not have accomplished half so much good in the world." Helen, who did not share her mother's view that administrative work was superior to scholarship, tried to convince herself that she would attain academic distinction some day, though she felt "as if life was not long enough" to get her back to her old self. Perhaps her place in the tripos would not adversely affect her reputation, "but it ought to have crowned it. That is the thing."[45]

Helen was right: a lectureship at Newnham was now out of the question. Four years of study in Europe had not enhanced her prospects in the United States, as they would, for example, for her contemporary Martha Carey Thomas. Thomas, also a Quaker, had chosen coeducation (at Cornell) and been frustrated by the paucity of opportunities for women to do graduate work. Excluded from seminars at Johns Hopkins, where she sat behind a curtain listening to Professor Basil Gildersleeve's lectures, she escaped, first to Leipzig, which did not grant the doctorate to women, and then to Zurich. In 1882 she received a Ph.D. summa cum laude. The presence of her father and uncle on the Bryn Mawr board of trustees no doubt helped her win an appointment there as dean and professor of English, though her pre-eminent qualifications were at least as important.[46]

Helen's mediocre performance in the tripos, an undergraduate honors exam, may have cast doubt on the significance of her doctorate, but equally important was the shattering of her self-confidence. Unlike Martha Thomas, who was "too practical to enjoy the equivocal illumination of self-doubt," Helen was unsure of her own ability. We do not know—nor could she—how much the agitation over Archer-Hind, isolation at Newnham, and inadequate preparation affected her or how well she might have done had she written another dissertation, where her thoroughness would have been an advantage, her lack of speed less of a handicap. All she knew was that she had not measured up, and in a society that rewarded only "superwomen," she doubted that she deserved a university appointment. Nor was she willing to succeed by abandoning all thought of marriage and single-mindedly abjuring entangling alliances with men. Unable to study to the beat of a pounding heart, she might well have neither marriage nor a satisfying career.[47]

Inconsolable about her prospects, Helen took some satisfaction from her role in expanding the educational rights of Cambridge women. The high score of a Girton student, Miss C. A. Scott, on the mathematics tripos in 1880 ignited protests that the young woman should receive a B.A. When the men's rankings were announced, women "interposed" (shouted out) Miss Scott's name in its proper place, remembering Anne

Clough's advice that the best way to get your rights is to take them: "Don't say very much about it my dears, but just take them." A Newnham memorial, circulated in the fall and signed by 8,000 people, asked the university to grant "properly qualified women" admission to examinations, official recognition, and the right to receive degrees. The cautious Henry Sidgwick, forever at odds with Girton, hesitated to go this far and instead urged Newnhamites to support a petition asking for some formal recognition short of the conferring of degrees. "Tactless criticism" of university policy, he believed, would hurt the movement. Before long the Cambridge syndicate appointed to review the policies of the institution had fifteen memorials to read, all but two requesting admission to degrees. In January 1881, just before Helen took her exams, the committee (Sidgwick was a member) issued a report advocating formal admissions to the tripos with a certificate granted to qualified women, their names to be printed in a list separate from the men. The committee declined to address the issue of granting degrees, "for reasons which its members felt unable to discuss." Within a month, in a resounding vote of 366-32, the faculty adopted the recommendation.[48]

Helen dubbed the vote a "Great Day for Newnham" and joined in the evening of dancing and rejoicing that followed the faculty meeting. She was not satisfied by the compromise, however, and joined other Girton and Newnham students who had passed the tripos in a petition to the vice chancellor and the senate. The "anomalous position" of women students at Cambridge, they wrote, put them *in* the university but not *of* it. Acknowledging with gratitude the "singular courtesy and kindness" of the faculty, the petitioners maintained that "the privileges at present enjoyed are held on a precarious tenure." The experiment of admitting women to the tripos, moreover, had been so successful that "the time may be considered to have arrived" to extend to duly qualified students of the women's colleges "the privileges of membership of the University and admission to its Degrees."[49]

The petition did not persuade the senate—women had to wait until 1923 for admission to degrees—but Helen's participation in the movement provided a sense of accomplishment. The first American woman to take and pass the tripos exams, she had had the courage to risk the displeasure of Henry Sidgwick by going beyond the recommendations of the syndicate. In time, women would be admitted to full membership in the Cambridge community, and future generations would owe some small debt to her.

In the spring of 1881, Helen Magill prepared to leave Cambridge. Her last meetings with Archer-Hind were bittersweet. She appreciated his expressions of confidence in her, especially after the tripos, but confessed:

"Alas, if he cared for me half of that confidence would be mine and I should be myself again." Since only his love could free her imprisoned self, his chaste kindness, so emblematic of his sterling character, tortured her. The two made a compact to exchange views on ancient philosophy, a subject in which Helen was sure to excel when she could "work after [her] own fashion ... no longer plagued by tiresome coaches and tyrannous examinations.[50]

As she walked around the Newnham grounds and "began to look about in that hopeless way in which one does," Helen may well have recalled a poem she had written two months earlier. "Sing to me, thou sweet Hope! One more day" was a summoning of the will of a still-proud woman who was returning home to an uncertain future. Determined to pursue "an energetic and systematic course, to trample despair under foot," she prayed to her muse: "Or false, or true, sweet Hope, / Sing on Today."[51]

NOTES

1. HM, *Diary,* Oct. 24, 1875.

2. HM to Mrs. Richards, Dec. 8, 1886. See also *Boston University President's Annual Report,* 1876–77, p. 31.

3. HM, *Diary,* Oct. 24, 1876.

4. HM, *Diary,* Jan. 25, 1876; HM to EC, Aug. 7, 1876. Girls who boarded in town, Eva Channing observed, "are rather scattered, and do not have any clubs or common boarding-places...." EC to HM, Nov. 25, 1874. For two recent treatments of the nature and value of social networks in the higher education of women, see Barbara Miller Solomon, *In the Company of Educated Women* (New Haven, Conn., 1985) and Martha Vicinus, *Independent Women: Work and Community for Single Woman* (Chicago, 1985).

5. HM, *Diary,* Feb. 27, 1877. See also HM, *Diary,* Nov. 3, 1876.

6. HM, *Diary,* Oct. 30, 1876, Nov. 7, 1876. See also HM, *Diary,* June 10, 1876.

7. HM to EC, Aug. 31, 1875. For B.U.'s arrangements with the Universities of Athens and Rome, see *Boston University Year Book,* vol. 4 (Boston, 1877).

8. HM to EC, Aug. 28, 1877. See also HM, undated ms. on higher education in England.

9. HM, *Diary,* Sept. 24, 1876, May 7, 1876.

10. *Boston University President's Annual Report,* 1876–77, p. 31; *Boston University Year Book,* 4:118.

11. HM to SWM, Feb. 5, 1878. See also *Woman's Journal,* 8, no. 37 (Sept. 15, 1877): 89.

12. The manuscript of this essay is in the HMW Papers, but I have not been able to locate it in back issues of the *Boston Advertiser.*

13. During the past two decades, feminist critics have explored in detail the

power of the observer and the vulnerability of the observed. See, e.g., John Berger, *Ways of Seeing* (New York, 1977).

14. HM, *Diary,* Jan. 11, 1876, May 7, 1876, June 4, 1876. See also HM to EC, postcard, ca. Summer 1876.

15. HM, *Diary,* Mar. 27, 1877.

16. HM, *Diary,* June 28, 1877.

17. See Rita McWilliams-Tulberg, *Women at Cambridge: A Men's University— Though of a Mixed Type* (London, 1975); Barbara Stephen, *Girton College, 1869–1932* (Cambridge, U.K., 1933); Martha Vicinus, *Independent Women: Work and Community for Single Women* (Chicago, 1985), pp. 122–62.

18. See McWilliams-Tulberg, pp. 13, 83; Vicinus, p. 126. The prohibition against granting women degrees was an advantage in one respect. Coaches depended on fees from their pupils, and since the main object of male students was to win a high place on the exam lists, coaches did little more than spoon-feed information to them. Because their names were not published, women were tutored more often by college lecturers interested in scholarship and woman's rights rather than fees and rote memorization. See HM, undated ms. on higher education in England.

19. See HM to EC, in "The Contributor's Club," *Atlantic Monthly,* 42 (1878): 637–39. Helen was angry that the *Atlantic* did not include her assertion that Harvard offered women half a loaf and required them to find the yeast and flour: thus was "the rose presented to the American public without its thorn." HM to SWM, Sept. 17, 1877; HM to EC, Sept. 29, 1878. Helen's parents had sent the letter to William Dean Howells for publication, and Helen insisted that it be printed anonymously and "above all that my Ph.D. does not accompany it. I will never let that be written till I have taken a good standing at Cambridge." HM to EHM Oct. 19, 1878. See also HM to Elizabeth Miller, Oct. 3, 1877; HM to SWM, Mar. 19, 1879.

20. HM, "The Contributor's Club," p. 637.

21. HM to Elizabeth Miller, Oct. 3, 1877. See also HM to Parents, Sept. 30, 1877, Jan. 13, 1878.

22. HM to EHM, Apr. 18, 1878; HM to EC, Jan. 5, 1878. See also HM, "The Contributor's Club," p. 638. As if to underscore how unattractive she was, Helen told her parents of a baby-faced undergraduate, with spectacles on his innocent nose ("Ug in arms," she called him), whom she met from time to time in public places "and who—but I forbear." HM to Family, May 1, 1878. Helen's tone may have been jocular because, as we shall see, she was in the midst of a love affair with Alice Lloyd when she wrote this letter.

23. HM to EC, Jan. 5, 1878; HM to EHM, Feb. 8, 1880. For a description of life at Newnham, see Vicinus, pp. 121–62.

24. HM, *Diary,* May 14, 1878. See also HM, *Diary,* Mar. 3, 1878, May 14, 1878, May 30, 1878.

25. HM, *Diary,* Dec. 3, 1878, May 30, 1878, Mar. 3, 1878, Mar. 17, 1879, Mar. 18, 1879.

26. HM to Parents, July 2, 1878; Vicinus, pp. 142–47, 160–62, 187–99. See also Solomon, pp. 99–101. Helen and Peggy apparently visited each other's rooms, possibly in the presence of others. More often, the two played tennis.

27. HM, *Diary,* Feb. 9, 1879; HM to SWM, Feb. 23, 1879; HM, *Diary,* Mar. 20, 1879.

28. HM to EC, Oct. 8–10, 1877; HM to Parents, Oct. 21, 1877; R. D. Archer-Hind to HM Oct. 10, 1877. For more information on Archer-Hind's career, see *Dictionary of National Biography, Supplement—1901–1911,* vol. 1 (London, 1951), pp. 49–50. Anne Clough spent most of her first sixteen years in South Carolina. Shy, awkward, ill-at-ease with boys, her isolation was, in some ways, similar to Helen's. See Deborah Gorham, *The Victorian Girl and the Feminine Ideal* (Bloomington, Ind., 1982), pp. 135–41.

29. HM to Parents, Oct. 21, 1877, Nov. 24, 1877. Amused that one of the dons would not allow ladies to attend his lectures without a chaperone, Helen vowed to get an old woman "to give me respectability." HM to EC, Oct. 8–10, 1877.

30. HM to Parents, Nov. 19, 1877; HM to SWM, Aug. 29, 1878; HM to Parents, Sept. 30, 1877; HM to SWM, Feb. 5, 1878, ca. February 1878. See also HM to Parents, Nov. 24, 1877, Dec. 15, 1877.

31. HM, *Diary,* Dec. 25, 1877; HM to EHM, Oct. 19, 1878; HM, *Diary,* June 5, 1878, Mar. 6, 1878.

32. EHM to HM, Nov. 5, 1880; HM to SWM, Sept. 19, 1878. See HM to EHM, Oct. 8, 1877, for a list of Helen's expenses.

33. HM to SWM, Mar. 19, 1879; HM to EC, fragment, ca. 1879; HM to Parents, Jan. 23, 1878; HM to EHM, fragment, ca. March 1879.

34. HM to EHM, Nov. 2, 1879, Jan. 3, 1880, Mar. 24, 1880, Apr. 19, 1880.

35. HM to SWM, Sept. 4, 1878.

36. R. D. Archer-Hind to HM, Aug. 11, 1879, Sept. 9, 1879. See also HM to EHM, Nov. 2, 1879.

37. R. D. Archer-Hind to HM, Mar. 22, 1880.

38. HM to EC, June 22, 1880; HM, *Diary,* Apr. 12, 1880; HM to SWM, Oct. 19, 1879; HM to EHM, June 18, 1880.

39. HM to SWM, Apr. 24, 1880; SWM to HM, Dec. 19, 1880; HM to SWM, May 22, 1881.

40. HM, *Diary,* ca. Oct. 1880.

41. HM, *Diary,* ca. Nov. 1880; HM to SWM, Jan. 23, 1881. Helen later changed the title of the poem to "Love Denied."

42. HM to EHM, Dec. 7, 1879; HM to SWM, Feb. 8, 1880, Sept. 2, 1880, Jan. 15, 1881, Feb. 15, 1881; HM to EC, Feb. 3, 1879, June 22, 1880. Another student, Isabelle Clemes, took the tripos before Helen and urged her to consult a physician as early as possible. HM to SWM, Jan. 28, 1881.

43. HM to SWM, Jan. 28, 1881; SWM to HM, Feb. 10, 1881, Mar. 2, 1881. See also RDAH to HM, Jan. 27, 1881, Mar. 5, 1881; HM to SWM, Sept. 30–Oct. 2, 1880, Mar. 7, 1881.

44. HM to SWM, Mar. 7, 1881; HM, *Diary,* Feb. 26, 1881; HM to SWM, Mar. 22, 1881; HM, *Diary,* Mar. 24, 1881. For a letter of commiseration from a Newnham student that attributes Helen's performance to fate and bad weather, see B. Swindells to HM, undated.

45. SWM to HM, Mar. 12, 1881, Mar. 20, 1881; HM to SWM, Mar. 22, 1881. See also EHM to HM, Apr. 19, 1881; SWM to HM, Apr. 25, 1881; HM to SWM, Feb. 6, 1881. One wonders how Helen reacted when her mother suddenly remembered Francis Gardner Magill, who had had no chance to distinguish himself: "Oh what a bright day it will be for us all when we sit once more together, an unbroken family circle, for will not our 'dear boy' be always present in our midst." SWM to HM, Mar. 27, 1881.

46. For a brief description of Thomas's education and early career, see Barbara M. Cross, ed., *The Educated Woman in America* (New York, 1965), pp. 31–37.

47. Cross, p. 31. For a brief description of superperformance as the "obvious approach" to professional status, requiring "hard work, outstanding ability, and the willingness to sacrifice traditional relationships," see Penina Migdal Glazer and Miriam Slater, *Unequal Colleagues: The Entrance of Women into the Profesions, 1890–1940* (New Brunswick, N.J., 1987), pp. 211–16.

48. McWilliams-Tulberg, pp. 73–80; HM, undated ms. on higher education in England.

49. HM, *Diary,* Feb. 24, 1881; Petition to the Vice Chancellor and Senate of the University of Cambridge, Undated.

50. HM, *Diary,* Mar. 21, 1881, Mar. 24, 1881; R. D. Archer-Hind to HM, Apr. 15, 1881. See also R. D. Archer-Hind to HM, Aug. 15, 1881.

51. HM, *Diary,* May 5, 1881, Mar. 3, 1881.

CHAPTER THREE

"Something better to do than accept second best"

During Helen's final spring at Cambridge, her father began to search for a job for her by writing to the presidents of Smith, Vassar, and Wellesley colleges. Sarah Magill, who promised she would not be "a maneuvering mamma anxiously looking about . . . for some eligible parti," encouraged her daughter to teach at one of the better females-only colleges: "*Real women* are sick of farces and pretensions [like the Harvard annex] and want something in education which has the true ring of the real metal." She thought an offer might well come after Helen met with President Caldwell of Vassar and presented her letters of recommendation.[1]

Edward's letters generated enthusiastic responses but no offers. No one doubted Helen's qualifications—in fact, the Vassar president asked her to lecture on "The Higher Education of Women Abroad" or "Opportunities for Post-Graduate Study"—she was simply in the wrong field. Unwilling to be restricted to the humanities and fine arts, women in the late nineteenth century began to study science and the newly emerging social sciences, practical fields more appropriate for careers in homemaking or public service. As students won the right to elect courses, enrollment in the classical languages declined precipitously. Faculty appointments reflected these changes in the curriculum and the message from women's colleges was always the same: professorships in Greek or ancient philosophy were not available; openings were not anticipated. Many women's colleges, moreover, preferred to hire their own alumnae. Coeducational schools experienced the same pressures on the curriculum, with few matching Boston University's willingness to hire women. All-male institutions, of course, refused even to entertain the idea.[2]

Of little help to Helen's pursuit was Archer-Hind's frank letter of recommendation. Although her reading was "necessarily not yet extensive," he wrote, her knowledge of Greek and Latin was sound, her literary sensibility commendable, her grasp of ancient philosophy "worthy of special notice" and comparable to that of the ablest Cambridge student. He added that if her health had not completely broken down in the tripos (she was "almost incapable even of the mechanical labor of writing out her answers"), she would certainly have had a second. Although he could not "too highly" praise her thoroughness, earnestness, and analytic powers, he had sown the seeds of doubt by calling attention to her collapse under pressure. She would, it seemed, have to settle for less—or wait, like Mr. Micawber, for something to turn up.[3]

Because he knew that college positions were not easy to secure, Edward Magill thought about starting his own school. His experience at Swarthmore demonstrated how few young people were adequately trained for a higher education, and a first-rate preparatory school might therefore find a ready constituency; and, in time, it might even grow a college branch. By staffing the school with his daughters—Helen as principal, Eudora in mathematics, Gertrude in French and English literature, Beatrice in art—he could bypass the vicissitudes of the job market. Helen's career could resemble his own, and the family could live and work together, until matrimony intervened. The plan was attractive, Helen agreed, if her father could secure financial support and find a suitable building in Philadelphia.[4]

While she waited, Helen lived at Swarthmore, serving as secretary to her father, keeping busy around the house, delivering lectures at women's colleges, and thinking often of Archer-Hind, "that funny little figure, with his short quick step, his whiskers streaming away on each side behind him, Plato under one arm, his umbrella held stiffly out in front by the other, and his eyes fixed upon different quarters of the heavens." Would she ever again see his "beloved ugliness"? And when would she do serious work in ancient philosophy? Frightened by their daughter's near-breakdown in Cambridge, the Magills were not at all unhappy that the fates had conspired to give her a year off. Helen said little about her year at Swarthmore, but the lure of family life and domestic chores—and, perhaps, fears about her health—must have made it difficult to concentrate on the classics. Uncertain about her future, she simply marked time.[5]

In the summer of 1882, Cyrus Elder, an old friend of Edward Magill, appeared at Swarthmore, had breakfast with the family, and offered jobs to Helen, as principal of the coeducational English Classical Academy in Johnstown, Pennsylvania, and Dora, as instructor of mathematics. With their father's blessing (he had not been able to secure financial backing for his own school), the two young women accepted. If Helen had qualms about administrative work, she said nothing, aware of the absence of alternatives and her sister's eagerness to begin teaching. High school teaching, moreover, was sometimes the first step toward a university professorship. Alice Freeman (Palmer), a University of Michigan graduate, for example, began her career as principal of a high school in Saginaw,

Michigan, then became head of the history department at Wellesley and, in 1882, president of the college. Helen, who was to work with Freeman in the Association of Collegiate Alumnae, may well have been inspired by her example.[6]

Although the appointment was not Helen's idea of scholarly life, it shook her out of her intellectual lethargy. Less than a month after Elder's visit, an article in the prestigious *North American Review* aroused Helen's ire. In "Woman's Work and Woman's Wages," Charles W. Elliott attacked the women's movement by calculating the social costs of employment outside the home. Technological improvements, he reasoned, had made useless such female occupations as spinning, sewing, and weaving and would soon replace cooking with commercial food preparation. The twentieth century therefore promised insufficient work for women, whose labor was worth "about one-eighth [that] of a man." For Elliott, the foremost question of the modern age was how to "secure for woman, or to restore her to, her normal position and value."[7]

Women could not successfully compete with men in physical labor, Elliott argued. Hard work made a woman "common, coarse, ugly, dirty— undesirable, except as a beast of burden," and tended to produce "diseased and deformed children." Even in tasks requiring dexterity rather than strength, female mill workers produced at about half the capacity of men, and typesetters, telegraphers, sewing machine operators, and bank tellers reported "indigestion, diseases peculiar to women, general debility." Doctors had discovered that the knee joints of women prevented them from standing for long periods of time, as did the wider female pelvis, which tended to "press the upper extremities out laterally." In Europe, Elliott acknowledged, women had to work in order to eat, but "enlarging the sphere" of women in the affluent United States was unnecessary and unproductive. Women simply were not good enough workers to support themselves. He reported that the *New York Times* had recently found that the average salary of female laborers in New York City was about four dollars a week. In the workplace, women lowered men's wages by dividing the existing work; they were "the least valuable of created beings."

According to Elliott, women were equally unsuited for intellectual activity. The great strain of the reproductive function, hundreds of doctors agreed, incapacitated all but the most exceptional women. Thus, because one fifth of a woman's life was—or, in Elliott's opinion, should be—devoted to maternal concerns, a man could devote 20 percent more of his time and energy to work. Since men were judged to have more blood and larger brains than women, their competitive advantage could not be overcome. Like Dr. Clarke, Elliott thought coeducation and professional aspirations were foolish and injurious to women's health. As with physical labor, women would merely divide the work, depress wages, and make it more difficult for men to support their families.

A college education and the vote, Elliott argued, would add the burdens of "thought, time, struggle, and perhaps service" to frail and vulnerable women already occupied with more important responsibilities. Women needed the protection that could only be secured through marriage, yet by competing with men for jobs, they engendered hatred and rivalry, making themselves "disagreeable" companions. Not surprisingly, he wrote, marriage was "growing more difficult for women and less desirable for men": women no longer knew how to keep well and handsome; nervous women made poor wives; "impracticable theories" stressed the desirability of self-sufficiency; many men could not afford to marry; the attack on marital laws had weakened the institution. The "true cure" for women and the nation, Elliott concluded, was neither suffrage nor higher education but marriage, the only institution wherein women could earn their keep—by helping husbands and children.

A conventional assault on the women's movement, this article hit the exposed nerves of an unmarried woman approaching thirty whose health had suffered as she competed in the tripos. Spurred by the prospect of a public debate, Helen immediately composed a reply. Angry at Elliott's deprecation of the intellectual ability of women, she nonetheless argued over means and not ends, for she, too, believed in the desirability of marriage and motherhood and did not advocate work outside the home for women after marriage. Her concern, not surprisingly, was with women who were waiting for the right men. Self-sufficiency for these women was not an impractical theory but an economic necessity that enabled them to strengthen the institution of marriage by entering unions based on love and common interests.

Helen began by disputing Elliott's reading of history. The old days, she noted, were anything but good, for women were forced to yield to the "brute-force" of men. Fathers and brothers often conspired with suitors to arrange marriages based on expediency rather than love. A family's responsibility to its female members was temporary, lasting only until one dependency could be traded for another. Support was a gift, a duty, a financial burden, and women had few options: they could be maintained by parents and relatives or sell their "motherhood to such a bidder as offered the least humiliating terms." In contemporary America, however, the status and circumstances of women were much better than they had been in the ancient world. Acting on their "natural desire" for self-development and individual achievement, many women now searched for alternatives to the doctrine and practice of female inferiority. As they gained economic self-sufficiency, women were free to marry for love, for the first time in history. If young people at times seemed reluctant to marry, they were simply being "more exacting in their demands." Now that they had "something better to do than accept second best," Helen argued, women refused to compromise their "ever nobler ideal of a worthy manhood." If men curbed their "self-indulgent habits" and stopped viewing women as ornaments who could not and should not work, the number of marriages would increase. The experiences of single women made them amenable to hard work and economy, willing to take on domestic duties and uninterested in a place on a pedestal. Men who could not afford to keep an "idol at home to receive everything and do nothing" need not worry, Helen wrote, for the new American woman, trained in the virtue of labor and the vice of an unwise indulgence, was ready to work and sacrifice for family, country, and race.[8]

Elliott's desire to close the world of work to all women was, according to Helen, a patent medicine remedy prescribed for the wrong illness. The crowding of the professions, the disappearance of handiwork, the decline of health attributable to tea, coffee, alcohol, tobacco, and high-pressure living, all were social evils that could not be cured by returning women to the home. Nor should the relatively greater productivity of the average male be used to discriminate against all women. By this un-American denial of opportunity to individuals, more able women would be forced from the field simply to make places for average men. Why not, Helen wondered wickedly, banish all single men to reduce the surplus of labor? Working single women, no doubt, would "agree to allow something for the maintenance" of these men, even though they deemed them unsuitable for marriage. This solution was at least as fair and practical as Elliott's, although Helen preferred laissez-faire, however harsh, to any arbitrary exclusion.

Professing no expertise on the subject of manual labor, Helen focused on higher education to counter Elliott's assertion that women were ill suited to intellectual activity. He knew "all that is worth knowing" about the academic activity of men, she wrote, but "appears to have taken little pains to inform himself" about the education of women. The testimony of virtually all presidents and faculties that admitted women, as well as the majority of physicians with "*practical* knowledge" of females, had demonstrated that higher education did not damage health. Helen, whose own experience confirmed that college students were healthier than those women "at the center of a system of social delights," offered herself as evidence in a misleading (if carefully qualified) account of the "terrible ordeal" of the honors exam at Cambridge, which often caused "vigorous men" to faint but did no permanent injury to women, many of whom ("especially the younger ones") studied "in fine health, from beginning to end." She concluded that she would rather face a tripos "than undertake the mingled mental and moral strains" often endured by a housekeeper.

A college education, the vote, and employment opportunities would, Helen maintained, assist women while advancing civilization, and the sad fate of societies that shut women out of public life and intellectual companionship with men suggested that these experiments deserved at least a trial. After all, she wrote, Elliott's gloomy pictures of the present, "mingled with half-regrets for the past and half suggestions," amounted to little more than complaints. Woman's rights were part of the inexorable march of progress, the light of hope "to guide and cheer our dark and toilsome way." Did Americans really want to turn their backs on the future?

By connecting the women's movement to the popular doctrine of progress and portraying woman's work as an antidote to the decline of marriages that some considered the prelude to Anglo-Saxon "race suicide," Helen made more palatable her call for "freedom and equality of position" for females. Employment outside the home was, in her mind, a temporary expedient, for single women ascribed to marriage and motherhood the deepest "moral and spiritual significance," the very "mainspring" of their being. Her plea to extend the sphere of women was really a plan to escort them to kitchen and crib, and she thus bemoaned the tendency of working-class women to go into factory work rather than domestic service, because the latter was an ideal training school for marriage. For middle- and upper-class women, the "natural desire" for self-development must at some time be suppressed, she argued, and an instinct for self-denial substituted for it. She knew when that was, but she did not know how, nor did she address Elliott's claim that the experience of individual achievement might become habit-forming, making women less interested in a subordinate role in marriage and less attractive to men.

In a sense, Helen wished the problem away by failing to take note, for example, of the movement to give married women a legal right to the wages of their labor outside the home, an issue debated in state legislatures (and in the pages of the *Woman's Journal*) throughout the 1870s. In good marriages, she assumed, wives rarely worked; those who did would have neither the desire nor the need to lay claim to their salaries. Even in the modern age, wedded women traded freedom for responsibility. "Only our failures marry," Martha Carey Thomas once defiantly proclaimed. Helen did not agree. For her, marriage remained the noble ideal of womanhood, though she had let the genies of aspiration and achievement out of their bottles.

Helen sent her essay to *The North American Review* and within a week it was returned—with a rejection notice. Charles W. Elliott was not Harvard president Charles W. Eliot, Helen's old nemesis, and many of her barbs had hit the wrong target. Amused, disappointed, but not deterred, she altered the manuscript and sent it without success to *The Atlantic* and then to Thomas Wentworth Higginson, who accepted it for *The Independent.* "Women's Work in the Nineteenth Century," by "Professor Helen Magill," appeared on October 5, 1882, shortly after Helen took over as principal of the Johnstown High School.[9]

A provincial western Pennsylvania city with about 8,000 inhabitants, Johnstown did not resemble the college communities to which Helen had become accustomed. Moreover, the townspeople did not warm up to the austere, direct, sometimes draconian spinster who, with the aid of two assistants, sought to impose discipline and order on the educated boys and girls, aged ten to seventeen, who attended the high school. The previous principal, Helen believed, had been popular in part because he was "disgracefully slipshod," keeping no records and paying little attention to the wayward habits of his pupils. Driving herself, her staff, and her students very hard, she taught German, French, English history, and literature, in addition to a numbing administrative routine. "I correct exercises and compositions and make out reports," she wrote to Eva Channing. "I write letters to parents in which I mildly but firmly refuse to let their young hopefuls have entire control of my methods of discipline and instruction. I glare at boys till I think my eyes will wear out. I am rather exhausted at night and on Saturdays and Sundays I darn my stockings." The Johnstown boys evidently tested the new principal, who established her authority with a firmness that may have been excessive. Soon, the "pretty severe things" she said to parents about their children began to be repeated all over town.[10]

Only Helen's missionary faith in coeducation kept her going in this unrewarding job, with "juvenile Johnstonians" forever blocking her from any sustained study of ancient philosophy. Encouraging letters from Archer-Hind also helped. Because he deemed the education of women "the most important question afoot just now," he urged her to persist even if her material was "somewhat raw" and the work often "uphill." After all, she had "a certain combativeness" native to Anglo-Saxons, which had had "much to do with making the fortunes of the said race." Helen must ignore those who viewed her as a "harmless fanatic," until, through coeducation, women's powers "were developed to the utmost and allowed free play."[11]

Try as she did, Helen could not keep the faith in Johnstown. At best she received grudging respect from the students, who were ill prepared and little interested in a curriculum laden with Latin and Greek. "Ignorant opposition" from Johnstown parents grew, moreover, with every effort to improve the quality of education. "I might spend twenty years working up a decent school here," she told her father, "and be worn out and rusty by the time I had broken the ground for the kind of work for which I am specially prepared. The children have no ambition, the parents have none for them, they are utterly undisciplined at home, and the majority of parents resent school discipline." Although Dora Magill thought her sister had been patient, Helen pleaded guilty to Cyrus Elder's charge that she had not been sufficiently conciliatory at first. She became more careful after she learned of the whispering campaign against her, but by then the damage had been done. Parents and scholars groaned because the term ended fully a month after the public schools closed, and a number of students left the school because of the "steady pressure for work and order." Many townspeople thought Helen was "a horrid old thing . . . [with] a sharp tongue and very decided ways." Yet with time, she believed, they might appreciate her impartiality and amiability. If she wished to make changes, however, she would have to continue to be "severe and rather inflexible on some points."12

Although, "considering the material," Helen saw some improvement among the students, she decided to leave Johnstown at the end of her first academic year. A social Sahara, the city contained few cultural attractions. Moreover, she had learned that the life of a female administrator was often lonely. Unlike teachers, who had colleagues, principals had subordinates who could not be companions. Helen spent a good deal of time with Dora, but as supervisor and surrogate mother; she loved and counseled, though did not confide in, her sister. Willing to instruct the children of Johnstown, Helen was neither equipped to essay the education of a hostile community nor prepared to back down to court popularity. Elder pleaded with her to change her mind. He had "blown his trumpet" in support of her reforms, and despite the difficulties he felt that significant progress had been made. His own prestige on the line, he fumed that Helen had no "missionary spirit": he would "never have anything to do with advanced women again." They parted good friends, Helen reported to her father, but we "do seem to be leaving him in a mess."13

Early in 1883, Edward Everett Hale, the famous orator and minister, had approached his old friend Edward Magill in behalf of some prominent citizens of West Bridgewater, a small town in southeastern Massachusetts. The group was establishing a nonsectarian high school for girls, in accord with the bequest of Capt. Benjamin Beal Howard, who had left $80,000 for this purpose at his death in 1867. Sounded out by Hale about his willingness to invest in and/or become principal of the Howard Collegiate Institute, Edward Magill revived his Philadelphia plan and recommended Helen for the position: "Helen is nearly 29—as old as the new Prest. of Wellesley [Alice Freeman]—her scholarship is second to that of no woman in the country, I can safely say, and she has had excellent success in organizing an English Classical Academy at Johnstown, Pa."14

The Howard school, Magill informed his daughter, provided "a Providential opening for thy work" and a splendid opportunity for Dora and Gertrude Magill to teach. With six or seven grades, it might eventually accommodate 200 boarders and day students. At the outset, the school would have a large preparatory department but might grow into "the first truly liberal college for women in the country, in the end!" Edward was not positive, at this point, that the trustees would accept a woman as head; nonetheless, he reminded Helen that the alternatives were few. The Orthodox Quakers who founded Bryn Mawr, for example, had little use for Hicksites like the Magills, "so I want thee to take the other girls, and head this '*Howard Academy!*' "15

Helen needed little persuasion. In the open field of higher education of the late nineteenth century, Howard's collegiate aspirations were not fanciful, although the competition for a still-small pool of qualified girls had grown fierce. With an academy for boys nearby, Helen could even hope one day to preside over a first-rate coeducational institution. In any event, with her father's agreement to invest in the school, the trustees gave Helen, sight unseen, a five-year contract as principal of an academy for young women of any denomination "to pursue their studies as far as at Smith College or Wellesley College." She would have "entire direction of the school," including appointment and payment of teachers and management "in every detail." The trustees pledged to furnish a boardinghouse for four instructors and forty students and to pay the tuition of any West Bridgewater girls who passed the regular course of study in the grammar school. Helen's salary was $1,000 a year, out of which she must pay advertising costs and other incidental expenses.16

As soon as the school year ended in Johnstown, Helen raced to West Bridgewater—and found confusion and chaos. The academy was to open in the fall, but buildings had not been completed nor students recruited. In constant touch with her father, Helen placed advertisements in *The Nation* and the *Woman's Journal* and put together a handsome brochure describing the Howard Collegiate Institute. Applicants for admission, it announced, must be at least twelve years old, able to read and write English "as difficult as Hawthorne's children's books," with a thorough knowledge of "common and decimal fractions" and a background in geography and history, "which will be tested conversationally." The academy offered a traditional course of study, with emphasis on classical and romance languages, English, history, and mathematics. Few science courses were available, and instruction in music and drawing was limited by requirements in the other areas. Although no college courses would be offered in the first year, "no pains [would] be spared" to prepare Howard students for any institution of higher education open to them in the United States; in fact, the upper grades used material from an ordinary college curriculum. Located in a desirable neighborhood, equipped with a boardinghouse that resembled "a comfortable home," where principal, instructors, and students lived together as a family, Howard provided an ideal educational setting. The residence was arranged on the cottage system, with each student (as at Newnham) assigned to a single room to encourage study and individual development. A number of luminaries, most of them friends and associates of Helen and her father, lent their names to the enterprise: Newnham's Anne Clough, Trinity's R. D. Archer-Hind, the poet John Greenleaf Whittier, Boston University president William F. Warren, astronomer Maria Mitchell, suffragist Lucy Stone, Swarthmore's William Hyde Appleton, University of Michigan president James Angell, and Cornell University president Andrew D. White. Widespread publicity, the Magills hoped, would fill the halls of Howard.[17]

Helen did not expect the Howard Institute to compete with Harvard for some years, but she did want to build a college worthy of the name. The problem with higher education in the United States, she believed, was that half of the colleges were, or tried to be, universities, while the others were, but tried not to be, high schools. Eventually, the Howard Institute would conduct students "through a carefully arranged course in essentials, allowing the element of option to enter only a very little toward the close." By admitting students as they emerged from childhood and surrendering them as well-prepared men and women, colleges would free universities to concentrate their resources on advanced research and study. As a model intermediate institution, Howard might lead the way to a more rational higher education in America.[18]

As the inaugural day approached, only a handful of students were in residence. This was not a cause for alarm, Edward Magill told his apprehensive daughter, because the sizable number of day students from West Bridgewater and its environs would compensate for the small number of boarders. Who, after all, would send a daughter away to an untried school? "Its work must begin on those near," he wrote. "There is a safe little nucleus. . . . " The scarcity of students fed on itself, however. When Mrs. Lothrop brought her three daughters from Sharon, Massachusetts, to West Bridgewater, she discovered unfinished facilities and few pupils. Only Helen's promise that the girls would be sent home if more students did not enroll persuaded Mrs. Lothrop to register them. Students would appear after opening day, Helen told herself, when public exercises and good speakers began to advertise the school.[19]

On October 2, 1883, Dr. Helen Magill presided over the opening of the Howard Collegiate Institute. Joined by nine boarders (one of whom was fifteen-year-old Marian Magill) and nineteen day students, the eight-member faculty of instruction and government (including Eudora Magill, instructor in mathematics, and Gertrude Magill, instructor in modern languages, English literature, and elocution) began the business of education. High prices for a school without a reputation (board and tuition was $350 a year) kept the enrollment down, but a steady flow of inquiries about Howard was encouraging. At the moment, however, the financial condition of the school was precarious.[20]

Helen's management of buildings and grounds was, from the outset, a source of concern for cost-conscious trustees. When she arrived in West Bridgewater she found a cesspool near the boarding hall. Afraid that living "on the borders of a lack of sewage" would expose students and staff to diphtheria and typhoid fever, she asked the trustees to drain it immediately, begged her father to "make a fuss" about it, but could not persuade the building committee to appropriate the funds. "How any body of men can be so wickedly negligent or so grossly ignorant I can't understand," she fumed. Openly critical of two members of the building committee, Benjamin B. Howard (one of Captain Howard's sons) and Charles W. Copeland, Helen took matters into her own hands, hiring contractors, establishing a garden, purchasing equipment, and exhorting Francis E. Howard to wrest control of the school's finances from his brother.[21]

Edward Magill counseled caution. To save money, Helen should conserve fuel and burn lights only when necessary. A trip to Swarthmore should be postponed to avoid losing "an unnecessary day—so much depends upon the impression this first year makes; and little things sometimes go a great way. . . . " Most important, Helen must explain to the trustees her desire to build an institution that "will be a great credit to all concerned with it." Accepting her father's advice, she held her tongue and tried by dint of hard work to win over several important trustees. On the janitor's day off, for example, she took the poker in hand every two hours, singing "Rake, rake, rake with care / Rake in the absence of the janitair." Even the flinty-eyed Mr. Copeland came to lavish praise on her budgetary acumen, noting "the remarkable business faculty of our talented principal." But if Helen hoped that her "troubles with gas-men and such like torments" were over, she knew she had not "reduced the trustees to a state of submissive subjection." They were beginning to listen, however, agreeing to her request to place a woman on the board, even if they did not appoint her candidate. Although Benjamin Howard remained a dangerous foe, unwilling to defer to a woman in fiscal matters, Helen anticipated a solid second year for the Howard Institute.[22]

At first things did seem better. The little boardinghouse was filled with students, and Helen persuaded the board to authorize her to raise funds to enlarge it. At times she seemed the perfect diplomat: assuring a worried guardian that tuition and fees covered a little dentistry or a call or two from a doctor; or bending the rules to grant a leave of absence to a student in accord with her parents' wishes. But Helen could not always stop herself from saying what she thought: telling Josephine Littlefield that her guardians only "pretended to love her"; or speaking severely to Dolly Burke when the girl failed to heed her instructions. Some parents welcomed such strictness, applauding, for example, Helen's swift and firm response to the young man who was doing all that he could "to cause meetings" with Alice Jones. Still, fatigue and the frequently unrewarding duties of a principal took their toll, as at Johnstown. Helen enjoyed teaching history but found that she could do little more than drill the students in elementary Greek and Latin. Plato lay unopened on her desk, a casualty of meddlesome trustees and "constantly shifting lesson-giving."23

More troubling was the fact that enrollment at Howard was shrinking. From hindsight, we know that the Magills' timing was exquisitely bad. Community after community in Massachusetts built public high schools in this period, and, as Reed Ueda has recently shown, parents began to exercise a preference for keeping children at home. New boarding schools like Howard had difficulty attracting students, in part because, with small staffs and tiny endowments, they could not offer the range of courses available at many high schools. By introducing modern languages and science into the curriculum, and not requiring Greek, Helen tried to keep up with educational trends. But the larger schools could offer the classical curriculum and the English curriculum *in addition to* the Latin-scientific course of study adopted at Howard. Some parents, no doubt, continued to prefer a classical curriculum for their daughters, for whom knowledge remained ornamental rather than utilitarian. Meanwhile, colleges were pushing preparatory functions down to the high schools: whereas only twenty-six colleges in the United States had no preparatory division in 1870, two decades later colleges had less need to supply themselves with students. The Swarthmore model of a college emerging out of its preparatory division was an anachronism.24

As enrollments declined, so did trustee confidence in the principal. Although Helen directed her most caustic descriptions of Benjamin Howard to her family ("Mr. B.B.H. is a fraud"), her contempt for him was well known. She accused him of covering up the drainage problem by carrying the board's reports on the matter to a vacation hotel in Bermuda. She sizzled when the building committee, at his direction, prohibited her from ordering anything without written permission from two of its members. Her principal ally, Francis Howard, was sympathetic but had neither the personality nor the power to bend the building committee to his will. Caught in a cross fire between his family and his principles, dismayed by Helen's testy suggestion that he be more aggressive, Francis Howard frequently fled for cover, taking refuge in the claim that he had done more for the school than anyone else. He knew that Helen worked hard and that she assessed priorities "from a different standpoint" than the trustees, but he also felt that she should lower her expectations and be more careful with money. The letters she wrote to him, he chided, had two one-cent stamps on them when a penny would suffice. With such support, Helen concluded that she was on her own.[25]

In 1884, Benjamin Howard turned his attention to the boys' school in West Bridgewater and Helen feared that the girls' institute would lose a substantial piece of the Howard bequest. Perhaps the two schools could be joined, she suggested to Francis Howard, if a merger would not lower admissions standards. Although he did not think that the time was right, he agreed to ask the board to put Helen in charge of the boys' school, after she promised to grant the boys "equal privileges with the girls." At the fall 1884 board meeting, a resolution authorizing Helen to select teachers for the boys' school was hotly debated. Benjamin Howard shrewdly argued that it would be a great injury to the collegiate institute if the two enterprises were mixed in the public's mind, as few parents would send their boys to an institution known "simply as a girls' school." In a stinging rebuke, the trustees voted 5-3 to deny Helen power over the boys' school.[26]

"The indifference and apparent coldness of the Trustees," who did not invite her to deliver any public addresses on education after 1884, was now out in the open, Helen wrote. Benjamin Howard wanted to see her proposals, in writing, for paying interest on improvements before he agreed to call a board meeting. He objected to her plan to use the dining room for dancing, thinking it might endanger property and suggesting instead that the little room adjacent to the dining room would be a sufficient music room. Although he expressed interest in having things "as agreeable as possible," while representing his concern as "simply about expenses," Helen felt that his sugar-coated praise for her "good work" did not cover his contempt. She nonetheless pressed on, perhaps hoping that trustee interference would turn to indifference, yet determined to be principal in fact as well as in name.[27]

Although several parents withdrew their daughters from Howard because it provided no teacher training, Helen turned aside suggestions that the institute become a normal school. With support from her father, who believed that "the way to make good teachers is to *teach* them well, and have them well grounded in what they are to teach," she agreed to arrange for a series of lectures on pedagogy, but she vowed to go no further. Fortunately, the only trustee who expressed interest in a normal school was Francis Howard, and he agreed not to press the issue. In return for his indirect support, Helen retained Rev. William Brown, an outspoken advocate of making Howard a normal school, as teacher of moral philosophy. Brown was rigidly orthodox and not very smart, Howard acknowledged, but he was a sincere man "who has given character to your school such as but few teachers are capable of doing." He was also one of only two instructors (Lydia Ferguson, instructor of physical sciences, being the other) over whom Helen had any real authority—she could not discipline or fire her sisters, Eudora and Gertrude, and the other instructors, Edith Copeland in drawing and painting and Sarah Washburn Ames in music, were daughters of members of the board of trustees. By cashiering Brown, the principal could send a message to the trustees that she intended to exercise what little power she had. But without Francis Howard's support, Helen knew she could not sustain her action in the face of powerful opposition from the board. And so she relented, with an almost fatalistic resignation. A paper tiger, she could draw blood but not really wound; the more she fought, the weaker she appeared. She could either give in to the trustees or challenge them; either way, she was certain to lose.[28]

Despite his daughter's discouraging reports, Edward Magill continued to predict a "regular, normal, natural growth" as the institute acquired a reputation for putting young women "under better influences" than any other school in the country. Still, in the fourth year of her contract, two events at Howard sealed Helen's fate. When the trustees proved unwilling to appropriate money for a gymnasium, she prepared to hold a "German," or dance, in the hall of the school building. "Aside from the possibility of injury to the ceiling of the room directly underneath," Francis Howard warned, in anticipation of his brother's wrath, "there is a great danger that the reputation of your school may suffer in the estimation of a class of persons whom it may not be good policy to antagonize." At the head of that class stood Benjamin Howard, who was miffed that Helen had not allowed her charges to attend a party he had given. But Helen could not be dissuaded from moving forward with her plans, and when the dancers damaged school property, Benjamin Howard was ready to attack.[29]

Olivia Whipple provided Howard's pretext to action. Accompanied by her father, Olivia complained to the trustees that the principal had responded with "unreasonable strictness or severity or unevenness of temper" to a minor infraction. If she left, Howard suggested, other students might leave as well. Even the usually sympathetic Francis Howard bewailed Helen's tendency toward "too much scolding." Discipline was necessary, he acknowledged, especially for some of the rather wild girls at the institute, and it often happened that those who were punished retaliated with unjust accusations against those in authority. But such complaints could not be ignored, given the school's small enrollment; nor could the principal's occasional intemperance in writing and speech. With Francis Howard neutralized and with Charles Copeland in tow, Benjamin Howard visited Helen and suggested that she resign. Suffering from headaches and shortness of breath, the beleaguered principal told her father that she was in a "pack of trouble" and enlisted his help in finding another job.[30]

Edward Magill conducted a spirited defense of his daughter, branding the charges against her trivial and the characterizations of her temperament "equally groundless." Good schools, he icily informed Francis Howard, are built by ignoring such complaints—"and never by giving them serious attention." At the same time, Edward canvased colleagues throughout the country who might know of openings in a college or university. President Rhoads of Bryn Mawr thought Helen might be a suitable assistant to Professor Woodrow Wilson in history, but negotiations ended when she indicated she was not a specialist in that field. An offer of a professorship in ancient languages and history from Evelyn college, the newly founded women's annex to Princeton University, came just in time, allowing Helen to resign from Howard and to release her rage at the trustees.[31]

When the board accepted her resignation (only Francis Howard dissented) without "one word of recognition" of anything she had done, Helen composed long letters of explanation to out-of-town trustees who had not attended the meeting. At stake, she believed, was her reputation. Although 1886–87 had been a lean year, she insisted that every new school experienced fluctuations in enrollment. The problem was not management but men (she "could not call them gentlemen"): Benjamin Howard and Charles Copeland had lied to pupils and parents about her and, "word by word," had composed the Whipples' complaint. The "unscrupulous" Howard, who had been "objectionable in his attentions" to one of the younger pupils, had ignored Helen's "pretty strong hints" that he desist, forcing her to ask the girl's guardian to remove her from the school to avoid a scandal. No display of administrative competence, she implied, could reduce Howard's animus against the person who had caught him in the act and who might, at any time, make public his transgressions. She also insisted that the tight-fisted Copeland feared the Magills would receive too high a share of the profits if the school prospered. "A man of his character," Helen concluded, could not see that she put money back, without interest, into improvements nor believe that personal gain was not her aim. These men might be made sadder by the responsibilities of running the school, but she didn't have much hope that they would be "either wiser or honest." Unwilling to subject herself to shameful treatment any longer, and grateful for the support of Francis Howard—who, unfortunately, was not a "fighting man"—Helen had decided to give up the Howard Collegiate Institute for a place where her "talents may be better employed."[32]

Defiant and at times self-righteous, Helen was nonetheless shaken and depressed by the four-year fiasco at Howard. As at Johnstown, she had been a woman alone, responsible for three sisters and a school, this time among ineffectual and predatory men. Her failure was a family disaster, leaving Gertrude and Dora without work, her father in debt, and her own reputation besmirched. Equally disturbing was the knowledge that her position and authority at Howard had depended on Edward's reputation and financial interest in the school—a fact the trustees never let her forget. When she sought to use a bequest of land to finance renovation of buildings and grounds, for example, trustee approval awaited Edward's written pledge to contribute $500 if Helen failed to secure $2,500 from the sale of the property. Although she could attribute her troubles to men who were "capable of anything in the way of effrontery and deceit," she concluded that, at age thirty-four, she was the Magill family albatross.[33]

Part of the problem was Helen's willingness to accept administrative work. She "wasted her talents" as a principal, wrote Ellen Swallow Richards in a letter of condolence and exhortation that seemed to capture Helen's own thoughts. The nutritionist and pioneer in home economics, who probably first met Helen at meetings of the Association of Collegiate Alumnae, believed that "those of us who are really pioneers in behalf of American women should fill the places in which we can really rise the highest and so break a path for others." She regarded her work as a "scientific woman" as more important than her work as a teacher, and "so it is with you," she told Helen. "There are few if any who can fill the professor's chair as you can," while many could serve as figureheads for schools. She was apparently unaware of the absence of alternatives or of Helen's belief that she could serve all women while building a college. Although she valued teaching, Helen agreed with her colleague's assessment of administration and scholarship. Might she have secured a position had she waited a little longer, or tried a little harder, or been a little smarter? Or could she now break "new roads" in ancient philosophy at Evelyn?[34]

Edward Magill thought that Evelyn College promised "congenial work, opportunity for study, hearing lectures," but he had different reasons for enthusiasm for his daughter's new job. He knew about Howard's precarious finances and the vulnerability of the principal to the winds of fate and the whims of trustees. Although low enrollments were the main problem, he traced some of the difficulties to his daughter's uncompromising, impatient, blunt honesty. A principal must be a good diplomat, willing to give way, keep silent, settle for half a loaf. That Helen lacked these characteristics so often associated with women seemed clear to Edward. Apparently, his daughter could not lead and would not follow; her assertiveness at times appeared to be self-destructive. At Evelyn, he warned, Helen must curb her tongue: "Do not go forward except by request—and never criticize—even in thy own mind, much less outwardly, the way in which the McIlvaines attempt the organization of *their* school." In a subtle way he pointed to a different future for Helen. An academic haven, Princeton also promised "a wholly different social life" from that at West Bridgewater, presumably more amenable to marriage.[35]

Named after a seventeenth-century English gentleman-scholar, Evelyn College was founded in 1887 by Joshua McIlvaine, once a Princeton professor and later a Presbyterian minister in Newark, New Jersey, as a means of support for his two unmarried daughters. Adolescent girls, McIlvaine believed, needed close supervision and a homelike atmosphere that could not be obtained in contemporary colleges. His daughters, who themselves lacked college training, would teach in a beautiful, large Queen Anne–style house about a mile from Princeton; their students, whenever they ventured outside, would be accompanied by chaperons. The founder expected that Evelyn, established without an endowment, would generate handsome revenues through tuition, for the college's appeal was sure to be enhanced by the participation of Princeton faculty, who could supplement their income while demonstrating their commitment to the education of women.[36]

From the outset Helen was skeptical about Evelyn's chances for success. James McCosh, the cantankerous Princeton president, was at best noncommittal about McIlvaine's school: he expressed concern about the influence of the college upon "his Boys" while assuring his good friend Edward Magill that he did not oppose coeducation. Edward knew better, as did Elizabeth McIlvaine, who thought "the whimsical old man," annoyed that Evelyn advertised itself as a Princeton annex and frightened by hints of coeducation, might try to do "serious harm" to the new school. The proprietors hoped that high enrollments would silence the scoffers and prevent the Princeton president from becoming a vocal opponent. When the McIlvaines boasted that applications to the school, built to accommodate fifty students, exceeded that number months before the scheduled fall 1887 inaugural, a cynical Edward Magill guessed "that story is founded upon the number of applications for *Catalogues!*—which is a very different thing—as we well understand." The Swarthmore president told Helen, who no longer bore responsibility for attracting students, to look to her scholarly work and the opportunity to teach more advanced students in her "own special subjects."[37]

Evelyn College made "a very small beginning," enrolling five boarders (two first-year students, one of whom had not yet decided to do "regular work," two preparatory students, and one special student) and twelve day scholars, only four of whom were preparing for college. Helen had seen it all before: a new institution, beset with competition but forced to charge high prices; and a preparatory school ("the greatest possible mistake"), an economic necessity perhaps, but always a threat to devour a college. In many ways Evelyn was less promising than West Bridgewater, where Helen had been the architect of educational policy. Committed to coeducation, she did not "altogether sympathize with the McIlvaines' ideas and methods" (like McCosh, they opposed coeducation), although she tried to believe they might be "better adapted to opening the way at Princeton" than her own approach. Only the social atmosphere was better than at West Bridgewater; the McIlvaines were congenial hosts, "genuine, good-hearted, generous people, cultivated, appreciating things intellectual." Even Helen, who hated "talking for the sake of talking" and often returned home from parties feeling as if she "had been drawn through a knot-hole," warmed to Princeton receptions, to "new faces and pretty rooms." At these parties she joined in the speculation surrounding the retirement of James McCosh, finding in each potential successor an attitude more favorable to the education of women.[38]

On the whole, however, Helen was "agreeably disappointed" with Evelyn. So close to the "very advanced and very thorough" classics faculty of Princeton, she was again occupied with elementary instruction. Unlike Princeton, Evelyn required no Greek, allowing the substitution of a modern language. Only one brave girl began Greek, but, "being very hard worked and not strong," she dropped it, leaving Helen with thirteen hours of preparatory Latin, six hours of elementary Latin, two hours of elementary Roman history, and four hours of general history in the preparatory division. With classes of only one or two students, she had few papers to grade; but to her dismay, the young women, content to skate on Princeton's frozen lakes, evinced little enthusiasm for language, history, or higher education.[39]

A few months into her first year at Evelyn, Helen became headachy, unable to sleep or concentrate and barely able to get through her classes. A pleasant social life could not overcome the sense that she was stuck in a school for spoiled females. She had, it seemed, traded an impossible task for an irrelevant one. Helen's experience at Cambridge, an anxious Sarah Magill wrote, was a warning that rest was the only cure for exhausted, anxious women: "I have not the slightest doubt that this trouble will give way to medical treatment aided by a mental quietude." Unwilling to admit that she suffered from "the female complaint" (an inability to withstand the pressure of work), Helen reminded her parents that her health had remained robust during the ordeal at West Bridgewater. Those four years of stress had no doubt taken a toll, but it was this new present without purpose, she implied, that fostered her foreboding about the future. More circumstantial than constitutional, her illness was not likely to yield to rest, the treatment prescribed for neurasthenia.[40]

Helen vowed to stay in Princeton, but brave words were not enough, and in March 1888, "seriously troubled," she returned to Swarthmore. Convinced that "some kind of nervous breakdown" was imminent, her doctor insisted that she leave Evelyn. Helen refused to resign but agreed to stay at home until she felt healthy enough to return. Unwilling to admit defeat, she had, ever since the tripos, become accustomed to disappointment. The McIlvaines allowed her a two-week leave of absence in addition to the two-week vacation to which she was entitled. With a month of the "rest cure"—quiet relaxation in the sun and no work, not even letter writing—she improved and, despite her doctor's protests, returned to Princeton.[41]

As we shall see, the causes of Helen's near-breakdown are not easy to isolate, but the consequences were, to say the least, "a little unfortunate." While she was ill, Joshua McIlvaine took over her classes, "enjoyed the work and found he could do it very well." Well read in the classics, he was knowledgeable enough to teach elementary Latin. Given the uncertain financial condition of the college, McIlvaine decided that Helen's services would not be needed in the fall of 1888 and that it would be years, if ever, before Evelyn had "enough real college work" to sustain a person of her calibre, at the salary she so clearly deserved. Happy to provide a testimonial—he called her "a brilliant scholar, and fully up in all the methods of modern scholarship and teaching"—McIlvaine bid Helen farewell.[42]

Although she knew that Evelyn was not likely to become a college, or even "a good school," Helen was deeply disappointed by her dismissal. A better position could not be obtained for the fall, even if her health continued to improve, and McIlvaine's news precipitated another round of nervous agitation so serious that it convinced her to take a year off. During that time she would "rub up the places [in ancient philosophy] where I am in danger of getting rusty" and look in earnest for a more satisfactory position. At first she resisted the advice of doctors, parents, and friends that she drop the study of Homer and Demosthenes in favor of a rejuvenating laziness. But, as in England, she became so "invincibly opposed to mental work" that she gave up Greek, succumbing finally to the efficacy of rest. Eva Channing, herself a recent victim of nervous prostration, lectured Helen:

> You will be crazy, I think, if you attempt to do any real work until you are a good deal better. Why can't you be sensible and use this "year off" in getting strong and well? Everybody who has had "n.p.," and anything approaching it will tell you that you *must* give up and rest if you ever want to be strong again. I shouldn't *think* of attempting any hard brain-work this winter, although I am so much better; and I am sure that what you will gain intellectually you will lose ten-fold in other directions, if you attempt it now. Do be warned!

Significantly, Helen still suspected that nervous disorders might be aggravated by yielding to them, but she had no alternative to offer and no one to support her position. So for a year she rested—restlessly.[43]

During that year at Swarthmore, Helen thought often about her options. She considered herself "damaged goods," with a record of illness that could not be swept away by the fulsome praise of Joshua McIlvaine. It seemed she was right back where she had started from when she returned from Cambridge: disqualified from most schools by her sex; in a field shrunk by elective choice; and unlikely, as a Quaker by birth and a Unitarian in practice, to pass the religious tests of denominational schools. Thus handicapped, Helen knew that if she expected to teach in the fall of 1889, assuming she was fully recovered, she could not land a position in a university or college, let alone in Greek or Latin. She remained active by writing papers on higher education for women at Cambridge (for a Philadelphia brunch) and a little piece for her suffrage club, but she stayed away from the classics and noted without further comment the apologetic letters from her father's counterparts: no one needed an instructor in ancient languages, though everyone had a good word for Helen Magill. Only one offer was made—as a teacher of physical geography at a high school in Brooklyn, New York, that had only a regular curriculum but planned to introduce college preparatory work in the near future. Helen may well have recalled the prophetic words of a former classmate, written during her convalescence. If, when she began regular work again, Helen found something "really congenial," Beth Finlay would be delighted, "but with your high ideals about classical work you must expect disappointments." Beth spoke from experience, having learned to be content "with just school room attainments . . . [and] with pupils who are merely school girls."[44]

Helen took the job in Brooklyn, but her heart was not in it. She was working for wages now, as an independent woman must, and she had to muster the energy to teach four classes a day (including psychology, language, and geography) and grade 180 papers every week or two. Barely ahead of the students in psychology and geography, she tried to teach herself to cram, but temperament and pride intervened. She worked far into each night planning lessons, abandoned the lecture format in favor of recitations, gave frequent quizzes and difficult exams—and was astonished at how much she could "do with the girls with [so] little result." Thinking, "and especially learning to think," took time, but even the most competent teachers were forced to cut corners, to use methods they knew would result in the stultification of their pupils. Perhaps she would write an essay about it, "Education That Does Not Educate," an exposé that would be anonymous, of course, if she were "still in the mill."[45]

What Helen did not dare tell anyone was that she was in love again and that the tensions at Evelyn, Swarthmore, and Brooklyn were due in no small measure to uncertainty about her suitor's intentions. She had allowed herself to contemplate marriage, and more and more it loomed as a resolution, a good reason to give up a career search that seemed forever futile. If teaching was a surrogate for parenthood, why not choose the real thing? She already had her answer and now waited, none too patiently, to be asked the question she most wanted to hear.

NOTES

1. SWM to HM May 19, 1881. See also SWM to HM, Apr. 19, 1881; EHM to HM, May 17, 1881.

2. EHM to HM, Mar. 14, 1882; L. C. Caldwell to EHM Apr. 18, 1882. For the decline of the classical course of study in women's colleges in the second half of the nineteenth century, see Helen Lefkowitz Horowitz, *Alma Mater* (New York, 1984), p. 28. Horowitz also documents the practice at the "Seven Sisters" of hiring their own alumnae. For the impact of the elective system on the popularity of a curriculum in the classics, see Mabel Newcomer, *A Century of Higher Education for American Women* (New York, 1959), p. 92. For career options for Helen Magill's contemporaries, see Roberta Frankfort, *Collegiate Women: Domesticity and Career in Turn-of-the-Century America* (New York, 1977).

3. Letter of Archer-Hind, Apr. 15, 1881. It is surprising that this letter was sent to Helen (I assumed it was since it is among her papers). She would, no doubt, have respected his honesty, even as she recognized the letter's effect on her prospects for employment.

4. SWM to HM, Mar. 23, 1881, Apr. 19, 1881.

5. HM, *Diary,* May 22, 1882. See also HM to EC, July 2, 1881. Helen

wished "very much" for a job at Smith because it was "a very liberal institution." See HM to EHM, Mar. 30, 1881.

6. HM, *Diary*, July 10, 1882, July 20, 1882. It is interesting to note that Alice Freeman promised not to marry until she repaid her college debts to her parents and helped her brother and sisters through school. When she married in 1887, she resigned from Wellesley, in part because her husband, George Herbert Palmer, feared for her health and perhaps because her creative work there was done. Five years later, in 1882, she became dean of women at the University of Chicago, under an agreement that required her to be in residence no more than twelve weeks a year. See *Notable American Women, 1607–1950* (Cambridge, Mass., 1971), 3:4–8.

7. Charles W. Elliott, "Woman's Work and Woman's Wages," *The North American Review*, 135 (Aug. 1882): 146–61.

8. HM, "A Reply to 'Women's' Work and Wages," undated ms. For a discussion of the movement to give women legal right to the fruits of their labor, see Amy Dru Stanley, "Conjugal Bonds and Wage Labor: Rights of Contract in the Age of Emancipation," *Journal of American History*, 75, no. 2 (Sept. 1988): 471–500.

9. HM, *Diary*, Aug. 1, 1882, Aug. 8, 1882, Aug. 11, 1882, Aug. 15, 1882, Aug. 21, 1882; HM, "Women's Work in the Nineteenth Century," *The Independent*, Oct. 5, 1882, pp. 3–4.

10. HM to EHM, May 13, 1883; HM to EC, Jan. 10, 1883.

11. R. D. Archer-Hind to HM, Aug. 20, 1882, Feb. 18, 1883.

12. HM to EHM, May 13, 1883.

13. Ibid.

14. EHM to E. E. Hale, Mar. 24, 1884. For information about the bequest of Benjamin B. Howard and the founding of the Howard Collegiate Institute, see O. Hamilton Hurd, comp., *History of Plymouth County, Massachusetts* (Philadelphia, 1884), pp. 918–19, 924–26. See also EHM to E. E. Hale, Mar. 17, 1883.

15. EHM to HM, Mar. 18, 1883, Mar. 20, 1883.

16. Agreement between the Trustees of the Howard Funds in West Bridgewater, Mass., and Edward H. Magill and Helen Magill, undated.

17. *Howard Collegiate Institute, West Bridgewater, Massachusetts*, 1883–84, 18-page brochure, located in the West Bridgewater Historical Society and Museum. See also E. E. Hale to EHM, Mar. 29, 1883. The nonsectarian Howard Institute required students "to attend regularly such form of Religious Worship as their parents or guardians may request." For a description of the cottage system at several women's colleges, see Horowitz, pp. 87–90, 110–11, 227–28, 230–31.

18. Helen Magill, *What Is a Collegiate Institute?* (Philadelphia, 1884). For Archer-Hind's disparaging remarks about high schools and his suggestion that Americans use the term "high school" ("'high' sounds august and 'school' sounds business like"), see R. D. Archer-Hind to HM, Nov. 8, 1884. For a discussion of the movement to make universities centers of research and of the enthusiasm for electives, which Helen underestimated, see Laurence Veysey, *The Emergence of the American University* (Chicago, 1965).

19. EHM to SWM, Sept. 14, 1883. See also EHM to SWM, Sept. 20, 1883; Gertrude Magill to SWM, Oct. 11, 1883. Sarah Magill spent the summer in West Bridgewater with her daughters. Edward Magill assured Helen that he would gladly back the enterprise "to the extent of the last dollar of my worldly possessions, were such a thing needful . . . for what are possessions except to support and strengthen and encourage our own." See EHM to SWM, Sept. 4, 1883.

20. *First Yearly Catalogue of the Howard Collegiate Institute*, 1883–84, pp. 5–7; F. E. Howard to HM, Feb. 5, 1884; Gertrude Magill to SWM, Nov. 10, 1883.

21. HM to SWM, Mar. 9, 1883. See also F. E. Howard to HM, Jan. 10, 1884.

22. EHM to HM, Dec. 14, 1883, Feb. 11, 1884; Gertrude Magill to SWM, Jan. 10, 1884; R. D. Archer-Hind to HM, Feb. 28, 1884. See also EHM to HM, Feb. 29, 1884; F. E. Howard to HM, Feb. 8, 1884, Feb. 11, 1884. Gertrude's claim that "everyone is taken with Helen" was a bit of wishful thinking. Gertrude Magill to SWM, Feb. 2, 1884.

23. HM to H. W. Littlefield, Mar. 4, 1887; Maria Towne to HM, Apr. 11, 1886; "Friend of the Family" to HM, Apr. 28, 1886. See also HM to Mr. Day, Jan. 24, 1886; Isabelle Clemes to HM, Jan. 22, 1886.

24. Reed Ueda, *Avenues to Adulthood: The Origins of the High School and Social Mobility in an American Suburb* (Cambridge, U.K., 1987), p. 42. See also Frederick Rudolph, *The American College and University: A History* (New York, 1962), pp. 280–86. For a discussion of the changing curriculum of the high school, see Edward Krug, *The Shaping of the American High School, 1880-1920* (New York, 1964). The proliferation of public high schools and the decline of college preparatory divisions came earliest and was quite pronounced in Massachusetts.

25. HM to EHM, undated fragment; F. E. Howard to HM, Feb. 8, 1884. See also F. E. Howard to HM, Oct. 8, 1883, Nov. 17, 1883; HM to ADW, June 9, 1888.

26. F. E. Howard to HM, May 23, 1884, Apr. 27, 1886; B. B. Howard to HM, June 22, 1884.

27. F. E. Howard to HM, Apr. 27, 1886; B. B. Howard to HM, Sept. 23, 1884, Sept. 25, 1884. See also Charles Copeland to HM, May 16, 1885.

28. EHM to HM, May 17, 1886; F. E. Howard to HM, June 14, 1886. Edward Magill had delivered lectures throughout Pennsylvania denouncing normal schools. They had had "a great run," he thought, but had "been generally a great humbug." EHM to HM, May 17, 1886. Helen was certainly not impressed by F. E. Howard's argument: "because it failed at Swarthmore, it is not proof positive that it should here." F. E. Howard to HM, May 17, 1886.

29. EHM to HM, Dec. 13, 1886; F. E. Howard to HM, Feb. 14, 1887. See also F. E. Howard to HM, June 2, 1887; HM to Mr. Ames, undated draft.

30. EHM to F. E. Howard, Mar. 12, 1887; F. E. Howard to HM, Apr. 26, 1887; SWM to HM, Mar. 5, 1887. See also EHM to HM, Apr. 28, 1887; HM to SWM, Jan. 23, 1887; F. E. Howard to EHM, Apr. 30, 1887. For another parent's complaint about discipline at Howard and Helen's "cold indifference," see H. A.

Lothrop to HM, Apr. 21, 1887. Mr. Lothrop also disputed the principal's computation of his bill.

31. EHM to F. E. Howard, May 2, 1887. See also EHM to F. E. Howard, Mar. 9, 1887, Mar. 15, 1887; EHM to HM, Apr. 25, 1887; James M. Rhoads to HM, Apr. 9, 1887; B. B. Howard to HM, May 2, 1887.

32. HM to Mr. Ames, undated draft; HM to John D. Long, undated draft. Helen's characterization of Francis Howard was confirmed when he told her that soon after she left West Bridgewater, he wrote a complimentary article about her but, after reflecting on the controversy it would cause, "which I thought wise to avoid," did not publish the piece. F. E. Howard to HM, Sept. 30, 1887.

33. HM to Mr. Ames, undated draft. When Helen resigned, Copeland and Howard tried to get the $500 from Edward Magill. Helen acknowledged that she had gotten only $2,100 for the property but pointed out that she had surpassed the fund-raising goal set by the trustees. Although the Magills never had to pay, the incident mortified Helen, who already felt that she had let the family down. See Indenture between Helen Magill and Edward H. Magill and Trustees of the Howard Trust Fund of West Bridgewater, undated; HM to EC, Dec. 23, 1887. Sarah Magill may have agreed that Helen should give up administrative work, but she was not sanguine about her daughter's ability to work under someone else. A teaching position in Philadelphia would have been disastrous, she thought, because Helen "never could have submitted to be ruled with a rod of iron and that is just what thee would have had to do in that case for Clem. Biddle would have crushed thee like a fly if thee dared to act in any way contrary to his dictations." SWM to HM, Mar. 17, 1887.

34. Ellen Richards to HM, ca. Summer 1887.

35. EHM to HM, Apr. 25, 1887. The future of the Howard Institute looked "dark" to Francis Howard. See F. E. Howard to HM, June 2, 1887.

36. See Francis P. Healey, *A History of Evelyn College for Women, Princeton, New Jersey, 1887–1897* (Ann Arbor, Mich., 1971); Patricia Alberg Graham, *Community and Class in American Education, 1865–1918* (New York, 1974), pp. 194–95; Adelaide Stirling, "Evelyn College," *Harper's Bazaar,* 26 (1896): 806–7.

37. EHM to HM, Apr. 20, 1887; Elizabeth McIlvaine to HM, July 18, 1887. EHM to HM, Apr. 20, 1887. See also Henry Jackson to HM, July 18, 1887; Julia Sharpe to HM, Sept. 18, 1887. For negotiations on Helen's appointment, see Joshua McIlvaine to EHM, Apr. 22, 1887.

38. HM to EC, Dec. 28, 1887; HM to Dora Magill, Jan. 29, 1888.

39. Ibid.

40. SWM to HM, Jan. 28, 1888.

41. HM to EC, May 8, 1888.

42. Ibid.; undated letter of reference from J. G. McIlvaine. Evelyn College, which lost $3,000 in its first year, limped along for a decade but was never able to compensate for its lack of endowment and closed its doors in 1897.

43. HM to EC, Aug. 6, 1888, Oct. 2, 1888; EC to HM, Oct. 28, 1888. See also EC to HM, Aug. 5, 1888.

44. Beth Finlay to HM, Oct. 31, 1889. See also HM to EC, Jan. 4, 1889, Mar. 5, 1889. For a typical flattering letter of rejection, see J. Taylor to EHM, Apr. 22, 1889;

45. HM to Dora Magill, Oct. 8, 1889; HM to SWM, Oct. 13, 1889; HM to EC, Dec. 29, 1889. See also HM to SWM, Nov. 1, 1889; HM to EC, Apr. 21, 1889.

---◦---◦◦◦◆◦◦◦---◦---

CHAPTER FOUR

"Now are you satisfied with your 'taming of the shrew'?"

In September 1887, shortly before the beginning of the inaugural term at Evelyn College, Helen had gone to Saratoga, New York, to deliver a paper on "Progress in the Education of Women" at the annual meeting of the American Social Science Association. Founded in 1865 to study, discuss, and act on questions relating to crime, pauperism, insanity, sanitary conditions, and other "matters of statistical and philanthropic interest," the ASSA had become an influential lobby in the making of public policy as well as an informal headquarters for civil service reformers. When Thomas Wentworth Higginson, chairman of the education committee of the ASSA, invited Helen to the Saratoga meeting, she accepted immediately, although she remained nervous about speaking in public.[1]

The sessions began with a paper by Carroll D. Wright, Massachusetts commissioner of labor statistics and federal commissioner of labor, on the problems of census-taking and evaluation. In the discussion that followed, Helen was attracted to Andrew D. White, recently retired as president of Cornell University, who carried himself "with much dignity." That evening she was introduced to White, a wonderful conversationalist who talked about his Yale classmate Edward Magill and the scenic attractions of Saratoga. He was, she thought, "very pleasant to talk to," always interested in what she was saying and able to coax her to express her views.[2]

The next day, after listening to a graceful address by Higginson on free text books and the elective system, and a "rather rhetorical defense of muscle and physique" by Mr. Blaikie, Helen mounted the podium, "hardly able to stand . . . having lost so much sleep lately, packing Sunday and copying last night till after one." For an hour, often departing from her notes, she analyzed co-education in America and Europe. Her talk went well, despite a mixed audience of knowledgeable gentlemen and some girls who found everything she said "technical, funny or stupid." Amid the congratulations that followed, Helen deemed only one review, that of Higginson, worth recording. A few terms should have been explained, he said, but Helen, irked by the indifference and ignorance of the females in her midst, retorted that she had explained "more than he thought" and could not, after all, take all her time addressing those who knew nothing about the subject.

Throughout the meetings Helen gravitated to the company of men and could not get her mind off Andrew White, a sympathetic man, she thought, but perhaps a little worldly and therefore unlike Carroll Wright, who "could be deeply devoted to a person or a cause, or "the kind and even grandmotherly" Higginson. Might he be capable only of kindly, but disinterested, affection to an individual or rational interest in a cause? Indeed, his comments on a paper on "The Criminal Type" gave credence to this view. Helen assented to his condemnation of a "dangerous softness" in the "pathological view of crime," but his tone, his constant reference to "those creatures," gave her pause. She almost spoke in favor of a strong, but humane and Christian, approach, yet she held back, unwilling to present a viewpoint that had not been fully thought out—or, one suspects, to confront his "little hardness."

When the meetings ended, Helen accompanied White on a drive to Saratoga Lake, where he reminisced about Matthew Arnold, Tennyson, and Ezra Cornell; they also chatted about literature, architecture, Europe, and James McCosh and Princeton. A short man with gray hair, White seemed vigorous, Helen thought, and resembled William Hyde Appleton in appearance. Yet she had the impression "of a profoundly unhappy man," someone "inwardly broken." Perhaps the burdens of administration had overwhelmed him; perhaps he had not recovered from the recent death of his wife. Drawn to this melancholy man, Helen grew self-conscious, fearful that he was "dreadfully bored" by her conversation, certain that drinking lemonade through two straws rendered her "undignified and ridiculous." The strain of "entertaining and seeming or being entertained" diminished as White returned her to her hotel, and she left Saratoga wondering what he thought of her.

White met Helen at a critical moment in his life. Cofounder and first president of Cornell University, retired in 1885 after twenty years at the helm, he was frail but restlessly active. Not content to rest on his laurels as the architect of a distinguished coeducational, nonsectarian university, the fifty-three-year-old plunged into Republican party politics, began work on a history of the warfare between science and religion in the Western world, and hoped to resume a diplomatic career begun with two leaves of absence from Cornell to serve as U.S. commissioner to Santo Domingo and minister to Germany. These well-laid plans fell by the wayside, however, when Mary Outwater White, his childhood sweetheart and beloved wife of thirty years—the "best wife that ever was"—died suddenly. Mary White had freely admitted that her husband's happiness was more important to her "than is all the world besides." She never had a thought, a family friend wrote, that was not his, "first, last and always": "In everything she did her object was, as she expressed it, 'to climb up level to see with your eyes' and when I said oh Mary you are as high as his heart and that is high enough for any woman she only laughed softly and shook her head as she used to do when she made up her mind and did not want to argue." She rarely chose to exercise her influence with "St. Andrew," preferring instead to free him for a life of public service, and it was her devotion that made even his most petty triumph great. After her death, which White attributed to overwork and anxiety in caring for the children and grandchildren, rearranging the house, and preparing for commencement receptions, he found himself unable to concentrate, unable to lose himself in work as he had done so often before. He journeyed to Saratoga with only a faint hope that a change of scenery would ease his "fearful loss."[3]

Andrew White was attracted to Helen Magill, though he "dared not acknowledge" to himself how much. He wrote to her frequently and invited Edward to bring his daughter to visit the Cornell campus. Anxious to get better acquainted before Andrew embarked on an extended trip abroad, Helen asked her father to take her to Ithaca. She entertained no "foolish" or "unbecoming" ideas about his "very kind attentions," insisting that he was a congenitally enthusiastic person interested in "a woman whom he supposed to be remarkable as a scholar." Although she thought it inappropriate for a woman to pursue a man, did not believe in second marriages, and doubted that someone she cared for would ever be interested in her, she could not deny that he aroused her feelings, sympathy, and intellect. Her father tried to combine encouragement with restraint. He agreed to visit a man who "stands very high in my esteem," while assuring his jittery daughter that Andrew's devotion to his late wife was not "at all inconsistent with anything that he has done, or is likely to do." That the widower admired Helen, her father wrote, he could "see well enough, and he plainly told me so, in so many words. To what that may grow in time, it is impossible to say...."[4]

The trip to Ithaca was followed by Andrew's request that Helen maintain a correspondence with him. Trying not to think "too much about what it means but frankly accept it as it is offered," she wrote him long letters that ranged across subjects literary, religious, and personal. When he teased her for not writing frequently enough or for "hedonism" in not prolonging her stay, Helen responded in kind. If he chose to keep his letters short (as he often did), she would do the same, for she was "vilely proud." As for her hedonism: "I suppose you think the next time I may be called upon to change my mind I shall think it best to yield in the first place, so as to hear no more of it: but if so, you are very much mistaken: I can do what I determine, regardless of consequences—even the reproach of Hedonism." She agreed to catalog her faults so that he might soon "have me painted as black as Nature made me or I have made myself," but to *his* list she entered a denial: "Anyway, you can not say I am rhetorical, and as for domineering, if you think I am I must be, for you ought to be perhaps a good judge of that quality."[5]

Andrew was enchanted by his new friend, whose every letter helped him recover his strength, combativeness, and sense of humor. When Helen did not write, he proposed "An Act to remedy certain abuses on Public instruction":

> Whenever any Quaker maiden holding a classical or philological professorship in an annex to a Presbyterian College shall have begun to enlighten the understanding of any ex-President of a College—the said ex-Presdt being in the service of the said United States as a Regent of the Smithsonian Institution—by means of correspondence—then, and in that case, the Quaker maiden aforesaid must and shall write no less than once a week—and no letter shall be less than 24 pages in length.

He saw in her letters "a quiet depth, a breadth, a clearness, a certainty—a touch, at times light, at times strong," that revealed more than literary genius. The "proper study of mankind is woman," he told her, finding her an object of endless fascination: "I don't know which of your moods is best—even your critical mood is good tho' I never had a particle of the critical faculty myself."[6]

Helen's religious faith, more than her barbed wit, helped Andrew through the worst crisis of his life. He wanted to believe that his wife's soul was immortal and that he would be reunited with his "dear one" in Heaven, but a lifetime of rationalism had persuaded him that the soul expired with the body. At best, his view of the future was "wretchedly clouded by doubts—by great thicknesses of doubts. I never had expected happiness—hardly dare think of it—tho there is one happiness I pray for every night of my life. That is not what is called 'salvation'—if my soul is worth 'saving' it will probably be 'saved'—if not, I don't know that I care for it. My faith in a continuous existence is weak and flickering. . . . " Mary had had faith, though perhaps not with Helen's clarity of vision or powers of description, and now Andrew found himself longing for a token of Mary's presence, something he could grasp with his hand or even his mind.[7]

Each week Andrew's hope nurtured by grief was bolstered by a message of faith, a blend of Quaker intuition and Unitarian reason. Helen told him of a time "long ago, it seems prehistoric," when she doubted the fundamentals of religion, when she wondered "why the pictures hung on the walls and why we ate with spoons," when "the blue sky above seemed a strange mockery." The absurdity of a futile existence, she recalled, brought her back to belief. Since logic and reason "are all the time eating themselves up," people need faith to avoid the dark alley of fatalism. In this way she reasoned herself out of reason, although, if pushed, she was prepared to admit that the arguments establishing religion were not conclusive: the only real light came straight from Heaven, shining most luminously in the person of Christ. In Cambridge, "on a dull little street on a dull evening alone," Helen suddenly *saw* the Divine Spirit in the world around her and understood that "true life is to live in and for all things, through Him," while death is the eternal life that removes self-consciousness, leaving "only enough self" to look out, with love, "into the wholeness of things." To recapture the experience in a letter was impossible, she wrote. "The thing itself was not words, nor exactly thought; it was a vision, an insight; I believe in it as much as I do in my own life." Since then, she had been able to accept the pain as well as the joy of life, having found "an inexhaustible spring of patience and hope." She recognized that the New Testament had been altered and even contained inconsistencies, though most of it "met a witness in [her] own mind." But the life and personality of Christ ("a friend of man, himself a man, yet living in that perfect spiritual union with God which is the destiny of all men to obtain") could not have been invented, nor could she have been blinded by the light.[8]

Helen was certain that only faith could save Andrew from "that terrible doubt, the only real death, the enemy of all true life, whether here or hereafter." Faith was a gift, bestowed upon all who would take it; it did not contradict reason but enabled one, when evidence seemed to conflict, to trust "the larger hope." She looked for the eternal significance in things and doubted that progress, his most cherished belief, had much meaning in a world that lacked permanent realities. She could derive satisfaction from work on projects whose benefits she would not see, but if everything was fleeting she could scarcely contemplate the prospect "of adding zero to zero in the vain hope of making a sum." Moreover, the permanency "of all that is true and beautiful and good" suggested to her that loved ones were "nearer to us than we often think." The mortal mind and body that encased each soul was a barrier to full communion. Death removed that barrier, but it could be lowered for those living persons who wrung from pain and doubt "their hard lessons" and subdued consciousness to attain "the peace that passes understanding." "I wish you could believe as strongly as I," Helen wrote, that in Heaven "you will take [Mary's] hand, instead of letting it go, and that, instead of a passage from light and love to darkness and separation, it will be the other way." Mary was not far away, Helen insisted, and she encouraged Andrew to "try to believe it, and spare no effort which shall help you realize it."9

A recurring dream indicated to Andrew that Helen might be right. He found himself standing in a room, face-to-face with a "happy, smiling, sweet" Mary who flung her arms around his neck. Although he knew that she was not living, she seemed "perfectly natural," Andrew wrote, except that "I distinctly remember that her cheek pressed close to mine was cold—cold as on that June morning—and yet she was not dead—in the usual sense. I was for a moment infinitely happy at the sight of her happy face—and I remember no more." This vision was, no doubt, "the result of natural causes," an assessment with which Helen did not disagree. The next world was not only a reality, she assured him, but one could live "*through* this world *into* the next"; all occurrences had natural *and* supernatural causes. For Helen, religion was an antidote to the dark side of human existence. One could never be truly united with loved ones or with God without faith that persisted even when "his face seems turned away to the outward part of our being, and nothing remains to us but that pure spiritual communion to which neither mind nor sense give any access." Andrew was seduced by her blandishments and admitted that he would not ordinarily accept theological dogmas "upon such a basis" but was impressed that intuitions of immorality had taken hold of so many people, "especially noble women." Helen was, he thought, a bishop "in the true Apostolic Succession," one who had confirmed him in his faith.10

Delighted that the "little hand" she held out had kept Andrew "from sinking into the abyss of utter hopelessness," Helen was dismayed that he attributed his conversion to "a woman's reason." Although he accepted what historians Barbara Welter and Ann Douglas have called "the feminization of American religion," Helen did not agree that intuition and emotion had supplanted reason and logic in her cosmology. With little interest in theology, she had an almost Jamesian will to believe, one that was, she thought, unflinching in its view of the world and the inconclusive evidence for immortality. Yet, what Helen claimed for herself she did not quite claim for her sex. Did more women than men really argue by saying, "I think it is so because I think it is so"? Perhaps, but she knew that, more than most members of either sex, she could "be reasoned in or out of convictions." Because she embraced the Unitarian view that revelation supplemented but never contradicted reason, she was not amused by Andrew's assertion that in literary and historical matters her "reasoning powers [were] inferior to her confirming powers: then *what* is your mind confirmed by—I hoped in the beginning it was a tribute to my reasoning powers." In fact, he had considerable respect for her intellect, although he continued to disparage it with a mixture of playfulness and prejudice.

Unquestionably, however, her intuitive, spiritual, "feminine" side attracted him most. They had come together, in a sense, over Mary Outwater's dead body, and Andrew, whose conversion to a belief in immortality was never complete, felt himself inside the sphere of influence of his "new advisor."[11]

Even as Helen pronounced gratitude "a word from which a friend must shrink," Andrew tried to say thank you by providing professional assistance. He knew that Evelyn College had lived down to Helen's expectations and wondered if she might be interested in directing Cornell's Sage Women's College. Guide, companion, and friend to the student residents, the directress would have no formal teaching duties, but voluntary lectures and special classes could be offered. Eventually, he hinted, an appointment as professor might be secured. In the meantime, he wrote to Thomas Wentworth Higginson for an assessment of Helen's professional competence. The reply was not encouraging. Higginson, who admitted that he had actually seen Helen for the first time at Saratoga, described her as a "strong and superior person, with a fine physique, high aims and purposes." Regrettably, however, she also had "a little distress of disposition" and "latent possibilities of temper." He made no mention of her response to his criticism of her lecture but remembered "sweeping and hasty remarks about the Harvard Annex," which gave him the impression of "a little impetuosity." Reports had circulated that Helen left West Bridgewater because she could not get along with the board of trustees, something Higginson promised to investigate further. He concluded his letter without making a recommendation.[12]

Andrew decided not to pursue the appointment, for he knew he could not hope to persuade his old nemesis Henry Sage, the lumber baron cum trustee who supervised the college at close range, to hire Helen without ecstatic testimonials to her character and temperament. His resolve, however, was probably as much a product of indecision about his intentions as it was a reaction to Higginson's letter. Andrew cared deeply for Helen. Always solicitous, he could also be flirtatious—when sitting with his friend in an art gallery or pouting when a week passed without an epistle in her exquisite handwriting. Yet he was loathe to dishonor his wife's memory with a hasty courtship. In his confusion, Andrew abruptly and mysteriously dropped all references to Sage College from his letters.

Out of such uncertainty Helen's anxiety was born. At first she tried to show indifference, telling her mother that it might be better if the position were not offered. However, Andrew's silence on a subject of such obvious importance was simply inexplicable, especially so since his interest was clearly more than professional. A "good many checks restrained him," Sarah Magill reminded her daughter, counseling patience toward a man of "unsettled mind" whose feelings seemed to be "leading him faster than his judgment." Andrew was lonely and sad, Helen agreed, but she had begun to get the impression that he consoled himself "by soft speeches and tender looks, taking care all the time, as in the way of flirts, to say *just enough* that is honest to give you the pleasing reflection, if you should find you had gone too far, that you should have known better, and have only yourself to blame for it." Perhaps she had revealed too much already, telling him of the isolation she felt, of the painful friendship she had had at Cambridge, of the frustrations at West Bridgewater and Evelyn.[13]

Helen tried to assess her enigmatic friend, making these notes on the back of an envelope:

—Always trying to be something different from what he is and succeeds to an extent that might deceive people considerably
—Appears to have little feeling; always pulling himself up for fear he will feel or show too much; really has quite a good deal of feeling
—*Extremely* egotistical: but not exactly vain
—Thoroughly a gentleman
—Coquettish
—As good as his word
—Executive
—Constant
—Persistent, but not too much so: knows when to stop
—Very self controlled: but sometimes acts very impulsively
—Fond of pleasure
—Firm even obstinate
—Likes his own way but is not interfering: when he does decide to carry his point succeeds
—A good deal of originality; has his own way of looking at things: not a man who follows
—Very fond of the beautiful
—Not sensitive: good-natured and kind-hearted: not imitable
—Never says sharp or mean things
—Not particularly ambitious but not the opposite
—Pretty even disposition, but a little inclined to despondence at times; or when that letter [about his late wife?] was written
—Often quite frank but can be very reserved

To discover how much he valued their relationship, Helen resolved to hold back, thinking he might reveal more if she revealed less. In turn, Andrew, who thought most women unable to control their emotions, gave Helen "credit for more imperturbability" than she actually possessed. Could she hope to outlast him in a contest to subdue feelings?[14]

Early in 1888 Andrew's conduct grew even more curious. He told

Helen that he was planning a European tour and hinted that he might ask her to accompany him as chaperon and director of studies for his daughter Ruth. But he also informed her that Professor Flagg, Cornell's classicist, was leaving and wondered if Helen was interested in the position. When she replied modestly that her scholarship might not be "deep enough" for a professorship at Cornell, he asked again about Sage, offering to arrange for her to deliver a lecture at the Fortnightly Club of Cornell so that she could meet the faculty. Helen framed a cautious reply. It had become increasingly clear to her that Evelyn College would not succeed, that the McIlvaines monitored the behavior of the students but had "no ideas about education at all," established no study hours, and permitted the girls to "waste their time fearfully." In any event, Dr. McIlvaine proposed to take the classical department during the 1888–89 academic year. Although the position at Sage was not really what she had in mind, "such positions are very rare for women," more so than she had realized before she began to look for them. Encouraged by his prediction that administrative work could be combined with some teaching, she asked for more information and told him that Sage was "in some ways very attractive." Edward Magill, who still thought that his daughter's ultimate destiny might be to have a school of her own, advised her to press Andrew "to say definitely whether Sage will be quite sure to need thee." If not, he wrote, she ought to apply for a position at the annex to the University of Pennsylvania.[15]

As Helen solicited letters of recommendation, Andrew informed her that Henry Sage was quite "sensitive regarding his prerogatives as the Founder of Sage College" and, in view of "certain temporary circumstances," he now did not think Sage worthy of her: "When you come to this University as women entered the lecture halls of Padua, in the good times of old—then I say come—and I don't think that day is very far distant from us." If the decision had been his, Helen would have carte blanche, a professor's title with all of its privileges and duties, "and a certainty of success." But without faculty rank, Andrew wrote, the place was not worth having. Helen could only speculate about his "real reasons" while trying to convince herself that he was right. At Sage she would have had to arrange "art talks or musical evenings," with no time to do research. Withdrawing her candidacy was an "immense relief," she told her mother, concluding bravely: "It cannot be, but well-known as my name has become, I can get some good classical position before very long."[16]

Helen knew that Andrew had played a part in the near-breakdown that forced her from Evelyn College in the spring of 1888. The air of Princeton may well have infected her with insomnia, but it was "uncertainty—the state of not knowing what responsibilities [she might] be called upon to meet"—that wore her down, and even daily doses of opium afforded her little sleep. She did not know whether her notions that his intentions were not romantic affected her health or whether her health caused them. Although she tried to cultivate faith and courage, she simply did not know what to think of Andrew. And his efforts to help her find a job, as she obliquely told him, had made matters worse: "I have a morbid dread, I believe, of ever seeming to ask for a grain more of regard than would be freely given. I always rate that of my friends as low, at least, as is at all warranted—for I should shrink from the possibility of any mistake in the other direction." Although freely offered, his aid, which she took as a token of his regard, had made her dependent on him, and now she had neither a job nor much reason to think he wanted anything more than friendship. She spent weeks resting at Swarthmore, forbidden to write long letters or do "anything much that an intelligent creature would do," feeling "moments of gloom" when she sensed that her "whole learning was a mass of fragments, hopelessly uncoordinated," when, paralyzed "into a kind of indifference," she knew she would never be a scholar. Her illness, she told Andrew, was caused by four years of care and worry at West Bridgewater. To say more was to invite his pity.[17]

Unaware of his role in Helen's nervous collapse, Andrew wrote frequently as he prepared to visit European cities he had enjoyed with his wife. He was becoming a suitor, though he tried to mask his intentions by posing as a curious friend. When he asked questions designed to discover what kind of wife she would make, Helen responded with a mixture of caution, affection, sarcasm, and indignation. She was proud, after all, that she was "not artful enough" to snag a man in the traditional way. "I don't mean anything disparaging to women who do have love affairs," she told Eva Channing (in a letter describing Andrew as "altogether a friend, my dear"), "but I have a theory that all men have to be managed and that I never could do." She did try to manage him, albeit by playing his game of ambiguity and obfuscation, but frankness came more naturally. With doubts about his intentions, and frustrated by dwindling job prospects, she was exasperated that she could not—and he would not—be more explicit about their feelings.[18]

Helen did not quite contain her anger that Andrew would leave the country at such a crucial moment in their relationship. What kind of friend could profess to find so much pleasure in her letters and her company and then embark on a long journey without saying good-bye in person? When he asked her to see him off, she hurried to New York without hesitation. Although he professed a desire to show her the cathedrals of Europe and told her he wished to see to the very bottom of her heart, she did not respond until she had returned to Swarthmore.

Had he the right to such a wish, she asked, when he did not reciprocate? And if he succeeded in enlarging her heart, might it "not be in some mistaken direction or in a degree quite beyond what was required—hearts are cranky things and dangerous to meddle with—and what should I do with the superfluity?... perhaps your other advice, which you gave at Ithaca, might be better: to cultivate a hard heart, or at least to rest satisfied with what I have, which is perhaps neither so small nor so cold as you imagine." She made no claim to a large or warm heart, leaving that judgment to others, but admitted that intense pride and shyness "might render the diagnosis difficult." She did not see how anyone could misunderstand her "simple motives," and as if to prove her point, she told Andrew of a dream, prompted by his "ghastly" discussion of the possibility of being lost at sea, in which she "received a dreadful little letter, directed in a strange hand,... telling me in telegraphic terms that you were dangerously ill." Morbid thoughts, which had accompanied her breakdown, returned during her convalescence, but now she imagined that he needed her and implied that her loving attention might preserve him.[19]

Andrew preferred to analyze Helen's needs rather than acknowledge his own. Attributing her health problems to overwork, he prescribed rest and asked her to join him in Europe as Ruth's tutor. He wanted to offer her a change and "to see her face and hear her voice more often than once in two or three months." Helen should not trouble herself about work—"there will be enough of it for you—and as to worry I schooled myself to give it up long ago." Sympathy, however, was accompanied by observations that offended her, even if she knew they were delivered half in jest: "How I despise the American sick woman! bah! Men—sick men are bad enough—but the ignoble army of martyrs known as sufferers from nervous prostration! Misery!" Helen responded cautiously to an offer that might be a suitor's opening gambit. What if she were wrong and he merely wished to be a friend? Would a hasty acceptance thrust her forward beyond the bounds of propriety? Might a demurrer, however polite, send the wrong signal about *her* feelings? After an illness that was sure to raise eyebrows, might an extended stay abroad be fatal to future employment—if she had to resume her career when she returned? In the end, Helen could not take the chance and so declined with thanks, taking the opportunity to contest Andrew's acceptance of current medical dogma regarding nervous prostration.[20]

Historian Barbara Sicherman has argued that neurasthenia was the illness of choice in late nineteenth-century America, especially for single women aged twenty-five to thirty-five. Often the result of concern for others, it struck sensible women who exhibited "a proper amount of illness," one doctor declared, and a willingness to do what physicians prescribed. For career-minded women like Helen Magill, however, the need to escape "from the contingency of the feminine role" was matched by the knowledge that illness was a risky proposition, likely to confirm male prejudices about working women. As we have seen, Helen did not agree that hard work caused nervous disorders, although she was unaware of or unpersuaded by the suggestion of a few of her contemporaries that culture, not biology, was at the root of the problem, that American society thwarted the legitimate aspirations of women. At West Bridgewater, she told Andrew, she had been "the little iron clad," a woman who worked recklessly with the conviction that she was invulnerable to illness. Her experience, moreover, indicated that excessive sympathy was not always kindness because neurasthenia could be aggravated by yielding to it. For this potentially radical analysis, Helen did not really have much evidence; in fact, although she had not had the rest cure prescribed by Dr. S. Weir Mitchell and others, a respite at home had been beneficial. Suspicious of a treatment that had helped, uncertain of the causes of her distress, Helen was more than a bit defensive with Andrew, who she thought too quick to leap from the illness of one female to derogatory remarks about women in general: "You ask me about my health—but why? If I am well, very good; but if I am not, you 'despise the American sick women'." Although she thought his remarks "a little hard," she had to admit that work was beneficial only when she felt free to rest when necessary.[21]

Not only did Helen chide her friend for his references to sick women, but she chastised him for branding females unreasonable. Andrew suggested she read a book of philosophy and then responded to her critique with the admonition that she beware how she tried to improve her mind until he came to guide her. His criticism was "irrational," she jabbed, since she was an "extremely docile" object of his plan to make her over and her defects could only result from his failure to be intellectually persuasive. To his comment that such sentiments indicated a desire to see her more than an assessment of her intellect, she replied: "And if you have anything to say about the nature of your regard for me that you can say plainly so that the most ingenious classical annotator could not pervert its meaning, then say it." Andrew's habit of putting his regard for her in the form of "a conundrum," as he so often did, was ill suited to a woman made for "a world of pure reason" who wanted "to understand everything and [wanted] everything to be perfectly understandable." Too rational to accept the intellectual inferiority of women, Helen wrote: "*Never* can you find arguments enough to sustain any such thesis—but let me hear them, such as they are—I am quite unprejudiced, and prepared to receive them with all the respect they merit. Even bad arguments employed in a bad cause will be received with that respect which I always think right to show arguments, or what consider themselves such. There is nothing bigoted about *me.*" From her own experience she knew that intelligence was hardly a male monopoly, and she relished the opportunity to puncture his prejudices.22

Both charmed and stung, Andrew countered that he argued playfully with her because he enjoyed the "pretty turns" in her responses and her "gentle and ingenious manner of extricating" herself from the dilemmas he posed. If conundrums annoyed her, he promised to be "as plain as a pikestaff." Of greater concern to him were Helen's often-stated fears for their friendship and her continuing bouts with depression. Their relationship, though still new and developing, was not about to "smash up"; nor was Helen, "the friend on whom I have relied to draw me out of the depths of depression," meant to be gloomy. Andrew renewed his prescription for good health: she must read comedy or old-fashioned melodrama where virtue triumphed and vice scampered down a trapdoor in disgrace; she must discard fatalistic novels like *Anna Karenina;* and, above all, she must avoid introspection and give in to her laziest impulses. Attracted to the *wunderkind* who could "drop into Greek, Latin, French, German, English, American and Quaker... at [her] own sweet will!," Andrew nonetheless preferred a more heavenly Helen, "the serene little Quaker woman whom I had imagined—the Platonist rising quietly above earthly trials and troubles—the gentle broad-browed seeress... Was she then a figment of my brain?" He hoped that when he returned from Europe, he would find his friend her old self again—sensitive and sympathetic, feisty but always feminine. If she did not remain optimistic, who could he rely on to dispel his tendencies to despair?23

To friendly exhortation, Andrew added questions about Helen's capacity to be a good wife and mother. Frequent discussions of architecture, literature, and music convinced him that she could develop the aesthetic sense of a child, but he was not certain that a woman with her training would be interested in or skilled at domestic work. Her ambiguous response was that advanced work in philology and philosophy could not eradicate "such natural feminine tendencies," at least not in one generation, and that she knew women who had done nothing but household chores all their lives and, she added maliciously, disliked the work intensely. With a virtual mania that his next spouse be a superior household manager, Andrew pressed the point. Helen parried by asserting that housekeeping required great intelligence in "what some people think a woman's only proper sphere" and that she welcomed it as a change from her ordinary vocations. She turned aside his not very subtle suggestion that she send a photograph taken in the midst of household chores, arguing that help was impossible to discipline, ovens were cranky and capricious, and Andrew would scarcely enjoy a picture of a woman wrestling with such conditions. She had never heard that "the saints made cake," nor would she send a photograph when Andrew refused to do so because he was too old to look "pretty enough"—she would accept one "taken in infancy, with your sleeves tied up with ribbands, and a smooth, unwrinkled countenance," even though she preferred a portrait that had "at least the appearance of wisdom." As Andrew chuckled, he was left wondering if Helen was willing to expend her mortal energies surrounded by cooks, kids, and crockery.[24]

When Andrew gingerly raised the subject of marriage, as a general topic of discussion, Helen's response was suitably self-effacing. That sacred institution, she said, should be reserved for people willing and able to sacrifice for the happiness of their spouses. To make someone "who is most dear to you depend so much on your worth" struck her as risky, "truly a thing to appal the bravest." She viewed marriage and family as the highest duties of womanhood, but she was too much a woman to claim that she would make a good wife and mother. Thus, she remained an intellectual without portfolio or prospects, a spinster in a society convinced that a woman could not be fulfilled until she was married. At times she professed to disdain marriage—"How people settle when they marry in this country! I think it is very uncivilized"—but more often she asserted that she did not want a career: "As for any call to write, indeed, or to express myself at all, except by such work as I may do in a quiet way, I don't think I have any." Yet, she informed Andrew, she regretted that she had not produced more and criticized less and she hoped that she had time to mend her schematic, scholarly ways.[25]

Women differed from men in temperament and inclination, Helen believed, yet she was hard put to pinpoint the source of such differences. She tried to sort them out and to remove the taint of inferiority from the woman's sphere, if only to make the abandonment of a scholarly career seem less like a retreat. As she was sewing a dress one evening, she mused about the preoccupation of women with clothing:

> It is an evidence of feminine inferiority that a woman reflects in that way, for I don't suppose a man ever does. . . . Is it because of your superiority, or is it because your garments are so hideous as to drive all possible sentiment to the ends of the earth. But then, do you believe Sir W. Raleigh mused over his ruffles or other gear. All posterity has, over his cloak to be sure. I dont know. . . . For it is undoubtedly the fact that, while I don't feel ashamed of such an attitude of mind in myself, I should not be pleased to think of one of your sex doing that kind of thing. . . . Is that because *you* think more about our dress and appearance—and is that perhaps a sign of

your inferiority. So what might appear your comparative indifference to dress is really *ours,* while our perhaps undue interest (on the whole) is yours. No: I myself know that I like to wear pretty things, mostly because they *are* pretty, and I consider the approval of my own sex, I *think,* more valuable than that of yours, because it is more discriminating.

We can almost see her twisting and turning in front of the mirror, trying on arguments in an attempt to embrace femininity without accepting male supremacy.26

If Andrew and Helen seemed ready to declare a courtship in the summer and fall of 1888, they retreated to friendship by the next spring. On doctor's orders, Andrew declared, he was prolonging his stay abroad. Although he wanted to return to his book on science and "get a chance to quarrel and dispute" with Helen face-to-face, "the Fates seem against it for the present." As he floated down the Nile, Helen suffered in Swarthmore, certain that her self-centered correspondent would have returned home if he had been in love. When she told her parents of her disappointment, they pledged his good intentions, remembered his "season of deep and painful trial," and begged her not to reveal to him "the animus of [her] expressions." Where suspicion "creeps in," Sarah Magill wrote, it destroys relationships.27

Helen found biding her time as difficult as biting her tongue. She told Andrew of her efforts to find a job and remarked that, although not fond of change, she would go wherever she found a college position, especially in Greek. In this case, honesty was the best strategy, and she probably did not intend to set a trap with the truth. "I am not in the 'barter period' ever with any friend," she claimed, although she certainly would not have objected if talk of work galvanized Andrew into action. If she went far away, she told him, "you may sometimes have the time and inclination to come and see me, though I believe it is rather more your idea that I should come and see you." She contrasted her steadfastness to fluctuations in his behavior: "As soon as I am *anything* to anyone, I am one thing always and invariably." Even as she forgave him for his fickleness, she announced that she had applied for a position in a large college in the Northwest.28

Andrew reacted in a curious way, telling her he could enlist his friend Leland Stanford in the search for a position. Stanford, after all, had consulted with him about the university that was to bear his dead son's name, and he might hire a female professor of Greek. But then he added that California was too far away: "You see that selfishness after all moves the world." If he thought his motives obvious, Helen deemed his efforts cruel, having raised her hopes only to dash them by taking no action at all. When she took the position in Brooklyn ("I cannot do better than accept what does offer"), she felt free to speculate about Andrew's "diabolism": "There is a detestable little hobgoblin, who whispers into my ear sometimes very unkind and unfriendly doubts of your friendship. You *must* recognize that you are very hard to quite understand sometimes." She then asked him to draw on his expertise in the history of religion to help her exorcise her devils of doubt.[29]

Andrew greeted Helen's announcement of her job in Brooklyn with "mingled admiration, regret and fear." He proclaimed geography a wonderful subject because it made children dream of places and people far removed from their often drab experiences, yet he worried that Helen was so prone to overwork, especially when she fretted about scholarship. "Let your Greek lie fallow," Andrew begged. Soon, he devised a better plan, reviving his request that she come to Europe as his daughter's director of studies. Ruth was, in the opinion of her father, a gifted musician but immature and unattractive. Deprived of her mother's influence, spoiled by Grandmother Lucia Outwater and Aunt Emily Outwater, who lived with the family, she might well remain unmarried. Margaret Wickham of Vassar, who had been hired as Ruth's tutor, lacked intellectual perception and was deemed unsuitable to accompany Ruth to Europe. So, without a companion, Ruth had remained in Ithaca. Now that Andrew had extended his stay, however, he wanted his daughter—and Helen—to join him. He suggested a trial visit for Helen at Cornell's commencement. Still, he urged his friend not to sacrifice her own needs to the plan, "as your life is more important in the world than [Ruth's]."[30]

Helen was tempted to accept the offer yet hesitant about giving up her job, even though the Brooklyn school was growing so quickly that she was almost certain to be rehired on her return to the United States. Although she disliked the idea of receiving payment for services rendered to her friend, she asked for a "fair salary" of $500 plus travel and living expenses. When a month passed without a definitive reply, her anxiety again turned to suspicion and then anger, finally spilling over in a letter written on May 22, 1889. She asked for prompt word of Andrew's wishes so she could evaluate a position in Indianapolis, which might take her far from home and him: "But why should I care so much for that? Have you not voluntarily—so far as I can see—put the Atlantic between us for more than a year, and who knows how much longer you prefer that arrangement?" The more she wrote, the more furious she became, as she remembered his insinuating question about her health: "Hysterics! *Of course* I never had hysterics." Nonetheless, she did not retract her acceptance of his offer, although hers was a sarcastic surrender: "I will go where you wish and stay where you wish, and do what you wish during your pleasure. . . . Now are you satisfied with your 'taming of the Shrew'?"[31]

Andrew was anything but satisfied. Before he received her letter he had written accepting her terms even as he objected to the proposed salary as too small and indicated that doubts remained about whether Ruth would leave Ithaca. Indeed, he may have delayed his response because he had not yet persuaded his in-laws to part with Ruth for a year. When he received Helen's missive, however, he decided to save himself the trouble. Defending himself against the charge of unscrupulousness, he lashed out at Helen's suspiciousness and her tendency to sacrifice friendship to her "skill in criticism." He had prolonged his stay in Europe because his doctor advised him that a return to the lecture circuit would injure his health, not because he wished to avoid her. Helen had, he remembered, declined to take charge of Ruth in 1888; she gave him no indication that a prompt decision was necessary. He was offended by her attitude, particularly because he had tried to help when he saw that she had not yet found a satisfactory position. Indeed, he had refused to call her a governess in deference to her education and intelligence. Andrew continued to believe that she would find "a fitting career"; if not, he promised to arrange an appointment as resident graduate at Sage College. At present, it seemed best to drop plans for a European reunion.[32]

Weary of ambiguity and delay, Helen was not mollified. In many ways Andrew's reasonable explanation missed the point. Even to ask whether she had been a hysteric was unforgivable, given the disorder's association with faulty heredity and moral turpitude. Although neurasthenics and hysterics shared many of the same symptoms, the former were usually refined and unselfish, the latter deemed suspicious, quarrelsome, introspective, independent, indifferent to the needs of others. It was possible, of course, to see either diagnosis in Helen's behavior; and, as Carroll Smith-Rosenberg has pointed out, physicians often used hysteria in the effort to establish male authority, by making women wary of their own assertiveness. Although Helen's anger gave credence to a charge Andrew had not quite made (but didn't he always argue through indirection?), she did not back down; rather, she made plans to return to Brooklyn in the fall. In her diary she wished for work in ancient philosophy or history "with college students where we could read something from the originals." Andrew's actions, she concluded, raised serious doubts about *his* character: "Is *he* that man of whom he once wrote to me who *likes* to make people suffer." With his response in hand, she wrote to him that she had decided to "close a correspondence which can only further distress you by explanations which will not explain." How he could mistake loyalty and confidence for distrust and criticism? The lack of trust on both sides seemed too deep for remedy.[33]

Within a month, however, Andrew broke the silence. Without Helen's spiritual and intellectual vitality, he was a melancholy old man. A diplomat, he evidently decided, should always keep open channels of communication. Pleased that he had taken the initiative, Helen assessed their relationship. She had sensed in him an indifference, a wariness, and had been offended by "the formal politeness" of his negotiations over Ruth. Thus, she had sought a way to enable him to break off their correspondence but not to make it necessary. While she sometimes stooped to "polite dissembling" with acquaintances, she refused to use "anything but the most perfect frankness" with friends. She confessed to "a cruel suspicion," based on a conviction that she did not merit his praise, that he had drawn her out because he wished to make a psychological study of her rather than out of a deep feeling. She now sensed that they were completely different, without the capacity to fully understand each other. Interestingly, she laid claim to the more masculine virtues, implying that *he* was impulsive and moody and citing his tribute to her critical faculties. Since she claimed she could no longer be deceived about his intentions and still liked him "pretty well," she was happy to write occasionally: "If we cannot be so good friends as before, and I don't believe we can, still we can perhaps make believe to be which is some consolation." She asked for his views about their correspondence, twitting the diplomat that his experience accustomed him, far more than it did her, to "*appear* contented."[34]

This time Andrew met frankness with frankness. If Helen had doubts about his sincerity, he was concerned about her sanity and about the morbid state that produced constant references to suffering. Nonetheless, he cared about her very much and expected to see her frequently when he returned to the United States in October 1889.[35]

Rapprochement quickly ripened into romance. Andrew visited Helen in Swarthmore and Brooklyn and promised her that leaving her job would not mean giving up the life of the mind. He needed her help in the preparation of *The Warfare of Science with Theology,* for he was "careless in composition" while she was neat and precise. Although she was "wonderfully well-fitted" to be a Greek professor, he thought her infinitely better suited to be a wife and mother. If she wished to read Greek with classes at Cornell, he would make the arrangements: "I foresee a Greek Club on our hill—and myself excluded as utterly unworthy of the society of the new Olympia Morata. How humble I shall be yet how proud."[36]

To assurances about intellectual pursuits, however, Andrew added his view that a wife's role was to make her husband content and in return to be "kept from all care—to be watched over—to be kept happy—to be guarded from fatigue." "Man's Lot Deprived of Woman," an essay in *The Philadelphia Times* which he clipped out and sent to her, summed up his views:

If there were no women men would have no object in life. There would be nobody to fight against being kissed, and then to snuggle up to a coat sleeve and take it as naturally as a cat does cream. Most important of all, there would be nobody to write against, to complain of, to love with all your heart and soul. Without women, men would never get to heaven, and without them they would never have a taste of the other place on earth. So when the bells are ringing in 1890, if Tom has any sense whatever, he'll put his arms around the woman he is fondest of, thank the good God for her, and wonder, as she does, what in the world he'd do without her.

One main purpose of Helen's existence, Andrew believed, was "to be sweet and beautiful in the sunlight which God gives it." She could throw off her cares in soothing him and abandon "fancied duties" by embracing a husband and her natural role.[37]

On January 5, 1890, Andrew White asked Helen Magill to marry him and was thrilled "far down in the depths of [his] heart" when she fixed her eyes upon him and said "Yes!" He then besieged his beloved with requests that she curtail her work or quit her job. He knew she loved to teach but to be fair to herself and to him, to reserve her strength for the "beautiful destiny" of marriage, he insisted that she see a doctor, get recreation, and hire help to grade papers. The head of the Brooklyn board of education was an old Cornellian who agreed to cut red tape to arrange a leave of absence. "Remember," Andrew told his fiancée as they discussed nest building, "your duties to the Brooklyn School Board are not your only duties."[38]

Helen never doubted that, if asked, she would marry Andrew. Like many of her contemporaries, she devalued spinsterhood because it blocked the "bright visions of usefulness" that dance in a mother's eyes. "Work first—love next," the credo of Charlotte Perkins Gilman, described Helen's life chronology but not her priorities. Like her parents and her future husband, she was troubled by the high percentage of unmarried female college graduates. Thus, she came to the collective bargaining that constitutes a courtship with material and psychological disadvantages. At thirty-five, this was probably her last chance at marriage and motherhood; yet without a fulfilling career, she was unable to make the professional demands on Andrew that Lucy Sprague had made on Wesley Clair Mitchell—in leaving Berkeley for New York, Sprague traded a deanship for a spouse and scholarship. Helen knew that teaching physical geography in Brooklyn was more a livelihood than a calling and not demonstrably preferable to opportunities at Cornell. Moreover, unlike many of her contemporaries, as described by historian Ellen Rothman, she was certain about her ability to love but unsure of her worthiness to be loved. Especially at the outset, at *his* moment of vulnerability, Andrew seemed the ideal man, the perfect contradiction in terms: aggressive and self-confident, yet solicitous, gentle, even deferential. In helping him, she assuaged her insecurity with palpable evidence of her worth. Throughout their turbulent courtship, she saw in Andrew many of the qualities she wanted in a husband: an academic, like Appleton and Archer-Hind, he was sympathetic and successful, far more worldly than they, with connections to the best and the brightest on two continents. Best of all, he was attentive and loving, interested in her intellect. The love of a man, Rachel Brownstein has suggested, often proves to a woman her value while serving as payment for it. Singled out among all others, a woman begins to realize an identity when she anticipates marriage. If a woman's primary power is the power to refuse, Helen did not exercise an option she could not contemplate.[39]

A clue to Helen's attitude can be found in her discussions of her relationship with Andrew. As we have seen, she was not drawn into the kind of circle that sustained so many women in Victorian America and that provided for some an emotionally satisfying alternative to marriage. Many women, Rothman suggests, were eager for friendship because they were wary of love; by contrast, Helen's fear of friendship may have made her more receptive to romance. It certainly left her alone in calculating gains and losses, in gauging her feelings. Her devotion to her four younger sisters was maternal: she gave comfort and counsel but did not expect to receive it. With Eva Channing, her lifelong friend and correspondent, she was reluctant to discuss affairs of the heart. She hesitated to call Andrew a suitor when she might be wrong, especially since both she and Eva expected marriage to disrupt and perhaps destroy their friendship. Each had predicted, almost as a pledge, that she would never marry. Eva suspected that Andrew was more than a friend but could only joke and wait for Helen to ask for her advice. Helen chose to confide only in her parents, the people most likely to encourage her to engage Andrew in passive pursuit. The Magills were proud of Helen's accomplishments: they had encouraged her to study and work when many middle-class parents ordered single women to spend their adulthood at home. But they never wavered from the belief that marriage was preferable, and they were ecstatic at the prospect of Andrew White as their son-in-law. At every turn the Magills met Helen's reservations with reassurances. Her father's counsel, "a man's judgment," was that Andrew was responding warily to a woman who might play a large part in his future; if Helen stopped criticizing a man who was, after all, already better than most, all would be well. Her mother also took Andrew's side, warning Helen to be neither suspicious nor assertive. Only with her parents did she feel comfortable discussing tactics. They told her what she wanted to hear, even though she sometimes could not make herself do what they asked.[40]

Andrew's proposal seemed to verify the Magills' advice, and for much of 1890 Helen's letters gushed. She was Mary Outwater redivivus, preserving the violets she wore on the day "when you first clasped me to your breast and I began to be a new woman." Their love was a flower, with the fruit to come later, "in a mutual life slowly matured" that would be ever sweeter, although it was difficult to exceed "this present joy." When her dearest was away she longed to see him: "I miss you so much. How glad I shall be when I need not be separated from you most of the time. You will be also will you not?" In letters filled with details about household linen and furniture, she also assured him that she would get along well with his children. She knew she had surrendered ambition and must subordinate independence to be the kind of wife he wanted. He had the power, she said, "of making me such a woman as I feel I was made to be: that must be one reason why I love you so deeply and feel that I need you so much." If misunderstandings arose between them, Andrew must come to her instead of writing. Her pen had been the emblem of her intellect, testimony to Emily Dickinson's observation that a letter was "like Immortality, for is it not the Mind alone, without corporeal friend?" Now that love made her dependent upon him for her "every existence," she was prepared to smother her rational powers in a forgiving embrace.[41]

Like the course of their courtship, the White-Magill engagement did not run smooth. To give him time to assure Lucia and Emily Outwater that they would remain part of the household and to explain to his children, Clara, Fred, and Ruth, that an ample inheritance still awaited them, Andrew wanted the wedding announcement to be postponed. He even entertained the idea of writing to Clara and Fred (Ruth was already fond of Helen) about his plans and then scheduling a ceremony before they received his letters. Ever solicitous of his children's sensitivities, he was not, in Helen's opinion, as mindful of her needs. Her "tone of reproach," he sighed, did not bode well for the future. At the slightest hint of trouble she seemed ready "to give up everything, read into my letters ideas that I never put into them, cannot sleep, cannot live!" Andrew had provided for her in his will, he kept telling her, and even if he died tomorrow she would not need to work for the rest of her life. Her mania about money was as unwarranted as her failure to understand his children's desire to protect their inheritance for their families. She must trust him and be patient with Clara and Fred, who were understandably reluctant to see their mother replaced. In the meantime, Andrew reaffirmed his love and his request to let things drift for a while, without setting a date.[42]

Although at first Fred and Clara refused to bless their father's remarriage, as he explained the provisions of his will and extolled the virtues of his betrothed, the "lions in the path" were tamed. Andrew was particularly eloquent in describing Helen's domestic talents. He reported to her: "I went slow on your Greek and Philosophy—dilated on your love of Literature and the value to the younger children [i.e., Ruth and the grandchildren] of having such a guide and counsellor, waxed eloquent on your moral perfections—fortissimo on your beauty of soul, sweetness of face and F.F. on your qualities as head of the household and your sympathy with me." When the Outwaters agreed to remain in the White household, the last obstacle was removed. The wedding was set for September 10, 1890.[43]

Helen was ecstatic, even as she worried about her lack of experience as a household manager and about having the Outwaters in her home. Her trepidation was fueled by Mrs. Fred White's report that the White establishment, as large as a small hotel and crammed from attic to basement with valuable things, "used up" even the most experienced housekeeper. Nonetheless, she cherished Andrew's confidence in her and was delighted that, finally, she could share her news. The engagement ring, once worn around her neck, now glistened on her finger. Her colleagues at school had suspected an announcement when, two days after Andrew's proposal, he had checked discretion at the door and kissed her in the front parlor, behind a curtain that did not hide his passion. She basked in their congratulations, content for the moment to suspend her concern that the prenuptial agreement shortchanged the children she hoped to have: "How short a time now it is before I shall be wholly yours; yet I am so even now: I have left behind me the time when I was quite independent and self-directed long ago. I do not regret it. I never shall for my own part: if only I am to you what I wish to be."[44]

Andrew had time for one more round of doubts. As the wedding day drew near, he began to sleep more fitfully, transported in his dreams to Swarthmore College to ask the residents if Helen Magill was sane. No one answered. The troubled groom-to-be related his nightmare vision to his fiancée in two hastily composed letters but held to his resolve, despite "painful doubts" about Helen's "want of get-along-attiveness," to make her his second wife.[45]

Helen Magill and Andrew White were married in a simple ceremony performed in the Quaker way. "May Heaven bless and keep us," he prayed. "My dear Helen is my choice, because of her inherent loveliness, sweetness and goodness as well as her remarkable intellectual gifts." Nonetheless, he reserved his love for Mary and continued to commemorate the anniversary of her death in his diary, where he made little reference to his second wife. For the remaining twenty-eight years of his life, Andrew had two wives: "dearest Mary," who had brought him only happiness, and Helen, whose rebelliousness sometimes approached that of Nora, the "utterly impossible character" of Ibsen's *A Doll's House,* which he read without pleasure four days after his marriage. The shrew had been caged—but not tamed.[50]

NOTES

1. Katherine Cowan to HM, Apr. 12, 1887. For a superb assessment of the ASSA, see Thomas L. Haskell, *The Emergence of Professional Social Science* (Urbana, Ill., 1977).

2. This account draws extensively on Helen's diary entries, labeled "Saratoga Sept 1887."

3. Jenny B. Lind to ADW, Oct. 5, 1887; E. E. (Mrs. E. P.) Evans to Mary White, July 9, 1872; ADW, *Diary,* June 13, 1887, all in ADW Papers. White thought his first wife "one more added to the thousands of martyred women, victims of a system which makes real 'help' in a household well nigh impossible." His old friend Evan P. Evans disputed the contention that domestic chores caused Mary's death. See ADW to E. P. Evans, June 23, 1887; E. P. Evans to ADW, Aug. 24, 1887, both in ADW Papers.

4. HM to EHM, Oct. 8, 1887, Oct. 9, 1887; EHM to HM, Oct. 25 1887. See also EHM to HM, Oct. 10, 1887.

5. SWM to HM, Feb. 14, 1888; HM to ADW, Nov. 28, 1887, Jan. 1, 1888, Feb. 6, 1888, ADW Papers. See also HM to ADW, Jan. 26, 1888, Feb. 3, 1888, ADW Papers.

6. ADW to HM, Mar. 5, 1888, Dec. 19, 1887, Mar. 8, 1888.

7. ADW to HM, Jan. 11, 1888, Feb. 8, 1888; HM to ADW, Dec. 15, 1887, ADW Papers.

8. HM to ADW, Nov. 28, 1887, Apr. 11, 1888, Aug. 12, 1888, ADW Papers.

9. HM to ADW, Dec. 15, 1887, Feb. 3, 1889, Feb. 14, 1888, ADW Papers.

10. ADW to HM, Aug. 18, 1888; HM to ADW, Sept. 4, 1888; ADW to E. P. Evans, Mar. 3, 1888; ADW to HM, May 14, 1888, all but the first in ADW Papers.

11. ADW to HM, May 14, 1888; HM to ADW, Apr. 11, 1888, May 15, 1888, ADW Papers. See also Ann Douglas, *The Feminization of American Culture* (New York, 1977); Barbara Welter, "The Feminization of American Religion," in *Clio's Consciousness Raised,* ed. Mary S. Hartman and Lois Banner (New York, 1974), pp. 137–57.

12. HM to ADW, Mar. 2, 1888; T. W. Higginson to ADW, Dec. 12, 1887, ADW Papers. See also HM to SWM, Nov. 13. 1887. Many years later, Helen responded to Higginson's reaction to frankness, "a variation from the attitude to which he was doubtless accustomed in the female mind: both his wives were hopeless cases of nervous prostration before they had been married two years: lucky he didn't marry me, or the nervous prostration might have been on the other side. *I* certainly should not have accepted it for want of speaking my mind." HMW to ADW, Sept. 14, 1900.

13. SWM to HM, Jan. 26, 1888; HM to SWM, Feb. 20, 1888.

14. Notes on ADW, written on an envelope postmarked July 14, 1887; HM to SWM, Mar. 11, 1888. Helen's view of Andrew would change a bit but would not deviate substantially (at least for very long) from this assessment.

15. HM to ADW, Feb. 1, 1888, ADW Papers; HM to SWM, May 13, 1888; HM to ADW, Apr. 29, 1888, ADW Papers; EHM to HM, Apr. 30, 1888. See also SWM to HM, Jan. 26, 1888.

16. ADW to HM, May 1, 1888, June 2, 1888; HM to SWM, May 29, 1888, May 30, 1888. See also HM to ADW, May 28, 1888, ADW Papers. Ironically, the recommendation of Edward Everett Hale, which Andrew received after he advised Helen to withdraw from consideration, was ecstatically positive, pronouncing Helen "a remarkable teacher . . . [with] a remarkable power in inspiring and guiding young women." See E. E. Hale to ADW, May 10, 1888, ADW Papers.

17. HM to ADW, Nov. 24, 1888, ADW Papers; HM to SWM, Mar. 11, 1888, May 30, 1888; HM to ADW, Apr. 19, 1888, April 11, 1888, May 15, 1888, ADW Papers. See also HM to ADW, May 28, 1888, May 31, 1888, ADW Papers.

18. HM to EC, June 3, 1888.

19. HM to ADW, July 8, 1888, July 26, 1888, ADW Papers. See also HM to ADW, June 22, 1888, June 26, 1888, ADW Papers.

20. ADW to HM, July 7, 1888, Aug. 25, 1888.

21. Barbara Sicherman, "The Uses of Diagnosis: Doctors, Patients and Neurasthenia," *Journal of the History of Medicine,* 32, no. 1 (1977): 41; HM to ADW, Nov. 28, 1888, Oct. 16, 1888, Sept. 13, 1888, ADW Papers. See also HM to ADW, Mar. 6, 1888, July 8, 1888, Aug. 12, 1888, ADW Papers; Elaine Showalter, *The Female Malady: Women, Madness and English Culture, 1830–1980* (New York, 1985), esp. pp. 63–65, 130–44; Suzanne Poirer, "The Weir Mitchell Rest Cure: Doctors and Patients," *Women's Studies,* 10, no. 1 (1983): 15–40.

22. HM to ADW, Mar. 6, 1888, June 10, 1888, ADW Papers. See also HM to ADW, Aug. 19, 1888, Sept. 6, 1888, ADW Papers.

23. ADW to HM, Sept. 18, 1888, Oct. 13, 1888.

24. HM to ADW, June 8, 1888, July 26, 1888, Aug. 19, 1888, Aug. 12, 1888, ADW Papers.

25. HM to ADW, Aug. 19, 1888, May 15, 1888, May 25, 1888, Feb. 15, 1889, ADW Papers. For a discussion of spinsterhood as deviant, see Lee Chambers-Schiller, "The Single Woman: Family and Vocation among Nineteenth-Century Reformers," in *Woman's Being, Woman's Place,* ed. Mary Kelley (Boston, 1979), pp. 334–50.

26. HM to ADW, Mar. 17, 1889, ADW Papers.

27. ADW to HM, Nov. 14, 1888; EHM to HM, ca. Apr. 1889; SWM to HM, Apr. 24, 1889.

28. HM to ADW, Nov. 24, 1888, ADW Papers. See also HM to ADW, Jan. 15, 1889, ADW Papers.

29. ADW to HM, Feb. 15, 1889; HM to ADW, Mar. 5, 1889, Apr. 26, 1889, ADW Papers.

30. ADW to HM, Apr. 26, 1889, Apr. 15, 1889.

31. HM to ADW, May 7, 1889, May 22, 1889, ADW Papers. See also HM to Eudora Magill, ca. Apr. 1889. For a discussion of Andrew White's delay in responding, see EC to HM, June 16, 1889. Andrew had evidently used the phrase "taming of the Shrew" in an earlier letter, which has not been preserved. Helen thought the reference "outrageously impertinent" yet claimed not to be as offended as she might have been because she "always had a good deal of respect for both of the parties in that little comedy." HM to ADW, May 22, 1889, ADW Papers.

32. ADW to HM, June 11, 1889.

33. Carroll Smith-Rosenberg, *Disorderly Conduct: Visions of Gender in Victorian America* (New York, 1985), pp. 197–216; HM, *Diary,* June 15, 1889; HM to ADW, June 30, 1889, ADW Papers; Showalter, pp. 130–40.

34. HM to ADW, Aug. 5, 1889, Sept. 13, 1889, Oct. 9, 1889, ADW Papers.

35. ADW to HM, Aug. 17, 1889.

36. ADW to HM, Dec. 5, 1889, Dec. 4, 1889. See also HM to EC, Oct. 13, 1889; HM to ADW, Oct. 9, 1889, Oct. 11, 1889, ADW Papers; ADW to HM, Feb. 5, 1890.

37. ADW to HM, Dec. 4, 1889, Dec. 31, 1889, Jan. 8, 1890. See also ADW to HM, Dec. 5, 1889.

38. ADW to HM, Jan. 6, 1890, Jan. 27, 1890, Jan. 24, 1890.

39. The "bright visions of usefulness" floated in Elizabeth Blackwell's head. See Ellen Rothman, *Hands and Hearts: A History of Courtship in America* (New York, 1984), pp. 195–96, 200, 249, 252–54. Joyce Antler, in *Lucy Sprague Mitchell: The Making of a Modern Woman* (New Haven, Conn. 1987), pp. 159–80, provides a marvelous description and analysis of the Sprague-Mitchell negotiations. See also Rachel M. Brownstein, *Becoming a Heroine: Reading about Women in Novels* (New York, 1982), p. xv. Charlotte Perkins Gilman is quoted in Ruth Bordin, *Francis Willard: A Biography* (Chapel Hill, N.C., 1986), p. 9.

40. Rothman, pp. 195–339; EHM to HM, Oct. 5, 1889; HM to SWM, Nov. 1, 1889. Helen didn't think there was "any mystery in my isolation. . . . I can't pretend to like things I abhor, or to be different from myself to please anyone. I try to like everyone honestly as much as I can. But oil and water will never really mix, no matter how much you shake them together. . . . Nobody wants the expressed essence of disagreement and disapproval in a transparent bottle always under their nose, no matter how tightly corked by polite toleration." HM to ADW, Jan. 26, 1888. For a discussion of the sustaining power of women's networks, see Carroll Smith-Rosenberg's now-classic essay, "The Female World of Love and Ritual: Relations between Women in Nineteenth-Century America," *Signs,* 1, no. 1 (Aug. 1975): 1–29.

41. HM to ADW, June 25, 1890, July 27, 1890, July 4, 1890, ADW Papers. See also ADW to HM, Jan. 8, 1890.

42. ADW to HM, Apr. 10, 1890, Apr. 18, 1890. See also ADW to HM, Apr. 14, 1890; HM to Edward, Sarah, and Dora Magill, Mar. 17, 1890. Andrew left Helen $60,000, about one-quarter of his estate, which would yield her an income of $2,000–3,000 per year. See ADW to HM, July 14, 1890; HM to ADW, Aug. 1, 1890, ADW Papers.

43. ADW to HM, July 11, 1890, ADW Papers. See also ADW to HM, July 7, 1890, July 31, 1890; HM to ADW, July 12, 1890, ADW Papers.

44. HM to ADW, Aug. 30, 1890. See also HM to ADW, July 12, 1890, July 17, 1890, Aug. 1, 1890, ADW Papers; SWM to HM, Oct. 17, 1890.

45. ADW, *Diary*, Aug. 4, 1890, Aug. 5, 1890, ADW Papers. No record of Helen's response to Andrew's dream has survived. While no stranger to suspicion herself, she may have met his doubts with equanimity, as they were frankly expressed and accompanied by assurances of love.

46. ADW, *Diary*, Sept. 10, 1890, Sept. 14, 1890, ADW Papers. See also Willard Fiske to E. P. Evans, Sept. 12, 1890, E. P. Evans Papers, Cornell University Library.

CHAPTER FIVE

"I suppose I must think of it all as a beautiful dream"

Helen Magill quickly learned that marriage to a public figure who seemed to know "all the people in the world worth knowing" could be as frustrating as it was fascinating. Although she enjoyed the attention of Andrew's friends, even when they almost smothered her with kindness, she had not anticipated a life of social distraction, preferring either the quiet of Ithaca or the culture of Europe. Her husband, she found, was a restless man, little given to contemplation and with an insatiable appetite for travel. He claimed to dislike social gatherings yet embarked on a "continual rash of giving and receiving entertainment." Even a "dreadful cough" did not exempt her from her duties as hostess: she planned a half dozen dinner parties from her bed, grateful for the assistance of a fleet of servants. If she had little time alone with her husband—the White household included Lucia and Emily Outwater, Ruth White, and a picture of the late Mary White in every room—she tried not to complain. Although no marriage could "be expected to be *all* plain sailing, even under the most favorable circumstances," Helen told Eva Channing that she was as happy "as any woman could possibly be, and I like it better and better."[1]

During 1890 and 1891, Andrew contemplated running for political office. He was offered the Republican nomination for a congressional seat in Tompkins County and later was touted as a gubernatorial candidate. Although Helen had little enthusiasm for the hurly-burly of politics, she urged her husband to do what he thought right: "I am ready for any decision: I live for you now: your good is mine." Although he ultimately declined the congressional opportunity and was not nominated for governor, his wife made clear that she would accommodate herself to his needs. Throughout their marriage she never mentioned teaching at Cornell, despite his hints about it during their courtship. Being Mrs. White was a full-time job, and a career was not compatible, she believed, with raising a family.[2]

Domestic duties, in Andrew's opinion, should keep a conscientious woman busy and happy, for they were at the center of the woman's sphere. He depended on Helen to serve as his social secretary, answering correspondence, entertaining guests, and purchasing gifts, and he did not hesitate to pepper her with instructions: "And now a matter of importance. Immediately after getting this—*the first thing*—write fully to Mrs. Hubbard thanking her and Mr. H. for their social kindness to us all and mentioning with special approval the *reception*. The Gilmans did this at once—and at length, immediately after reaching home. Do not fail. *Thank Mrs. H. also for so highly recommending Va. Beach and give some account of your life there. Don't delay this.* I ask it as a favor especially. I should be exceedingly mortified to have the matter wait longer." Andrew was delighted when Helen purchased dog whistles for the grandchildren and reminded him that she was qualified by sex to choose a shawl for Ruth. "A lady must buy these," she told him, "as you might easily be deceived about genuineness." Most important, however, Andrew hoped that Helen could be a mother to Ruth and diplomatically counter the influence of the possessive and extravagant Outwaters. Fortunately, stepmother and daughter shared a love for music, and great affection quickly grew between them, which Helen took as a sign that she was ready to bear a child of her own.[3]

Helen became pregnant, probably late in 1890. A dream she had then suggests that she viewed marriage and family as virtually simultaneous events: "I dreamed that I was making ready for my wedding—yet I had the baby. There was nothing wrong, but it seemed a little strange in the dream." She awoke, "oppressed with forebodings," and was comforted by her husband, although she did not reveal the content of the dream at the time. It is possible, of course, that Helen was experiencing guilt over sexual relations before marriage, although the couple's correspondence suggests that they shared nothing more than a few passionate kisses late in their courtship. Perhaps her forebodings reflected a subconscious sense that motherhood was her main motive for marriage and her uneasiness that love alone had not brought her to the altar. Without settling on an explanation of her dream, she shrugged off her anxiety and settled into her pregnancy.[4]

Unfortunately, Helen suffered a miscarriage. Although she wondered what the baby would have been like, she professed some relief, because during the early months of her marriage Andrew's "way of loving [her] seemed strange." She did not elaborate, but her discomfort at setting up a household in front of the Outwaters is as easy to imagine as Andrew's ambivalence at seeing his beloved Mary displaced in the kitchen and the bedroom. The newlyweds had for a long time been set in their ways, and much of their courtship had been by correspondence; moreover, Andrew's aggressive sexual behavior made Helen uneasy. Although she viewed marriage as a platonic ideal of devotion and love, and even dreamed of a virgin birth, she did not recoil from sexual intercourse (despite acknowledging that it was fully a year after her marriage before she began to enjoy it "the way [she] should have"). Her sexual inexperience and reticence account in part for her husband's episodic affections, but his moods, she was learning, simply had to be endured. In the spring of 1891, when she learned that she was pregnant again, she tried to be more optimistic, predicting that Andrew's love would endow the child with "a very happy constitution."[5]

On December 26, 1891, Helen gave birth to a "very strong baby," a girl. Giving voice to Helen's own thoughts, Andrew exclaimed: "Now my own wife, we are wedded indeed with this dear sweet tie to bind us. You are right; childless marriages are poor indeed compared to those blessed by offspring." The proud father wanted to name the baby Helen, but the flattered mother insisted on Hilda. Pregnancy had weakened Helen, and Hilda's unusually large head had made the delivery difficult, prompting the Whites to hire an excellent nurse, a six-foot Swede whose skill with infants exceeded her command of English. Helen could forgive Sophie for spoiling Hilda and for expecting the baby to like her nurse better than her mother. Nonetheless, to wean herself and her child from Sophie, Helen insisted on nursing her baby. She seldom gave much milk, at times almost nothing, but the experience of nursing was so sweet that she could not imagine how any woman could willingly forgo that happiness. The child flourished, gaining almost 3/4 of a pound per week, which Helen took as a sign of health. She refused to allow Andrew to call the baby "pudgy" ("you may call her mother 'pudgy' . . . but for her you must find some other epithet"), preferring to describe Hilda as "decidedly tall and stately."[6]

Hilda had large, dark blue eyes, a small chin, a well-developed turned-up nose, soft, golden brown hair, very fair skin, and fat, rosy cheeks. She slept all night, every night, without waking and did not need to be fed between 7:30 P.M. and 6:30 A.M. She was, Helen thought, "very conversational" and, if anything, too bright and active in the daytime; she was also quick to exhibit a high temper when aroused, issuing forth with a powerful soprano that left "much to be desired for harmony." In all likelihood a precocious child, as both of her parents had been, Hilda would require careful supervision, a task for which her mother felt uniquely qualified. Indeed, her daughter's birth provided a reason for Helen to return to study: "I must rub it [Greek] up for Hilda. I shall not want her to find me ignorant."[7]

When Hilda was about a month old, Andrew Carnegie invited Andrew White to accompany him on an extended tour of Mexico and California; the two would combine a little business with pleasure, further advising Leland Stanford on his ambitious new university in Palo Alto. Andrew agreed and at first contemplated taking his new family with him, then concluded that the trip would be too strenuous for a newborn. Might Helen consent to leave the baby with her mother or one of her sisters? As he probably expected, Helen was tempted but "would not give Hilda for the whole of Mexico and California." Instead, she gave the six-month journey her blessing and agreed to move to the Magill home in Swarthmore while her husband was away.[8]

Actually, the trip put Helen in "a doubting and despondent mood." Because Hilda was so precious to her, she trembled that something might go wrong and suspected that Andrew's departure was a belated vote against the shattering of peace and quiet that came with a second family. His recent actions, moreover—he had arranged to be buried next to Mary White, which reminded Helen of his interruption of their honeymoon to place a bust of his late wife in the Cornell University Library—raised doubts about his affection for her. The couple had not been particularly companionable: Helen's expectation that they would read, study, and even work together had been dashed because Andrew preferred "practical" to aesthetic or excessively literary works and could not accommodate himself to his wife's "slow turn of mind and willingness to linger over detail." In essence, Helen was too much the intellectual for her husband, although she sometimes blamed herself for the distance that was growing between them:

> I don't think you are very anxious, even when you are with me, to open your mind and thoughts to me—perhaps you think I am not able to appreciate them. I remember you intimated as much once—nor do you take much pain to draw out mine—but I fear, indeed, they are not worth it. I am sorry not to be more to you—you are so much to me—and if I don't understand or appreciate your ideas . . . it is not because I do not sympathize with you and try to understand you as much as I can. And perhaps this is a good deal better than you realize. I don't readily express what I most deeply feel. So often I think of things that I would like to say to you, and then I am somehow impressed that you would not care for it. And perhaps you would not. So many things that I and the world generally find interesting in books meet with indifference or even disdain from you. It is a curious experience for me, who never realized my intellectual insignificance until I was married. I suppose it is good for me; but I would rather have learned it in some other connection.

Helen's tone, only slightly more defensive than defiant, recalls the turmoil of her courtship, a turmoil unresolved by marriage and motherhood. Heaven had made her dear to Andrew, for "reasons unscrutable," she acknowledged on occasion, and "I am filled with wonder and thankfulness day and night, when I think about it." Yet she also guessed that her husband would love Hilda, as he did her, "very much in general but not very much in particular."[9]

When Andrew was away Helen felt isolated, a prisoner to his affection, someone who had left behind "the time when [she] was quite independent and self-directed." Hers was the double bind of educated women in Victorian America described by historian Martha Banta. If they married and took "the angelic gamble" by withdrawing from professional activity to serve their families, women risked becoming "moral bores or cultural excrescenses." But, as Helen found out, if they sought positions in the white-collar world of men, they risked failure, isolation, and criticism that they had forfeited "their special power as ideal forms." Even in death she contemplated a lonely existence, for Andrew might not put her remains in Sage Chapel, next to Mary and the place reserved for him: "It makes me feel so dreadfully lonely to go there even now: how much more so if I should be left alone. And if Andrew, more than twenty years her senior, died first, a sad life would be left to Helen, who "never had any happiness" and never would, except in his love. In her dreams, she depicted her fear of abandonment by rendering her husband "very ill and dying:"

> I sat beside you and we talked a little: but you said you did not know that you cared about another life: and then I was dreadfully hurt and said I should think you would care to live, to meet me again, if you really loved me. You said you loved me, in a very weak voice, but you would not say any more, or express the least hope. And then I thought we were going to walk together, and I stepped back to attend to something, and when I went on I could not find you, but went up and down long stairways and through halls and corridors looking and looking for you.

Searching for Andrew, she passed through a picture gallery, stopping in front of a painting of a mother and child, laid out for burial. As she looked at it, she heard someone wonder aloud if Mrs. White thought "her baby would die in the hospital." She moved away and continued to look for her husband. Dreams "go by contraries," Helen believed, but she did not hesitate to give Andrew the "sad" details of a neglect that was akin to murder.[10]

Andrew got the message. He inundated Helen with affectionate letters, lamenting their separation, detailing his grievance against Hilda for keeping Helen in the East, and contemplating a summons to San Francisco from her "suzeraine and liege lord!" With loving humor he comforted his spouse: to her demand that he substitute long letters for businesslike telegrams, he dubbed her a "perverse unthankful wife—you dear little foolish wise woman! You preposterous child-wife! Darling, consider yourself kissed again and again. I find myself counting not merely the days but the hours." In Hilda's "savage temper" Andrew saw his wife's peculiarities perpetuated, a sufficient reason for Helen to curb her "Quaker ferocity." When he returned, his "soothing influence" might have "a happy effect" on the baby and perhaps even Helen.[11]

This time Andrew calmed without arousing. Helen agreed that bringing Hilda to California was impractical, given her own inability to nurse and the difficulty of getting milk on railroads. Nor could she contemplate leaving the baby with her elderly mother or her busy sisters. She laughed at Andrew's jokes because they were accompanied by passionate declarations of love (in letters too sacred for "eyes other than ours") and were replete with promises that he would never again, as long as he lived, permit so long a separation. A "deep longing" overcame him, he wrote, as he talked with the Stanfords about their university: "At times I feel that I must break away at once, that life is not worth living alone; then I try to think of other things and so gradually get into a more sane condition—but the trouble returns, more and more intense; the longing to see your face, to hear your voice, to be by your side and kiss you and the baby. Dear sweet wife, dear sweet mother, dear sweet baby,—both mine." Such familial images relieved the disquiet of Helen's dreams. "My darling husband," she wrote, "you have made my life so sweet—I never imagined anyone could be so happy as I am."[12]

Andrew cut his trip short—but only when the resignation of Charles Kendall Adams, his successor as president of Cornell, necessitated action by the board of trustees. He found Helen worn out, her digestive system upset by pregnancy, nursing, and the drugs "and other trash" used to treat her. To give her a rest, he proposed a vacation in Saratoga, where he was to deliver an address. Helen was reluctant to leave Hilda with Sophie or with her mother, but since the baby seemed healthy, though a little "out of sorts" because of her teeth, she finally agreed to visit the place where she and Andrew had met. As the Whites relaxed in Saratoga, however, a telegram summoned them home: Hilda was gravely ill. Leaving their baggage behind, the couple departed the resort at midnight but arrived too late.[13]

Death came to Hilda White without warning, brought on by an embolism. Although the doctors could not determine the cause of the "stasis of the circulation in the sinuses of the brain," they were certain that no one could have saved the infant. Nonetheless, Helen's grief was mixed with guilt: she had a gnawing sense that bottled milk had something to do with the tragedy. Moreover, she felt she had abandoned her baby to be with her husband—though she said nothing to Andrew about enticing her to Saratoga, perhaps preferring to hold herself responsible. Even as she tried to take solace in the six months of happiness she had shared with her child, her melancholy seemed to Eva Channing almost suicidal. What kept Helen from leaping to join Hilda in "the other life," however, was duty to her husband. As long as he lived, she would "remain here but here I shall never be happy again." Never would her suffering cease; never again would she have "the same bright hopes" for a child. This "crushing experience" had altered forever her "relation to the things of this world." For the rest of her life, Helen kept close at hand Hilda's little pillow, white with embroidered forget-me-nots and a lace ruffle.[14]

As if to divert attention from a mother in mourning, President Benjamin Harrison appointed Andrew White minister to Russia just ten days after Hilda's death. A post in St. Petersburg was hardly Andrew's first choice; he preferred Paris or Berlin and for some years had had reason to think he might be secretary of state. Nevertheless, he accepted the position because it might lead to a more important role in the making of foreign policy, especially if Harrison gained re-election in 1892. Although no record of Helen's reaction to her husband's appointment survives, culturally forlorn and climatically forbidding Russia was probably not the change of scenery she might otherwise have welcomed; in addition, if she became pregnant again, she might have to settle for the primitive medical facilities of St. Petersburg. Nonetheless, her place was with her husband. To combat loneliness, Helen took with her Marian Magill, her youngest sister, who could be a companion to Ruth White as well. The party traveled in stylish leisure, lingering in London and promenading in Paris, all to the delight of Marian, who found her brother-in-law extraordinarily "entertaining, kind and thoughtful."[15]

Andrew's resilience in shrugging off Hilda's death, in sharp contrast to his reaction to Mary's demise, seemed almost sacrilegious to Helen. Victorian women, Ann Douglas has suggested, used grief as "therapeutic indulgence"; as they domesticated death, they enhanced their influence by stressing the value of "insignificant" lives. To Andrew, however, work and even worldly pleasure were morally superior to protracted grief. Thus did the gulf between husband and wife widen, as Andrew's lusty appetite for meals and museums, his apparent imperviousness to pain, marked him in Helen's eyes as callous, less devoted to his second family than to his first. One night in a Paris hotel in the fall of 1892, Andrew made a sexual approach that Helen rebuffed, precipitating an argument that lasted into the morning. Anxious to become pregnant again, she viewed his insistence on interrupted intercourse as emblematic of a self-centered indifference to her needs. When he stormed out, she assessed their relationship in a remarkable letter.[16]

Helen wrote to her "beloved husband" because he refused to "listen to or weigh with judgment" what she had to say. Although he treated her with an impatient and "undeserved harshness," sometimes proposing to cast her off, she loved him nonetheless and always would. Willing to shoulder some blame for their quarrels, she tried to provide a context for her attitude toward sexual intercourse:

> Let me write plainly and read what I have to say. That which gives you pleasure also give me pleasure, as I must have shown you again and again the moment I felt I could accept that pleasure without danger of permanent injury to me, which would result, sooner or later, in loss and dissatisfaction to you. My confinement was a hard one and my recovery is far from complete. . . . That which is very sweet to me always (when I have it fully) does not seem to hurt me but rather to do me good, if I have intervals of repose of some length. But when it is too frequent, and especially when it is not complete, it always seems to put me backward. . . . If you could only know how I feel my whole physical being comforted and refreshed when I received what I desire, and compare this with the wretched disappointed feeling that in spite of some pleasure at the first, comes over me sooner or later when I am deprived of it (sometimes not till some time after when I quite think I have escaped it, so it can not be imagination), I am sure you would not be so impatient with my prudence. If I dread to become an invalid, like so many women, it is always because I feel it will be so wretched for you: nothing else could give me the force to offer you a resistance so intensely distressing to me. You *must* have seen how happy I am when I can give you pleasure. . . . Nothing else, except my love for the baby has ever given me perfect happiness. Since she is gone, one half my life is pain and now it seems that it must be wholly so.

"Sweet intercourse" was "very dear" and probably beneficial to her health, Helen thought, if taken in moderate amounts and fully consummated. Although "somewhat in the dark" about the male constitution, she considered Andrew's sexual regimen "reckless": he was "*mad* to put such a strain" upon himself as would even endanger a much younger man. Self-restraint would strengthen his "very elastic constitution" and probably prolong their "unspeakable happiness for *years* to come"; of course, she felt compelled to add that she would continue to love him when he lost his vigor entirely, "as in the course of nature you must." Because she valued affection far more than intercourse, her love would not "change with outward circumstances, perhaps not [even] with injustice and cruelty, if I should suffer these at your hands."[17]

To preserve "the precious privileges" of sexual pleasure, Helen proposed that they have intercourse only once or twice a month, a plan she preferred even if it decreased the likelihood that she would bear another child, though that, too, might result "in a good and seasonable time." She also forgave Andrew for the reproaches that burst from his "cruel passion."

Then she offered to make the final—and for her the ultimate—sacrifice if he did not return her love:

> I think we must try to get along perhaps and make a good public face now till we get back to America. Then if I really seem to make you more unhappy than happy I will go away and take up my old life, though it can never be the same, of course, as it was before you came into it and thought you loved me and made me so happy for a while with this mistake, and with the dear joy of motherhood which came of it. I suppose I must think of it all as a beautiful dream—but the waking from such dreams is a very hard one. Yet, unless on your account, I can never regret it.

Like many of her contemporaries, Helen feared that sexual excess endangered health, but her attitude confirms historian Carl Degler's observation that a belief in temperance "should not be confused with repugnance or distaste." When allowed to reach orgasm, Helen found intercourse "sweet"; she objected to coitus interruptus, it is interesting to note, because it denied her sexual pleasure, not because it made procreation impossible. Clearly, she was reticent about sex, a topic she did not discuss with her parents or with Eva Channing. Still, she tried to write a wifely letter, couching her complaints, suggestions, and resistance as concern for her husband's welfare and happiness, which she valued "more than my life a thousand times, or my health or anything else."[18]

Helen must have known that, despite her protestations, her tone was provocative, and so she decided not to send the letter. Might discussion of Andrew's "less worthy feelings and impulses," of his "cruel passion," of his declining vigor have fueled the flames of his rage? Might he have been angered by the audacity of her proposal? Might Helen have been embarrassed about giving voice to her own sexual desires—or worse yet, afraid he would accept her offer to leave? Did she now confront how much marriage had reduced her independence? Whatever her reasons, Helen put the letter in an envelope, sealed it, and wrote "For A. D. White (after my death) H.M.W." Had she decided, melodramatically, to risk her health rather than confront her husband, to martyr herself to his passion but then remind him, from the grave, that he had callously caused her death? Did she practice what Phyllis Rose preached a century later in a study of Victorian marriage: that inflicting guilt is the revenge of the less powerful? Keeping the letter, unanswered and unanswerable, Helen not only got the last word, she could revisit her triumph by rereading it. We can only guess at the nature of the Whites' reconciliation and of their subsequent sexual experience. Alone together in Russia, Helen occupied herself with the household while Andrew set up his diplomatic shop.[19]

St. Petersburg was dreary and depressing. Helen had a cold when she arrived, and it seemed to take up permanent residence in her body. If lucky enough to return home alive, she wheezed, "you will never catch me going in further expeditions of the kind, or coquetting any more with the North Pole." She judged most Russians to be as cold and dull as the weather, with little desire to socialize with foreigners, and she found the morals of government officials offensive. If she refused to see anyone who kept a mistress, Helen informed her mother, she would exclude two-thirds of the "best" society of St. Petersburg, a prospect most inviting to a Quaker lady but quite impossible for a diplomat's wife.[20]

Early in 1893, Helen discovered that she was again pregnant. Lame and sore, with quite a bit of blood in her urine, she was adamant about leaving Russia. Both she and her unborn child would have "ten times the chance" of surviving in the bracing air of Helsingfors, Finland, she told Andrew, who thought the trip unnecessary and expensive but relented nonetheless. On July 9, three days short of the first anniversary of Hilda's death, Karin Andreevna White was born. The delivery was far easier than had been feared. The maid, Margot, wakened Beatrice Magill, who had replaced Marian that spring, at 4:30 A.M.; six hours later the baby was born. Although Helen was weak, she was in no danger; neither chloroform nor instruments had been used in the delivery. The doctors thought Helen would not be able to nurse Karin, but she found that she had almost enough milk and, with a wet-nurse to "finish off," brought her baby to her breast five times a day.[21]

Helen, who worried constantly about Karin's health, asked Beatrice to sleep in the room with her and her daughter to provide relief during the "concerts" Karin gave every night, and the sisters struggled even more when Margot departed in August to attend to family problems. Like Hilda, Karin wanted to be juggled constantly; used to Margot's experienced attention, she wailed when handled by her mother and aunt. When Karin was ill, Helen grew desperate, frustrated that Finland had no homeopathic doctors and ready to ask Andrew to come from St. Petersburg. This time, she vowed, she would remain at her baby's side.[22]

Although she disliked being separated from her husband, Helen dared not risk Karin's safety by returning to Russia, where the "pestilential climate" produced an enormous death rate, "especially of children." As if the recent outbreak of cholera were not bad enough, anarchist-inspired violence, directed against czarist officials but indiscriminate in its victims, sustained her resolve. For the duration of Andrew's term of office, Helen, Karin, Ruth White, and Beatrice took up residence in Dresden, Germany.[23]

Pressed with official business, vexed by an inefficient staff, Andrew thought his wife an alarmist. The baby was likely to have her "ups and downs," he wrote, and Helen must not risk her own health by worrying.

As before, he prescribed a traditional remedy: "quiet, equanimity, freedom from care," achieved through fresh air, strolls in the park ("take your book or even sewing there, if you *must* read or sew"), and adequate sleep. Because Helen had gained a considerable amount of weight in the last two years, he recommended exercise, pointing out that a robust mother could supply wholesome milk for Karin. But most of all, he tried to be supportive and loving. "How sweet and good you seem to me when I think of you as a mother!" he wrote, as he sat alone in front of the fire, "unable to stand" being apart from his family. A silver cup from the time of Peter the Great appeared in Dresden on Helen's fortieth birthday, a gift from a "lover on instinct" who had not *remembered* the occasion but "*divined* it." Andrew claimed he dared not think too much of his desire to join his wife, for "to do so would keep me in a sort of a fever." Never again, he pledged, as he had before, must they be separated "before our final separation comes."[24]

Try as they both did, absence only made their hearts grow harder. Andrew posed as a forlorn bachelor, but Helen sensed that he accepted their separation with equanimity and even relief, ill prepared at sixty-one for a bawling baby and weary of her lengthy discussions of Karin's condition. At every turn, moreover, he manifested little respect for her intellectual interests. He resented her criticisms of his work on the warfare of science with theology and disdained her "Epicurean testing of various literary and artistic pleasures." To her proposal that she settle in Ithaca after his death, he lectured her about Mrs. Nott of Union College, whose house had become a center of disaffection against her husband's successor as president—her likes and dislikes "held with a conscientiousness which is only seen in women and college professors." To save Cornell from the catastrophe of "one gifted woman's criticisms," Andrew suggested that Helen return to Swarthmore when he died. This exchange reminded her that she was a wife without a home, who meant little to her husband "and likely [would mean] less and less in the inevitable effect of time." Feelings of "settled loneliness," the clouds of her married life, closed around her, and the best she could do was resolve to try to make their life together "as acceptable as possible."[25]

Helen considered it her duty to ensure that Andrew provided adequately for his second family. Convinced that the prenuptial agreement she had initialed shortchanged Karin, she pleaded with her husband to change it. With the exception of Ruth, she argued, his children could take care of themselves and had already been the beneficiaries of their father's largess. Furthermore, if anything happened to her, he should provide for Karin's material needs but give "*absolute control*" over the girl to the Magill sisters, who would "train her wisely and conscientiously" and "love her truly and unselfishly." Helen hammered home the point with Karin as a stand-in for her long-suffering mother: "If she is like her mother she will need, before all things, to be loved really and truly, and I believe I could kill her with my own hands rather than let her be dependent on anybody who would merely tolerate her and very likely misunderstand and despise her, and who will dislike and get rid of her in any way they [*sic*] can if she seems likely to cause them the least trouble." If Andrew died first, Helen would need a substantial sum of money to enable Karin "to be independent." With Fred White managing the family finances, trying to preserve a large inheritance for his own children, she anticipated a difficult widowhood, unless Andrew's will recognized need as well as equity.[26]

Andrew became impatient with Helen's hectoring, which persisted throughout their marriage. He claimed that he had left her $80,000 in cash and $40,000 in real estate and provided property for Karin that would be worth as much as or more than the sum provided for his grandchildren. The attitude of his children, Andrew believed, was understandable. In "distress and terror" they feared that their father, mesmerized with love, might forget their own children, and "naturally they tried to protect themselves." What parent would act differently? His will was just, yet he had received "no thanks—but many reproaches" from Helen, who, in his opinion, maintained an extravagant style of living and seemed unwilling to keep track of expenses. Andrew gave his wife $12,000 a year to run a household in Dresden, an inexpensive city where the demands of society were small, and she was forever drawing on their bank account without telling him what she was buying. She might think an unexplained bill of $50 "a little matter but a grain of dust in an inflamed eyelid is a severe infection. . . . " *He* had not married *her* for wealth or honor, he wrote, hoping to shame her into silence with a reminder that she had, and would always have, more than enough, and certainly far more than she could have had, had she not married a wealthy man.[27]

Andrew expected Helen to defer to his judgment, deeming suspicion and criticism in a wife a betrayal of her marriage vows. Her inconsistency in weighing his behavior undercut the logic of her arguments: sometimes her scale rose, sometimes it sank, but the balance in her instrument had to be defective because "when your side rises mine rises, and when your side falls mine falls." Since the problem was in her head and heart, it was up to her to will it away. To enter into the "aims, plans and tastes" of a husband was not to spoil him, Andrew thought, so Helen must subdue her inclination to thwart him by adopting a "superior, hypercritical not to say rather snappish" tone, quick to "pooh-pooh" his feelings and opinions. When she was knowledgeable about a subject, the music of Wagner, for example, he did not contradict her. Could she not reciprocate in his sphere, by bowing to his financial acumen and embracing the validity of his point of view on science and religion? Above all, she must cast aside her unwarranted doubts about his motives and "trust to the larger hope," as she had advised him to do years ago.[28]

With a baby to tend, Helen allowed the squabble to subside, and when she returned to a sphere whose boundaries she did not accept, Andrew thought her a "very nice, tidy little hen—clucking about her chicken," generally kind, though occasionally severe with "the father of said chicken." Karin grew prettier each day. She did not have Hilda's exquisite coloring or striking blue eyes, but she was a bright child who crept everywhere. Because the doctor thought speech at an early age excited the brain unduly, Karin's inability to talk did not bother Helen. Nursed five times a day, the child also drank boiled milk and ate concoctions of food whose odor made her mother sick. Helen envied people who knew nothing about germs and gave babies real food, though her bravado barely hid her concern for Karin's health. She attributed her daughter's happier disposition to good milk and good training.[29]

Just as Andrew knew Karin was in good hands, he was especially gratified for Helen's affection toward Ruth. The two spent much time together in Dresden, listening to *Siegfried* and *Die Meistersinger* and browsing in art galleries under the tutelage of Beatrice Magill, a talented painter. Andrew attributed Lucia Outwater's charge that Ruth had grown lonely because Karin took all of Helen's attention to the older woman's desire to have her granddaughter returned to Ithaca. Although he did not subscribe to Helen's view of Mrs. Outwater as the "evil genius of Ruth's existence—a selfish, brainless old woman" who had brought up her invalid daughter Emily to be "as inane as herself," he recognized that his former mother-in-law spoiled Ruth and kept her from her peers. Andrew marveled at Helen's patience with Ruth, whose "unfortunate manner" and "unpleasing exterior" made her an improbable object for a man's affection, and he was quite pleased that, under Helen's watchful eye, Ruth had met a young man in Ithaca and exchanged letters with him from Europe that hinted at matrimony. Andrew knew that love as well as duty motivated his wife's treatment of Ruth and that he could rely on her to care for Ruth when he was gone.[30]

Helen rejoined her husband in Russia, probably in the spring of 1894, and did not hide her delight when he resigned his post that September. Andrew felt he had been a diplomatic exile, without compensating social pleasures. Although he enjoyed walks and talks with Leo Tolstoy, he had met few other distinguished men of science and literature. Helen still thought Russia without redeeming virtues and vowed to commit to paper her impressions of the "absurdly" overrated Nevsky Prospect and the Winter Palace, that "perfect acme of hideousness." The quais and the interior of the Hermitage did little to brighten "the sordid ugliness" of St. Petersburg, she wrote. "It is enough to make a nihilist just to look at it."[31]

Happy to leave, the Whites were not at all certain where to live or what to do. As long as the Democrat Grover Cleveland remained in the White House, an ambassadorial post was out of the question. Andrew's book, *The Warfare of Science,* would soon be finished and published, leaving him to wonder how he might spend the few years that remained to him. Helen, of course, had Karin to raise, Ruth to look after, and a household to run, but she hoped as well for an intellectual outlet. She offered to help Andrew with his book, but her view that theology *was* a science, that it was neither the only nor the most significant threat to science, that the book sacrificed correctness to convenience, curtailed collaboration. Andrew nonetheless encouraged her to write, agreeing that she was "by no means a contemptable literary critic"; in fact, he teased, she could make a fortune as an essayist on moral questions, despite—or because of—her "crotchety" tone. In a more serious vein, he suggested that she use his research notes to write a brief biography of Fra Paolo Sarpi (the seventeenth-century Venetian who would be one of Andrew's *Seven Great Statesmen in the Warfare of Humanity with Unreason*) and that she help him gather material for his memoirs. He knew that Helen the perfectionist often became Helen the procrastinator, and as she prepared her lecture on Russian society for delivery at Swarthmore, he exhorted her to work steadily lest "wrecked or hurried and late."[32]

Although not averse to literary activity for Helen, like so many academic men, Andrew saw his wife as his intellectual assistant, helping with proofreading, research, and writing, available to undertake or complete projects he had abandoned or postponed, or recording her impressions of Russia for a largely female audience. He acknowledged, but did not quite admire, her literary taste because her aesthetic sensitivity had not produced serenity. Andrew thought a return to the classics might impair Helen's health and interfere with her duties as wife and mother, and she did not disagree. She could rub up her Greek a bit for Karin's sake, but she considered an original interpretation of Plato beyond her.

Reluctant to return to Ithaca, where Andrew might look over the shoulder of the president of Cornell and where Helen might clash with the Outwaters, the Whites drifted for months, traveling through Italy, at times together, often separately so that Andrew could visit old friends unencumbered by Karin. As always, the couple sparred when separated, with Helen pointing out that Andrew showed how much he cared by the company he chose. In the summer of 1895, this time with his wife's blessing, Andrew went home, leaving the entourage in the bracing air of northern Italy. A transatlantic passage in hot weather, Helen thought, might risk the health of a teething two-year-old, "just now in for her worst spell." In the fall, Helen brought Ruth and Karin to Ithaca, bristling at her mother's suggestion that Andrew return to Europe to fetch them: "How perfectly absurd. . . . Marriage has not made me quite such a helpless person as that."[33]

Another summons to public service was not long in coming. To settle a boundary dispute between Venezuela and British Guiana—and thereby assert the Monroe Doctrine—President Cleveland appointed a "nonpartisan" investigatory commission. As a member of the commission, Andrew spent much of 1896 in Washington, supervising research and writing the report. He managed to find time for presidential politics as well, writing pamphlets for William McKinley, denouncing William Jennings Bryan, pillorying the Populists. When McKinley was elected, Andrew received his reward: appointment as ambassador to Germany, a post he had coveted.[34]

Shortly before Andrew's appointment to the Venezuela commission, Helen learned she was pregnant. As always, when Andrew thought of "the mother—prospective and actual," his love became "infinite"; he wrote, "I longed to tell you of it & to kiss you while I tell it." For Helen, the news may not have been cause for celebration. Early in 1895 she had told her mother that, despite her desire to have a boy, her constitution could not support another delivery; alluding perhaps to differences with her husband, she added that "it would not be right" to try again. Perhaps the Whites succeeded without really trying. In any event, about the time she became pregnant, she took to bed with a "catarral affection of the head" and "obstinate constipation." Apprehensive and melancholy, she suffered through her pregnancy, little buoyed by her husband's cheerleading from afar—"Be a good, strong, brave woman, keep up your courage. Remember that the temperament of another human being whom we are both to love depends upon your self control now"—and without "the woman's world around the birthing bed" (the importance of which has been documented by Judith Walzer Leavitt). Andrew was in Washington and busy with the campaign, and her mother was too sick to journey to her side; only Marian, who probably arrived shortly before the birth, kept her company. As Helen lay in bed, images of Hilda intruded, uninvited, and she could not shake the conviction that her husband was indifferent to her fate and that of her child.[35]

On July 10, 1896, Edward Magill White was born and died. The only account of the delivery comes from Marian, who informed her mother of the "fatal mistake": "It is strange, too, after Karin came so easily—but then I suppose she was much smaller. . . . we hoped so *much* that H. was spared the dreadful trial of knowing just how it was and that she was unconscious and the doctors let her think it was born dead. It is too dreadful to think of that your life had been spared only through the death of your own dear child, who already seems a person to one by that time." In later years, Helen rarely referred to Edward, nor revealed how much she knew about the circumstances of his death. The depth of her grief needs no documentation, yet fragmentary evidence suggests that she subsequently blamed herself for the tragedy. First through Karin and then a friend, she explained that "she loved sweets and goodies and finally got diabetes. The baby was a heavy, big one and . . . could not be turned and it seemed that with knives the baby died and was removed." From Swarthmore, Sarah Magill offered a mother's consolation: "It is not absolutely necessary that we [women] should be happy but it is laid upon us to live holy and thoughtful and trusting lives." A mother lives not for herself but for her children; fortunately, Helen had a daughter to mold into "something better than the purposeless existence of a worldly and self-willed and self-seeking woman." Helen's response has not survived, but it is doubtful that she took much comfort in Christian doctrines of duty and submission.[36]

While Andrew campaigned for McKinley, Helen rested at Virginia Beach. Her health remained precarious throughout the fall and winter, and her sagging spirits contrasted with the buoyancy of her husband, who relished combat with Populists and free-silver Democrats. Six years of marriage, separation, pregnancy, and death had taken a toll. At times Helen lashed out at Andrew, for forgetting their anniversary in 1896 and for his reluctance to go "a little beneath the surface of daily happenings and business matters." But she was weary now and a bit defensive, often admitting that their problems were perhaps her fault. She was no less direct, but defiance was giving way to resignation, as if she felt her fate was to fight and lose. After the presidential election, the couple prepared to assume their posts as ambassador and ambassadress to Germany.[37]

Since college, Helen had yearned to live in Germany. She now found Berlin to be a cultured and cosmopolitan city, and as ambassadress she hobnobbed with the royal family, diplomats, and intellectuals. A superb conversationalist, she sparkled at dinner parties, bedecked in the latest fashions in a luxuriously decorated apartment. In Berlin, Karin learned about music, opera, and art with every breath she took. When she had time, Helen helped Andrew prepare a history of the Reformation in Germany from lectures he had written decades before. The Quaker had become an American Queen, sought after, praised by princes and professors, with a large staff at her disposal.[38]

Andrew D. White in 1890, the year of his marriage to Helen. Author's collection.

Beatrice Magill and Hilda White, ca. 1892. Courtesy of Department of Manuscripts and University Archives, Cornell University Libraries.

Helen Magill White with daughter Karin, 1894. Courtesy of Department of
Manuscripts and University Archives, Cornell University Libraries.

Helen Magill White, as ambassadress to Germany, ca. 1900. Author's collection.

Andrew, Helen, and Karin White, 1905. Courtesy of Department of Manuscripts and University Archives, Cornell University Libraries.

Helen Magill White, widowed in 1918. Author's collection.

Although Andrew appreciated Helen's skills as a hostess, the couple battled constantly, often in front of the servants and Karin, whose "perversity," both parents agreed, owed much to their example. This time Andrew initiated the combat, usually by lambasting his wife's extravagances. He was amazed that "the thinking members of [her] sex" wasted so much time and money appeasing the "chronic condition of 'nothing to wear' " and furnishing ambassadorial residences in a style ill suited to republican simplicity. Living costs in Berlin exceeded those in Ithaca, and Helen seemed to know no limits. Andrew made suggestions, but they were usually ignored, prompting him to declare, "I might as well make a request of a brazen image." To Helen he was a "household tyrant" who brooked no disagreement, no explanation, however reasonable. Throughout his career he had held his temper and moderated his views to avoid conflict with the Cornell board of trustees and the U.S. State Department. In fact, his public life, "singularly free" of quarrels of any sort, had been marked by "acquiescence for the sake of peace." But at home he expected to be the master; his family should never question or challenge his authority. If Helen remained intractable, the couple could not be compatible, for in families, as in nations, sovereignty was indivisible.[39]

As the Whites took turns being irritated and irate, Sarah Magill unwittingly broke the cycle of recrimination and resentment. She became ill just as her daughter left for Berlin, then suffered a stroke. Uncertain about the chances for her mother's recovery, Helen awaited a summons from Swarthmore. In the spring of 1898, Beatrice informed her sister that the end was near. Helen took Karin and left her husband, sending from the ship an expression of disenchantment with her married life. Andrew replied that he found temporary bachelorhood a placid existence: "Contrast this with my life last year. Always alone at breakfast—the house up to 11 o'clock and noon a pandemonium. You breakfasting in bed; with Alvina, your maid, your masseuse, your German teacher, Carl, August and myself running to and fro to do your bidding—people waiting in the vestibule and elsewhere on appointments [which] you had not kept—all my work interrupted by summons to your room." He found signs of her "selfishness" everywhere: she rarely met him for breakfast; she did not keep an appointment book; she did not keep track of expenses; she did not take regular exercise, especially after the birth of their children, "to keep down [her] flesh." Inevitably, his love had died, and Andrew, at first indifferent to Helen's return, now regarded it with "repugnance." "Spasmodically critical, harsh, exciting," she exercised anything but a "quiet, wifely influence." As if outbursts massaged her taught nerves, Andrew wrote, Helen craved conflict: "We cannot travel together we cannot drive together we cannot walk together we cannot sit together . . . without the most bitter personal quarrels." Unless she promised to change, he asked that she remain at Swarthmore. Perhaps, in a year, affection might return; or, Helen might seize "the opportunity to pursue [her] chosen studies." No doubt she would send "reams of well-stated arguments" to prove him "outrageously unjust," but a reasoned defense would only "make matters worse."[40]

Helen framed a detailed rebuttal. She claimed that in all things she tried to please her husband and that she gave "regular minute and conscientious attention" to bills. Andrew jumped to the conclusion that she had not returned silk patterns to the dealer when, in fact, she had painstakingly packed them for parcel post. She kept not one but two memorandum books of all appointments and spent most evenings recording and filing. She regretted that she could not join her husband at breakfast but thought he understood that household chores and social calls kept her busy from 10:00 A.M. until the early hours of the next morning. Sleep was a duty, more important than the pleasure of his company, for he would suffer most if her health gave out. As for exercise, she regularly took long walks, often with him, though she had had precious little time to do so in Berlin. In sum, Andrew's portrait of a selfish, self-indulgent wife was a libel: "I should have thought you might find a hundred images of me as an affectionate wife, a devoted and careful mother and householder, trying faithfully to discharge very onerous duties. . . . " It was doubtful, she decided, that he would come to see her in this "truer light," and so to avoid the "shame and disgrace" of separation, an arrangement that would kill her mother and destroy her father, she promised to linger in Swarthmore until December but begged for permission to return in 1899: "I shall try hard to correct the faults that distress you. I shall not ask for your love, but to be tolerated for the sake of my child, and of those dear to me, to whom such a shame and mortification to me as to be thrust out of my rightful home would be a dreadful blow." They should commune across the Atlantic for three consecutive Sundays, Helen suggested, to think things over, seek Divine guidance, and perhaps find a way to resume their life together.[41]

In one sense Helen's brief defied her husband, whose respect cum dislike for her rational powers conflicted with contemporary notions of feminine capacities. At bottom, however, she was a supplicant to a sovereign who could send her into exile and disgrace. Part of her believed that a woman was "largely responsible for the kind of affection she inspired"; though Andrew's bill of particulars was riddled with errors, his larger point, that she had brought it all on herself, struck a responsive chord. Helen seemed willing now to settle for the appearance of a happy marriage; to return to scholarship was impossible and to be separated, shunned by society, without the resources to raise her daughter, was a prospect too dreadful to contemplate. She could do nothing more than submerge herself in an appeal to her husband's sympathy and sense of justice.[42]

Helen's abject advocacy, accompanied by an offer to return the clothing she had purchased for Karin and herself, reminded Andrew of their early courtship, when he had "dreamed of a sweet, serene, restful old age" with a loving wife to comfort him. Such a view of marriage was selfish, he knew, but "natural" for an old man. To show her that he was not obsessed about money, he bought an adornment for her boudoir and withdrew his objections to her expenditures. As he communed Sundays, however, he wondered whether she could ever pass up opportunities to exhibit her gifts in the art of sarcasm. When she struck, he freely confessed, he erupted angrily. If the marriage was to survive, they needed rules for a cease-fire and an honorable retreat. Andrew could not promise quiet compliance "under the regime which a lady Preceptor would administer to a pupil," but he was willing to try. In September 1898, the month that Sarah Magill died, he informed Helen: "We are to resume our life together."[43]

Andrew's criticisms indicate that he would not countenance a "balance of power" in marriage and did not cede control of the domestic sphere to his wife. In the economy of consumption of the nineteenth century, women made the purchases but men usually retained the power of the purse. As the breadwinner of the family, Andrew felt free to review expenses, adjust the budget, and dictate when Helen arose and whether she exercised. He did not let her forget to whom she owed her extravagant life-style. At forty-five, without an active career beyond the home, Helen could not envision a life outside marriage. She prepared to return to a sphere that she would superintend at her husband's sufferance.[44]

As if to seal the agreement, Helen checked into a sanatorium in Dansville, New York, to begin the work of weight reduction before returning to Berlin. Opened just before the Civil War, the Dansville health center was one of the most famous facilities of the nineteenth century. Under the care of Dr. James C. Jackson and his large, well-trained staff, the predominantly female patients recovered health and fitness through a combination of rest, exercise, diet, and the water cure. Helen's initial examination revealed some anemia, an excess of phosphate, "nerve waste," as Dr. Jackson called it, and a little too much uric acid, perhaps an indication of gout.

The Dansville regime filled the day, and Helen was a dutiful patient. At 7 A.M. she received a stiff massage and then breakfast of grapes, a little fish, crusts of bread, and one cup of postum. She prayed, listened to a lecture on the principles of hygiene, then hurried to "the infernal regions" of the "torture chamber" where feet, arms, legs, and body were shaken and stretched by a strange machine. After a nap and a walk, "a very sparing dinner carefully regulated against starch" was served and patients were permitted to read the newspaper. Every other afternoon Helen had a "Moliere": shut up in a hot box, with only her head sticking out, she sweated, sponged off, and took to her bicycle for a two-hour ride. Supper was light, primarily skim milk and "educators," a form of hardtack that was, she guessed, designed to enlighten body and mind. After each meal patients drank a weird concoction made out of bone marrow. Not a scrap of fat could be found at Dansville. Still, she was disappointed by the results. Her tight dresses fit a bit more comfortably, but after shedding five pounds the first week, she could not coax the scale to drop below 150. She did not give up, however, and shipped a bicycle to Berlin, a purchase Andrew undoubtedly approved.[45]

Helen had lost some weight and regained her husband. Never again would the Whites approach the precipice of separation, but like Helen's diet, their reconciliation was not an unqualified success. Squabbles and sarcasm reappeared during the last two decades of their Sisyphean ritual, an unsatisfactory union that was, for both, acceptable only in the absence of alternatives.

NOTES

1. HMW to ADW, Sept. 30, 1890; HMW to EC, April 9, 1891. Throughout her marriage, Helen never breathed a word of criticism of Andrew to her friend Eva.

2. HMW to ADW, Sept. 30, 1890. Even the feminists of that generation, William Leach points out, did not deny that "mothers should not work during the years of childbearing and child rearing." *True Love and Perfect Union: The Feminist Reform of Sex and Society* (New York, 1980), p. 195. According to Thomas Wentworth Higginson, no woman should "be self-supporting at all during her career of motherhood," even if it lasted for decades (quoted in ibid.). By the time Helen completed her child-rearing responsibilities, she would be fifty.

3. ADW to HMW, Mar. 20, 1896, ADW Papers; HMW to ADW, Sept. 26, 1894, ADW Papers. See also HMW to ADW, May 10, 1894.

4. HMW to ADW, Mar. 13, 1892.

5. Ibid. Margaret Trevor Ford to author, Sept. 30, 1986, author's files.

6. HMW to ADW, Feb. 3, 1892; ADW to HMW, Feb. 3, 1892; HMW to ADW, Mar. 13, 1892; HMW to EC, Mar. 15, 1892.

7. HMW to ADW, Feb. ?, 1892. See also HMW to ADW, Mar. 13, 1892; HMW to EC, Mar. 15, 1892.

8. HMW to ADW, Feb. 13, 1892.

9. HMW to ADW, Feb. 22, 1892, Mar. 5, 1892, Feb. ?, 1892.

10. HMW to ADW, Feb. 13, 1892, Feb. 15, 1892, Mar. 13, 1892. The phrase "the angelic gamble" has been used by novelist Iris Murdoch. See also Martha Banta, *Imaging American Women: Ideas and Ideals in Cultural History* (New York, 1987), p. 440.

11. ADW to HMW, Mar. 16, 1892, Mar. 14, 1892, Apr. 1, 1892. See also ADW to HMW, Mar. 21, 1892, Mar. 22, 1892.

12. ADW to HMW, Apr. 25, 1892; HMW to ADW, Apr. 30, 1892. See also ADW to HMW, Mar. 28, 1892.

13. HMW to ADW, Apr. 16, 1892; ADW to Willard Fiske, July 19, 1892, ADW Papers; ADW to F. W. Holls, July 19, 1892, ADW Papers; ADW to E. P. Evans, Aug. 22, 1892, ADW Papers; HMW to EC, July 26, 1892.

14. Joseph Bigler to HMW, Aug. 24, 1892; HMW to EC, July 26, 1892, Sept. 8, 1892. See also HMW to ADW, Sept. 29–Oct. 1, 1900, ADW Papers.

15. Marian Magill to EHM, Sept. 18, 1892.

16. Ann Douglas, *The Feminization of American Culture* (New York, 1977), pp. 242–72.

17. HMW to ADW, ca. Fall 1892 (written on the stationery of the Paris hotel at which the Whites stayed).

18. Carl Degler, "What Ought to Be and What Was: Women's Sexuality in the Nineteenth Century," *The American Historical Review,* 79, no. 5 (Dec. 1974): 1467–90. For women's sexual attitudes in courtship and marriage, see Ellen Rothman, *Hands and Hearts: A History of Courtship in America* (New York, 1984), pp. 185–86, 255–62. Peter Gay, in *The Bourgeois Experience: Victoria to Freud.* vol. 1: *Education of the Senses* (New York, 1984) and vol. 2: *The Tender Passion* (New York, 1986), challenges the view that nineteenth-century Europeans were reticent in sexual attitudes and/or practices. For the contradictory consequences of women's moral influence in sexual matters, see Nancy F. Cott, "Passionlessness: An Interpretation of Victorian Sexual Ideology, 1790-1850," *Signs,* 4, no. 2 (1978): 219–36.

19. Phyllis Rose, *Parallel Lives: Five Victorian Marriages* (New York, 1983).

20. HMW to Marian Magill, Nov. 28, 1892; HMW to SWM, Dec. 30, 1892/Jan. 11, 1893 (Helen frequently double-dated her letters to account for the Gregorian calendar). To monitor government officials, an annual review was conducted, Helen wryly noted, where each Russian "leaves his mistress or his gambling for a week or so, confesses, is absolved, gets his certificate and goes merrily on again for another twelve months." HM to SWM, Jan. 17/29, 1893.

21. HMW to SWM, ca. June 1893; Beatrice Magill to SWM, July 16, 1893. See also HM to SWM, Mar. 27, 1893 (fragment); Beatrice Magill to EC, undated. For a discussion of the benefits and dangers of instruments in child-birth, see Judith Walzer Leavitt, *Brought to Bed: Childbearing in America 1750-1950* (New York, 1986). Leavitt stresses the importance of "the woman's world around the birthing bed" (pp. 87–115). Helen's desire to have Marian and then Beatrice with her no doubt reflected her desire for companionship during pregnancy, delivery, and nursing.

22. Beatrice Magill to SWM, Aug. 9, 1893, Aug. 13, 1893; ADW to HMW,

Aug. 7, 1893. When Helen was a child, Beatrice remembered, "she always imagined she had all sorts of diseases." See Beatrice Magill to SWM, Apr. 20, 1894.

23. HMW to SWM, Dec. 10, 1893. See also ADW to EHM, Jan. 23, 1894. Beatrice thought Helen's concern about cholera exaggerated. The epidemic was confined to the lower classes, she told her father, although she admitted that her analysis stemmed in part from a desire to visit the art galleries of St. Petersburg. See Beatrice Magill to EHM, Sept. 10, 1893. Andrew told his wife that Russia was, in fact, safer than the United States, "where the anti-social people have everything pretty much their own way" because they knew it was almost impossible to apprehend and convict them. ADW to HMW, Jan. 12/Jan. 24, 1894.

24. ADW to HMW, Aug. 14, 1893, Nov. 16, 1893, Oct. 9, 1893, Nov. 1, 1893, Mar. 6, 1894.

25. ADW to HMW, Oct. 1, 1894, Nov. 8/29, 1893; HMW to ADW, May 10, 1894, ADW Papers. See also HMW to SWM, Dec. 10, 1893; ADW to HMW, Apr. 11, 1894.

26. HMW to ADW, Sept. 26, 1894, ADW Papers. See also HMW to ADW, July 13, 1900; ADW to HMW, Nov. 30, 1893.

27. ADW to HMW, Sept. 9, 1893, Dec. 16, 1893, Dec. 18, 1893. See also ADW to HMW, Sept. 2, 1895, Nov. 30, 1893. Andrew had ordered his son to provide Helen $750–1,000 a month in Dresden, though he hoped she would not use so much. See ADW to Fred White, Dec. 18, 1893, ADW Papers.

28. ADW to HMW, Jan. 19/31, 1894, May 14, 1896. See also ADW to HMW, Mar. 15, 1894, Feb. 1, 1897.

29. ADW to HMW, June 2, 1894. See also Beatrice Magill to SWM, Nov. 6, 1893, Apr. 13, 1894; HMW to SWM, Apr. 2, 1894. For a discussion about concern for mortality and nursing and feeding practices in Victorian England, see Patricia Branca, *Silent Sisterhood: Middle-Class Women in the Victorian Home* (London, 1975).

30. HMW to Magill Family, Apr. 1893 (fragment); Fred White to ADW, Oct. 27, 1893, ADW Papers. See also HMW to ADW, May 10, 1894, ADW Papers; ADW to HMW, Oct. 29/Nov. 10, 1893.

31. HMW to SWM, Sept. 28, 1894; HMW to ADW, Apr. 8, 1896, ADW Papers. Helen was irked that she could not learn Russian but blamed her difficulties on the language.

32. ADW to HMW, Jan. 20/Feb. 1, 1894, Nov. 21, 1895, Apr. 1, 1896. See also HMW to SWM, July 25, 1894; HMW to ADW, Oct. 16, 1894. Andrew completed *The Warfare of Science* "in spite of [Helen's] latest deliverance against my work." But to "pay you off," he told her, "I have stricken the world 'dogmatic' out of the title." ADW to HMW, Nov. 23, 1893. For an assessment of White's work as minister to Russia, see Glenn C. Altschuler, *Andrew D. White: Educator, Historian, Diplomat* (Ithaca, N.Y., 1979), pp. 192–201.

33. HMW to SWM, July 26, 1895. See also HMW to ADW, Apr. 9, 1895, Apr. 11, 1895, June 1, 1895, ADW Papers; ADW to HMW, June 14, 1895, July 12, 1895.

34. For a fuller description of White's activities in 1896, see Altschuler, pp. 223–29.

35. ADW to HMW, Jan. 31, 1896; HMW to SWM, Jan. 29, 1895; Joseph Bigler to HMW, Dec. 17, 1895; ADW to HMW, May 23, 1896, ADW Papers; Leavitt, pp. 87–115. See also ADW to HMW, May 21, 1896, ADW Papers. Marian had married two years earlier and lived in Nashville, Tennessee. Much younger than Helen, she was helpful but not close to her sister.

36. Marian Magill to SWM, July 23, 1896. Margaret Trevor Ford to author, Sept. 30, 1986, author's files. Mrs. Ford mistakenly dated the baby's death as occurring before Karin's birth. See SWM to HMW, Sept. 24, 1896.

37. HMW to ADW, Oct. 14, 1896. See also ADW to HMW, Oct. 16, 1896, Oct. 17, 1896.

38. HMW to SWM, Dec. 30, 1896–Jan. 5, 1897, Mar. 11, 1898; HMW to Beatrice Magill, Apr. 14–16, 1897.

39. ADW to HMW, June 10, 1898, Apr. 1, 1897, Feb. 1, 1897.

40. ADW to HMW, July 13, 1898, July 16, 1898. See also ADW to HMW, June 27, 1898, July 15, 1898, July 21, 1898, Aug. 1, 1898; HMW to Beatrice Magill, Apr. 14–16, 1897.

41. HMW to ADW, Aug. 1, 1898. See also ADW to HMW, Aug. 6, 1898.

42. HMW to ADW, Oct. 20, 1896.

43. ADW to HMW, Aug. 8, 1898, Aug. 12, 1898, Sept. 17, 1898. See also ADW to HMW, Aug. 9, 1898, Aug. 12, 1898, Aug. 15, 1898, Aug. 24, 1898, Sept. 22, 1898.

44. Women who were public figures established a different "balance of power" in their marriages. See Rose, *Parallel Lives,* and the essays on Harriet Beecher Stowe, Julia Ward Howe, Elizabeth Cady Stanton, and Juliette Lowe in Mary Kelley, ed., *Woman's Being, Woman's Place* (Boston, 1979). Helen's efforts to extend her sphere, by asking to learn about investments, for example, did not succeed even though she justified them as a logical extension of her responsibility to provide for Karin when Andrew died. For an interesting analysis of the decline of domesticity and attempts to rationalize and commodify the home, see Glenna Matthews, *"Just a Housewife": The Rise and Fall of Domesticity in America* (New York and London, 1987).

45. HMW to Beatrice Magill, Oct. 27, 1898, Nov. 8, 1898. For a discussion of the Dansville approach, see A. O. Bunnell, ed., *Dansville Historial Biographical Descriptive* (Dansville, N.Y., 1902), pp. 27–31, 97–101; Jane B. Donegan, *Hydropathic Highway to Health: Women and Water Cure in Antebellum America* (Westport, Conn., 1986); Harvey Green, *Fit For America* (New York, 1986), chap. 4.

CHAPTER SIX

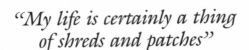

"My life is certainly a thing of shreds and patches"

Helen returned to Berlin to complete the task of turning the White's commodious second-floor apartment into a "diplomatic establishment." Before she left for Swarthmore, she had redecorated, "renewed" the floor, and refit the apartment with electricity and water. In 1898 she journeyed as far as Dresden, London, and Paris for the most fashionable furniture and upholstery, which was sent in padded wagons to Berlin. Although money went "frightfully fast," Andrew gave his wife a free hand to make their home "one of the most brilliant social establishments" in the German capital. With an annual ambassadorial expense account of $18,000 at her disposal, supplemented by Andrew's income, Helen rarely let a week go by without giving a dinner party, boasting to her husband that the $200 she spent on each occasion was less than a third of that spent by the French ambassadress, with no discernible difference in quality. At times she viewed these affairs as a duty, supplemented as they were by an endless round of diplomatic calls, made every day, rain or shine, from 3 until 6 P.M., except Monday and Tuesday when she received visitors at home. Helen did not seem overly concerned that there was little time reserved for reading. Superb theater and music in Berlin were de rigueur for diplomats, and she enjoyed the performances as well as the attention she received as the ambassador's wife, dressed in the latest Paris fashions and complimented by nobles and intellectuals.[1]

Helen considered herself superior to the unworldly Mary Outwater White, who had not supported her husband "in the proper way" during his first tour of duty as minister to Germany (1879–81):

> My private opinion is that the first Mrs. White, lovely and distinguished-looking and practically efficient as she doubtless was, in many ways, was undoubtedly a little *dumm:* I cannot otherwise explain the virgin soil I find in his mind in respect to many things which he *should* have learned from women. He hasn't the least confidence in me, and worries by croaking over everything I propose and undertake. Then he finds that it is a great success, and admits I have "some head," but the next step I want to take meets with the same discouragements.

As far as she was concerned, Andrew remained an "ingrained old Puritan" who worked constantly, had little appreciation of music and painting (with the exception of chorales, ethical sonnets, and historical styles of art), wore "all sorts of tweeds together and a soft hat that has got the crater-of-an-extinct-volcano shape," and knew less about women's clothes than "a barefoot friar." In social matters he was "a sucking babe" who had to be saved from his own naïveté. When a Mrs. Friedlander invited the couple to lunch at a fashionable hotel, Helen persuaded her husband to decline. She thought it "too cheeky for words" for Mrs. Friedlander to cultivate their acquaintance "in that public and sensational manner, for of course it would have been in all the newspapers." If Andrew raised his glass with a social-climbing Jew, she insisted, the Whites "could never look the English people in the face again." Helen viewed herself as without prejudice and supported her husband's efforts in behalf of the Jews when he was minister to Russia, but she took seriously her role as guardian of social conventions, insisting in a letter to her family that she had saved the ambassador from a serious mistake.[2]

Although she pretended to have little ambition "in a social way," Helen was delighted to be the pre-eminent American woman in Berlin. The idea that she was a society woman was funny, she told her family: "I know all the time that I am not a bit of one inside, but I will not deny that I enjoy the sense of power and try to use it in good ways as far as I can." How could she resist the lure of small, select parties or fail to notice that all Americans waited until she rose to leave a room? Who would not be flattered when asked to be photographed for a book on the Court of William II? If, when the camera flashed, Helen regretted that she had not ridden her bicycle more regularly, she could not sustain self-deprecation, not in a "yellow silk embroidered with nasturtiums trimmed with Venetian lace."[3]

Proud of her social sophistication, Helen tried to help her husband with his writing projects as well. She wrote to Professor George Lincoln Burr, Andrew's friend and former student, for information on the ambassador's literary plans. Burr suggested that she read German history and applauded her efforts to learn shorthand. Nothing could help Mr. White more, he said, than research, secretarial, and editorial assistance.[4]

In subtle ways, Helen also moved closer to her husband's political positions, abandoning the whisper of radicalism in her antislavery youth much as he had many years earlier. Ambassador White was an important man: selected by President McKinley as head of the U.S. delegation to the first international peace conference at the Hague in 1899, he was occasionally mentioned as a running mate for the Republican incumbent in 1900. Andrew thought of himself as a statesman, one whose idealism was tempered by a hardheaded assessment of human nature and historical context. In letters to her family, she echoed his political pronouncements and promoted his candidacy as a "fitting cap" to a distinguished career. Like her husband, she now believed that much good had "come of privilege and even of slavery in earlier stages of the world's development." If she did not think the United States should "go in largely" for imperialism, it was out of a conviction that the nation "was *too civilized* to deal with uncivilized nations as they should be dealt with." While Andrew encouraged German initiatives in the Far East, Helen praised England, the most imperialistic country in the world, as "the *most free, without* exception."[5]

War itself was a legitimate last resort, she asserted, in defense of the limited agreements hammered out at the Hague. The experienced delegates "knew that they would go further by not going too far—*on paper*—a thing that any club of Screamers can do." Compulsory arbitration of disputes between nations, for example, would never pass a Congress conscious of its duty to protect national sovereignty and promote the Monroe Doctrine. A chastened, evolutionary pragmatism was the only way to introduce national principles to international affairs.[6]

In domestic politics, Helen adopted her husband's views as well. American cities, boss-controlled and infested with criminals, were unsafe and unsavory. Unless the political power of ignorant foreigners were checked—through immigration quotas or literacy tests for voting—corruption would spread, threatening democracy in America. Even her ardor for woman suffrage was dampened by the recognition that reform would double the immigrant vote and thereby strengthen the Democratic party. That Edward Magill could contemplate voting for *"such a man"* as William Jennings Bryan left her aghast. Whatever he decided to do, Helen begged her father not to write to Andrew about politics.[7]

To a great extent, Helen's views were the product of her isolation inside the closed circle of the ambassador's political universe. With only a sketchy knowledge of foreign policy, immigration, and urban affairs, she deferred to the experience and expertise of her husband, whose friends and colleagues shared the genteel Republicanism characteristic of their social class. Faith in education, moreover, made her reluctant to enfranchise the ignorant. Had she heard other voices, things might have been different, as her reaction to Anna Shaw's lecture on woman suffrage in 1911 suggests. Although she had heard that Shaw was "extreme," she thought her "sane and sensible" and wavered when she learned how well suffrage was working in Denver. But it was too late: to Shaw's assertion that twelve million literate and only three million illiterate women would win the vote, Helen countered that the "proportion of fools to wise" was quite different.[8]

For the moment, other problems were more pressing. Neither Andrew nor Helen was terribly disappointed when President McKinley chose Theodore Roosevelt as his running mate. Close to seventy, Andrew was content to end his career in Berlin. Family affairs also occupied the couple. In the late summer of 1900, Ruth White married Erwin Ferry. Andrew crossed the Atlantic to attend the nuptials, but he thought the weather too hot to risk passage for Helen and seven-year-old Karin. If Helen was disappointed, she kept silent. She had great affection for Ruth, she told her family, and feared only that she would not be "finely fitted out for the daughter of a wealthy man" because Andrew knew so little and Ruth's sister, Clara, was the "idea of scrumpiness and indifference." To Ruth, Helen offered gifts instead of criticism, and she made certain that her stepdaughter received her fair share of the White family china. Well before the ceremony, Helen sent a beautiful piece of lace, costing $750, to her favorite White child, a token of affection designed as well to show the family the standards of taste appropriate to the wedding.[9]

Ruth's wedding was soon followed by the remarriage of Helen's widowed father, Edward, to Sarah Gardner; the couple took their honeymoon with the Whites in Germany. There was little inclination to celebrate, however, since Andrew was forced to spend time and money helping Clara White separate from her philandering husband, set up a household in Ithaca, and fight off a dependency on drugs born of despair. In November 1900, Lucia Outwater passed away and suitable quarters had to be found for her daughter Emily. Most devastating, however, was the suicide in July 1901 of the chronically ill and depressed Fred White. Helen, who tried to help Andrew through these family travails, was not close to Clara and Fred, yet she knew how useful Fred had been to his father (he managed the family's investments) and sensed that Andrew felt more pain than he showed. For once, she refrained from asking him to change his will, perhaps because she knew that he had to. Instead, she exercised a quiet influence, strengthening his resolve to retire in 1902 and counseling him to rest so that he would have time for his work, his wife, and his youngest daughter.[10]

Helen shared in the accolades at Andrew's retirement, for almost everyone praised the White residence as a magnet for princes, politicians, and professors. The last four years in Berlin were the best of her marriage, she later recalled. A social success, she received the deference of the ambassador in things domestic and once again was "a noble, absurd, sweet, ridiculous, wise, preposterous, hickory, prelactical Quaker! whose husband loves *grand meme* better than she deserves." Their marriage was far from idyllic, of course. The two squabbled, all the more frequently after Andrew's retirement, when Helen spent money like the ambassadress she no longer was. If they conversed more than they had in their early years together, they revealed little to one another, given Andrew's preference for the concrete and Helen's enjoyment of the abstract and aesthetic. Nonetheless, in Germany they had found satisfaction in shared diplomatic duties.[11]

To be sure, Helen got along by holding back, an approach that worked best when she felt constructively occupied. After 1898 she altered her expectations of marriage, shifting her concern to public perceptions and those of posterity. In death, she feared, Andrew might humiliate her by choosing to be buried next to his first wife or by denying Helen a sum appropriate to her widowhood. In Germany, with the help of a diary, she managed to contain her emotions. One entry is particularly revealing: As she strolled through a cemetery in Fohr one day, Helen came across the grave of a woman who was buried next to her first husband. On the tombstone was an account of a second marriage full of "the vicissitudes of this life," and Helen could not help thinking of herself: "Neatly put isn't it? I recommend it to people not satisfied with their second trial. Somehow it strikes me as more telling to reflect on your second than on your first: I don't know why: the latter might seem like hitting a man when he is down, perhaps. From an epigraphic point of view then it is better to have your worst experience last—especially if you survive him: 'last of all the woman died also.' I never realized what an advantage this was." Having the last word was particularly important to her, as she demonstrated in the letter she left for Andrew; now she trembled at his power to have the final say, even if he died first. Thus, Helen prepared for retirement without enthusiasm but with a certain amount of equanimity.[12]

What was a retired ambassadress to do? Reluctant to return to Ithaca, ostensibly because the harsh winters might damage Karin's delicate ears but probably because she did not feel quite at home there, Helen thought Italy conducive to literary endeavors and child rearing. Eventually the trio settled in a villa in Alassio, where Willard Fiske, Andrew's Cornell colleague, lived. Without "the necessary preparation" to do research for Andrew's *Seven Great Statesmen,* Helen made plans to do her own work while tutoring Karin in French and Italian. Extensive travels in Fohr might be converted into lectures and a manuscript, a project she had started in Berlin. In an almost idyllic two years—Alassio was "perfect," Karin informed her cousin—Helen did more writing than she had done in a decade, completing a series of lectures that were delivered to Saturday Circles in Italy and Germany and later at Swarthmore. When Italian summers grew unbearable, Switzerland beckoned. Neither of the Whites wished to be an expatriate, however, even in Paradise. Helen, a diplomat's wife almost from the moment of her marriage, missed her family and the chance to have friends she chose: "In America if I must suffer, it will be among those who love me. . . . " In 1904, they returned to Ithaca, Andrew to write and advise the trustees and president of Cornell University, Helen to give her daughter an American education.[13]

A passionate commitment to Karin both explains and is explained by the diminished intensity Helen brought to her marriage. At times, no doubt, she shared her sister Beatrice's wish for two mothers in the household, one to put the child to bed and the other to spend the evening with her husband. Andrew, however, rarely requested his wife's company, so Helen poured her attention upon Karin in an effort to exist for and with her, as advisor and counselor, companion and friend. Success at motherhood, she believed, would negate the failures of her early years. Her daughter allowed her, in essence, to have the final word, to leave proof that her life had been worthwhile.[14]

While in Germany, Helen hovered over little Karin, protecting her against disease and assuming personal control over her education. The White residence was a schoolhouse with a teacher who gave lessons in reading, writing, and arithmetic and did not neglect the aesthetic or the domestic: before she was seven, Karin danced, sewed, and scratched at the violin. To teach the child Italian and French, as well as English, Helen, Andrew, and the nurse each conversed with Karin exclusively in one language, "so she would never get them mixed up." A loving mother, however, must also be stern, and Helen recorded conduct marks in a little book, "red, blue and black, occasionally double red" for a little girl who was not "very fond of guiding." In at least one area Karin had to toe the line: to learn to walk like a lady, she exercised daily by turning out her toes.[15]

A precocious child, much like her mother had been, Karin had an active intelligence that was alternately delightful and disturbing. When Aunt Beatrice, whom she adored, left Berlin, Karin claimed that she had not cried: "Too babyish: but I can tell thee, I came very near it." When told to leave the room, she planted herself in a chair and begged to listen to the adults "because I'm very curious and if you want me to go away you would better begin to speak French." The same independent turn of mind shaped her response to religion. If Helen smiled at her daughter's conventional fear that she was not good enough to ascend to Heaven, she squirmed when Karin announced, at the age of eight, that she did not believe in "those legends about everlasting burning." Had she snuck a glance at the *Warfare of Science,* Andrew's effort to preserve the essence of Christianity by discrediting the myths that had grown around it? The child thought too much, Helen feared, perhaps because she had no companions her own age and was constantly among intellectuals.[16]

More unsettling were signs of selfishness and little "real regard or consideration for anyone." Although her father sent letters and cards whenever he was away from home, Karin wished he were dead so she would be spared the bother of writing to him. Helen tried not to spoil the child: she established a pay scale for schoolwork and household chores but could not induce her "to take the slightest pains to earn a cent of money." Karin sensed that her mother could not bear to deny her anything; marks of double red for "willful and absolute indifference" to the wishes of her parents had little sting because punishments were rarely sustained. Like her father, Helen did not believe in whipping, preferring appeals to reason. Karin, however, was "not at all judicial" about her desires: "she bites and scratches like a little wild animal when her *will* is crossed." Strict with the children of others, Helen could not be a "firm authority" to her daughter. Too often her commitment to discipline gave way to the indulgent impulses born of her newly acquired wealth. Any attempts to restrict Karin, moreover, turned temper into tantrum. Punishing the girl, Helen told her husband, was like "whipping a very nervous horse." If Karin responded neither to reason nor restraint, how could she be taught to be responsible and caring? And if her inheritance of American individualism, at its stubborn worse, was "already far too great," how would she fare when she had her compatriots as companions?[17]

When the Whites returned to the United States, Helen contemplated sending Karin to a boarding school. Discipline meted out by experienced strangers and contact with her peers might foster the girl's moral development. Reasons could also be summoned, however, to the cause of keeping her at home. The curriculum of most schools was "systematic stultification," a drastic departure from "nature's school." Helen could not bear the thought "of shutting Karin up in *any* house the best of the day—no matter how well ventilated or with what gymnastic exercises. I think she would wither with confinement of any kind." To Helen's good reasons for keeping Karin at home we may add a real reason: a dread of relinquishing responsibility and of being left alone with an often indifferent husband. The White household, then, became a school, staffed by tutors in arithmetic, Latin, and piano, run by a veteran principal who served also as teacher of Roman history and geography.[18]

For Karin, Helen's institution did not resemble "nature's school." She felt smothered, as much by constant attention as by her mother's high standards for study. Helen's desire for an intimate, a friend, crashed into Karin's preoccupation with privacy, a prerequisite for identity and independence for Victorian adolescents, symbolized by a room of her own. An unlocked door separated the rooms of mother and daughter, and Helen did not wait for an invitation to enter. She opened her daughter's mail, chose her attire, investigated the background of every playmate. In a not-at-all atypical letter, she showed a concern that could be exhausting, exacting, and exasperating, perhaps amusing to everyone but Karin:

> I trust thee got home comfortably and to bed—since that was expected, that all is going well with thee, and that thee is carefully taking thy medicine and using the nasal drops *every evening*. The pills were every three hours, I believe. Have they any marked taste beyond that of the spirit used to dissolve as to make the tincture I should say. All pills taste of that when freshly medicated. Do not fail to be *regular* about following this out: remember how much may depend upon care now: it is no light matter to have one's hearing seriously impaired, especially so young. Be assured I shall spare no pains to guard thee from it. Be careful about exposures, and uneven temperatures and about having cold drafts blow *directly on thy head,* at night or anytime. Thee cannot afford to take the risks so many girls do without serious consequences—*or seem to:* results of wrong or careless habits are sometimes obscure, and do not declare themselves at once. I don't like the cold feet: but I would try *any way* in preference to artificial heat. Dr. Weir Mitchell told Miss Austin to wrap her feet in a flannel petticoat. Thee has little other use for the good provision of those I gave thee. I really think thee would do well to wear the light summer weight ones in the evening when thee makes so great a change. Warmth about the abdomen is very helpful, and many serious ailments are cured by wearing a woven band. Thy underwear is so light. I believe so much in keeping the whole body at an even temperature. I am sending out to thee a box containing Thy old muff (take care of both sets)
> Hair brush
> Black ribbon for *three bows*
> Black tie knitted silk
> Dk. Blue tie Scotch imported (return if not liked)
> 1 pr. Black silk stockings—new.
> Three bar stockings, one pair which are lisle, faced with silk, and *I* think good enough for *most* occasions: Silk stockings are a great luxury: they should be used with care, aired after wearing and not washed each time of course. I keep mine on a nail in my closet, but should advise thee to air them and put them away in a *safe place.*

On and on she went, adding two paragraphs of reminiscences of silk stockings.[19]

When Helen took Karin to New York City to see *Die Welkure, Siegfried,* and *Gotterdammerung,* the girl chafed—"Ugh!!!!"—at the interminable explanations that preceded and followed each opera. When Karin did not do her homework, Helen flew into a rage. The two fought for little reason or no reason, over noise at the dinner table, a dress, or a bath. Karin admitted that she sometimes provoked her mother—for instance, by defending Anna Karenina against Helen's charge that she was a "sensuous animal," even though Karin did not "admire or respect A.K." any more than her mother did. When Karin played house with her cousins, she re-created her home life as she knew it: "They were my two terrible children, I was their desperate mamma."[20]

At bottom, Karin blamed "Frau Mutter" for the family friction. Helen raised her in "fits and starts—too indulgent, then too severe." Her "beastly" intolerance and that "virtuous martyr act" made Karin "white-hot" with rage: "If she weren't my mother, I'd knock the nonsense out of her, but she isn't Maria [the maid] so I have to endure it." On occasion, the two did exchange blows, as on the day Helen requested that Karin, who was working on a Greek lesson, be fitted for a dress. Karin asked her mother to write an excuse for her homework, which Helen refused, probably because the exercises had been left for the last minute. The two argued and Helen rushed her adversary, with clenched fists aimed at her head. Karin parried, grabbed her mother's wrists and held them. "Oh! I hate her," she told her diary, adding the unkindest cut of all: a preference for maternal tantrums over displays of affection. "To hate one's mother" was unnatural, she recognized, but she blamed Helen for giving her a cold and suspicious temperament that probably meant a lonely spinsterhood: "I shan't marry—I should be most wretched and so would he."[21]

Conflict between adolescent girls and their mothers is, of course, scarcely unusual, but Karin's view of Helen was especially relentless. She did not, for example, respect a woman who had lost the love of her husband and depended so much on the love of her daughter. She clashed with her father but claimed to "care a great deal about him," even if he was "*so* obnoxious sometimes." In contrast to Helen's "narrow-narrow-narrow!" perspective was Andrew's tolerance. Karin pitied her mother, whose life had been hard, but felt as if she "had but one parent." When her father was ill, Karin contemplated the prospect of life with mother: "Oh my God, my God, if I lose him what have I left? . . . Oh, he *must* live—many years yet." On the rare occasions that she praised her mother, her tone was stiff. While visiting relatives in Michigan late in the summer of 1906, Karin felt feverish, "as if a small stove were burning" inside her. Helen spent the night at her daughter's bedside, fanning her and putting cold compresses on her head. Effusive in her anger, Karin was spare in her gratitude: "Awfully good of her, I'm sure." One searches in vain, through years of diaries faithfully kept, for other hints of affection.[22]

"Almost numb with hopelessness," Helen scarcely knew what to do about her daughter. Karin went out of her way to treat with a "lofty contempt" things that Helen valued: her garden, her view of music, her taste in clothing. She was "just shallow enough," Helen thought in moments of despair, to dismiss her mother because she was not "beautiful and impressive in appearance." Brought up to despise such worldly preoccupations, Helen felt herself becoming almost indifferent to an intelligent but ungovernable teenager whose interests did not extend beyond the latest fashions. If Karin saw her as little more than "a necessary evil," Helen could only pray, look after her own physical needs, and consult her husband about the best way to influence their daughter's character.[23]

Far less patient than his wife, Andrew did not look forward to sharing his declining years with a tempestuous teenager. Although affectionate, he had little interest in Karin's studies and kept his inquiries to the state of her tennis game. Most of all, her presence in the house disturbed his mood of quiet contemplation. Like most wealthy Victorian fathers, Andrew expected his daughter to give off "sunbeams to make everything glad." But as Karin sat day after day, "drumming drumming drumming [on the piano] in that dark parlor—making the same mistakes in the same piece [which] she has been stumbling thro for weeks," Andrew's nerves tingled. Urging her to sample the fresh air on a beautiful afternoon, he stormed out of the house when she turned a deaf ear toward him, "hurt to [his] very soul" by her "chronic recalcitrancy." Had he asked her to practice, "she would have insisted on going out." In all likelihood, Andrew cast his ballot for boarding school.[24]

Thus, in 1909 Karin was enrolled at Rosemary Hall, a boarding school in Greenwich, Connecticut, and at the Lanier Summer Camp in Eliot, Maine. Nothing changed, though, as Helen buried her daughter under a volcano of advice: pages by the dozen on how to avoid being kidnapped; exhortations to study hard, avoid physical strain, "and take what comes philosophically"; orders to economize; angry responses to failures to account for allowance; pleas that music courses be retained because they were important for women. Karin countered with promises to do better, coupled with threats to leave school if money was not supplied. Helen agreed with Elizabeth Lanier that in many ways the daughter resembled the mother: both were bright but "dangerously critical," with strong wills and a craving for independence. She endorsed but did not adopt a plan to teach Karin "the law of duty" and develop her "affectional nature" by first satisfying her craving for freedom. No demands should be placed on Karin's affection, Helen advised, while constant assurance was given that she was loved and respected. So in need of assurance herself, so stung by "the stabs of Karin's indifference," so determined to fulfill her role as a mother, she could neither accept her daughter's declarations of independence nor lavish unrequited love.[25]

Out of frustration, Helen blamed Andrew for Karin's shortcomings, especially her tendency to "present an unmoved front to the clearest logic." Like her father, Karin could not be reasoned with nor commanded. If she had been raised in an "atmosphere pervaded by more devoted affection," of mutual sacrifice and patience rather than subservience on one side, she might have learned the give and take of caring. Nor, according to Helen, had Andrew ever discussed public affairs with his daughter, who after all might soon have the vote; only when men were at the table did the ambassador's conversation sparkle. Andrew had the worst possible combination of attitudes toward Karin: a lack of sustained interest, a short fuse, and a penchant for urging his wife to be patient. "Try *her* way from time to time in minor things," he counseled, though he rarely took his own advice. Like so many modern American fathers, he retained Karin's affection *because* of his absence and indifference. A consequence of the replacement of authority by love in nineteenth-century families, none of it seemed fair to Helen, who could not refrain from telling her daughter: "Thee loves thy father; I've done a great deal more for thee than *he* ever did! It's thy duty to love." But for Karin, her mother remained "a perfectly unintentional kill-joy," an "incompetent" who "badgered and baited," while her father was a remote, occasionally affectionate old man with sense enough to leave her alone. Envious of Andrew, Helen could not bear his criticisms nor abide his threats, when he was irked, to disinherit Karin. When he attacked, she defended, insisting that Karin was "much liked and admired," invoking parental duty and pledging "patience and hope to the end." A mother could only persist, even if she was a martyr to a lost cause.26

Not surprisingly, Karin's choice of a college disappointed Helen, who hoped that she would select Swarthmore or some other prestigious coeducational institution. As we have seen, Helen did not value schools where "the *feminine* predominates: they must be *narrow:* women *are.* " Yet when Karin settled on Vassar, because it was immensely popular with fashionable young women, Helen probably stunned her daughter by turning cooperative, after initially pointing out that all-girls' schools were "not quite normal." She helped prepare Karin for college and even arranged a dinner for her daughter and President Taylor to provide "a friendly footing." Perhaps at Vassar, Helen told her husband, Karin might train her intelligence and enlarge her horizons so as to "retain the interest and affection of a worthy husband"—or, failing that, to have "something to fall back upon in the vicissitudes of life."27

It did not take long, however, for mother and daughter to settle back into their old routine, Karin spending and Helen sermonizing ("Pay bills *at once. Save all thee can*"). There were telegrams from Ithaca ("on the state of my *teeth,* if you please,—*telegrams—four* of them"), silence from

Poughkeepsie, explosions from Ithaca, and threats to cut off Karin's allowance. Worst of all, from Karin's point of view, after "making a scene to split one's eardrums," Helen invariably tried "the kiss and hug business." Karin was particularly distressed when her mother asked about her direction in life. A good student with considerable talent in music, she was too restless to be a scholar or a musician. In one way, however, she resembled the young Helen Magill: no man had entered her life, largely because, as a girl "brought up in absolute loneliness," she had not learned to get along with her peers. Karin did not want to marry because she had "nothing better to do." "Untrained, unmastered [and] headstrong," she was "an anchorless, rudderless craft" in need of a mother who could "shake off prejudice and preconceived plans and *see,*" a mother who would leave her "to work out her own salvation—or damnation. If it's Hell-fire I'm headed for, why at least let me go and not be graded." The tragedy of this relationship was that Karin could not reach out and Helen could not discern what her daughter needed. Although she wanted Karin to stand on her own two feet, Helen could not let go. Historian Joan Jacobs Brumberg reminds us that possessive love can be psychologically debilitating for parents and adolescents, and when the child becomes an adult, it can be disastrous. Furthermore, women without female friends may be especially prone to mother-daughter hostility. What Helen thought was advice emerged as criticism to "a dependent who could not leave, who could not call her soul—or her purse!—her own." The two acted and reacted upon one another like dynamite, shaking any building they were in.[28]

As graduation from Vassar approached, Karin realized that she was "good for nothing in particular." If she returned home, she would probably "go to pieces—mentally and morally," but few alternatives presented themselves. After much soul-searching and some investigation, Karin applied to a postgraduate program for nurses at St. Luke's Hospital in New York City. She knew little about nursing but thought it an opportunity to sweep the cobwebs from her brain and cut the cord her mother had tied to her. "Mother will kick like the deuce," she predicted, "but she'll just have to kick."[29]

Helen did just that—and she cried and cajoled too. In the early twentieth century, historian Susan Reverby has pointed out, "nursing had few advantages to offer a young woman." Frequently overworked, nurses were saddled with menial duties, exposed to disease, and subject to the arbitrary authority of head nurses. Before the United States entered World War I, nursing schools were forced to accept "less worthy candidates," immature and undisciplined young women in flight from farm to city. A profession that could not attract genteel, educated women was inappropriate for Karin, Helen believed. The irregular hours of nurses were ill suited to her daughter's insomnia and, more important, "a kind of conventical life," where she met only patients and doctors, would make marriage distinctly less likely. Before committing herself to nursing, Karin should meet the family claim, as Helen had, by returning home to work as secretary to her father while taking courses in cooking and farming in the College of Agriculture at Cornell. Every woman ought to learn "how to run a house and make it into a home," Helen insisted, as she recalled how she had been "pitch-forked into house-keeping on a large scale" in Berlin and learned how to "grease the [establishment] with grey matter." Self-support after four years of "intellectual strain" at Vassar might endanger Karin's health, Helen argued, and she proposed a year or two of food, rest, and handwork, supplemented by music (which Ruth White Ferry had found to be her "best hold matrimonially and socially"). After a decent interval, Karin could begin a professional, wage-earning life, if necessary.[30]

Helen's ideal future—to live in a large city each winter and in the summer on a farm where she could bring nature's elevating influences to poor children—included Karin, for eighty-three-year-old Andrew would not live much longer. With him, Helen was "so much alone in mind and spirit"; without him, life looked "dull and sad and uninteresting." Karin's decision thus left her with no hope: "and if someone were to tell me it would be soon all over, I should be rather glad—tho, as long as I can be of any *use* to papa, I'm willing to stay: But I don't feel that is much. A good housekeeper, who would make him comfortable, would easily take my place with him." Now that Karin had become as uncaring as her father, Helen made explicit what was self-evident: "But perhaps I shall find some nice girl whom I can help to get the kind of education I had hoped thee would care for and who will appreciate what I can do for her, and be some kind of daughter to me." If not, she would be "alone to the end."[31]

Karin held firm to her decision, and on June 9, 1915, the White family celebrated commencement at Vassar. Andrew's presence on the platform, resplendent in his scarlet and crimson robes, made the occasion special: as Karin walked past "His Grace" to receive her diploma, the old man rose to shake her hand and kiss it. On her wrist Karin wore a beautiful gold bracelet watch, her graduation present. The day was almost perfect, marred only by Helen's weepy lament that Karin was not returning to Ithaca. "Now keep quiet—keep *quiet,*" Karin told herself, as she managed to refrain from saying that home meant being a "subject" to "Lady" White and that nursing for her was an escape.[32]

A heavy cost in guilt and insecurity was attached to Karin's resistance. Why, she wondered when she arrived at St. Luke's, was a young woman with music in her "heart and soul and fingers," a sharp, if undisciplined, mind, and "money, talent, education, friends" in a nurse's "convent"? Now more than twenty years old, her marital prospects seemed bleak, and her mother's ideas about marriage likely deepened her doubts. "Having been an old maid ... with much satisfaction to the age of thirty-six," Helen advised Karin to take her time and make a careful selection. Above all, she should not marry in order to have children, for to do so, except as a result "of an ideal relation is to do them a great injustice":

> We cannot always know when we are doing this, but we can at least make sure that our own contribution is as nearly genuine devotion as possible. . . . So many relations prove so different from what one or the other or both of the parties expect, and the self-control and delicacy which should make it possible for such unions to have any results—are quite lacking in most men from their utterly incorrect early training. Perhaps the world would be but sparsely populated if it were not so—but the race would be a noble one.

Although the prospects of a happy union were uncertain at best, Helen remained convinced that Karin must do her duty as a woman and take the gamble because, as she pointed out, an old maid "still is I fancy a failure even greater" than an unhappy wife.[33]

Who can blame Karin for her uncertainty? Her mother's advice about marriage and career must have seemed self-serving. In fact, Helen did not really know the path to the good life for a twentieth-century woman of privilege. With her acquired wealth and social status, she was caught between pretensions to gentility and a middle-class endorsement of success through achievement. Neither economic necessity nor the need for recognition would fuel professional aspiration for Karin, who was too selfish to understand noblesse oblige. Moreover, because Helen had tasted the fruits of failure, she could not share the optimism behind the great expectations her parents had had for her. She failed as a mother because she had given Karin everything but a vision, a goal. Out of her confusion came advice that abounded in contradiction: all at once she praised independence, discouraged ambition, worried that hard work jeopardized health, called Karin home to learn cooking and farming, disparaged marriage as a "lottery," pronounced even Clara White's ruined marriage better than none at all. As Karin sorted it all out, she should make family her constant, her parents her profession, for they might well be her best chance at love.[34]

Karin persevered for more than a year in the care of strangers, completing graduation requirements and passing the New York State board examination for certification in nursing. But then she wavered. Nursing was "too absolute a separation" from the social world she had enjoyed at

Vassar. Uncomfortable taking orders from anyone, she felt victimized by a head nurse. Besides, her father was frail and her mother was desperately in need of companionship. "I'm all she's got now," Karin realized, "now Papa has withdrawn into old age." A year or two at home, relaxing, studying music, might not be so bad, and at Cornell she could learn to cook and prepare for a career in teaching. She knew her mother would continue to nag and pester, but she thought she "could live with H., so as not to leave her utterly alone—and yet have work, and a certain amount of money, and a life of my own—all that's stupid, up there [Karin's diatribes against her mother]. I'm right fond of her, she and I have quite enough in common for a working basis—I'm silly to make a useless fuss." For now, the revolution was over, though the rebellion had not been put down. Everything was as it had been before: endless skirmishes over which sorority Karin would join, a broken shade, a slippery rug, a letter not attended to. Mother and daughter were locked in a lonely union, shackled together by the bonds of familial duty.[35]

Mothering still consumed Helen, but it took less of her time as Karin became a distant presence in and out of Ithaca. Helen kept busy, though she had no center, no identity to replace her role as ambassadress. In the United States her life was "certainly a thing of shreds and patches," full of motion, sound, and sometimes fury, but it signified little, she often thought.[36]

Correspondence and gardening constituted her principal activities. Writing graceful, informative letters was a duty as well as a pleasure for which "telegraphic apologies" could not substitute. When her sister Beatrice wondered how any busy woman could find time to write, she bristled: "Why *woman*? the beautiful—or the best expression of what one is, is one of the principal things we live *for.*" Although it might be presumptuous to think she had much worth saying, she scorned self-suppression as a kind of "underhand management" associated with women that actually undermined relationships. For Helen, writing letters provided intimations of sovereignty: "So I'm going to find a corner of time occasionally to say what I feel like saying—and to give the run to my mood and to my pen—*coûte que coûte.*" Her expression was not really free, however—she never criticized her husband to Eva Channing and almost never to her family—but her letters allowed her to frame and refine insights, ruminate on public and private issues, and, as it turned out, explain herself to posterity.[37]

Hours at her desk were usually followed by afternoons in the garden, the meeting place of physical and mental activity. Music had never let Helen "fully inside her gates," although she rejoiced "in the echoes which reach me outside"; but the garden responded to her touch and did not debate design. At first, Andrew disparaged the time and expense she lavished on her garden, prompting a peremptory defense: "Gardening is my activity—everyone must have some, and you could hardly have thought when you made my acquaintance that keeping a clean house and providing comfortable eating would be likely to be the sum of my mental activity." He should pay florist bills gladly, she thought, "putting up prayers of thankfulness" that his wife did not spend his money on cures and doctors, as did so many "really nice but foolish and poorly bred women." The benefits on her health and spirits were so much in evidence that his derision soon became delight, and he encouraged her plans to expand her garden and advise Cornell University landscapers.[38]

Aware at some level that the garden compensated for nurturing instincts that found no fertile ground in the family and for intellectual energies stifled by housework, Helen thought it the perfect metaphor for her feelings. When Andrew was away, the garden looked "parched—like the heart of a wife who is deserted eight months out of twelve—but struggles still to make some cheerful show of geraniums and the hardier blooms." Only a long-suffering wife and mother, she implied on another occasion, could wait five years for small tulips to bloom: "Mr. White would certainly say life is not long enough." Her garden rewarded patience and diligence, whereas human beings often did not. More and more, she found solitary contentment in the garden; she forever talked about it and took note to improve next year's flowers.[39]

To her surprise, Helen found much to cultivate at Cornell outside of her garden. When she returned from Berlin she took classes in Greek, audited a course in Dante, and danced with the Sage College women. Her "desultory life, with all the interruptions of a feminine existence," including responsibility to proofread, edit or "restore" her husband's prose, made systematic study difficult, but she persevered and managed to prepare a lecture on the early history of the Society of Friends for the Unitarian Church. Most important, she attached herself to the students at Sage, serving as patroness at dances and concerts, attending Saturday afternoon sewing circles, and reading literature with the young women. She provided valuable support for the Department of Domestic Economy established by Martha Van Rensselaer and for the establishment of Prudence Risley Hall. At all official receptions, the students insisted on her presence, next to the wife of President Jacob Gould Schurman. No woman, Helen claimed, "had ever been to them what I have," and she could not fathom her husband's proposal to send a picture of himself and his first wife to the Risley lobby: "If you are going to immortalize yourself *with any Mrs. White* in Risley, it should be with me." Despite such contretemps, she reveled in the respect of the young women of Sage and seized opportunities to teach them, chaperon them, cajole speakers to address them. "I will look out for the girls any way," she wrote, "if no one else does."40

Helen believed that the cultivation of an elite class, imbued with a sense of noblesse oblige, promised a civilization superior to that produced by egalitarian principles or run by those who "scraped together" wealth in one generation. Not much could be done for the lower classes, for "the stream cannot rise higher than its source" and public schools should serve only those "families who can afford nothing better." Privileged women should nonetheless do what they could for the children of the poor. Acts of charity ennobled the philanthropist even if they did not fundamentally change the recipient. Thus, she invariably included some "unfortunates" in her annual Christmas celebration, believing that such occasions helped the students at Sage learn a sense of responsibility while binding together the social classes. In addition, she worked hard on public school reform, traveling often to Albany to lobby for higher salaries and pensions for teachers. Because normal schools could not hold their best instructors, the least-valuable men and women taught the teachers of the next generation. When a pension bill passed the legislature, Helen rejoiced even though she had little faith that the public schools could do more than teach the rudiments of civilization and provide manual training for workers. Schooled by life to work on in the face of failure, she was glad, in "the midst of what seems something of a wreck in other directions," to engage in worthwhile activity, even "in one small particular."41

A full schedule—hosting the Mothers Association of New York, entertaining the Roosevelts, watching Isadora Duncan dance, taking exercise and Bulgarian buttermilk—brought moments of unselfconscious enjoyment in these years but could not overshadow disappointment with Andrew—or the terror of a life without him. During the early part of the century, he was healthy enough to travel but preferred to do so *en garçon*, often giving the impression, Helen thought, that he was ashamed of his wife. His friends believed that she was "a sort of caravan and a deadweight"; if such "grotesque impressions" came from her husband, she pleaded for "an economy of prevarication" when he went off to flowery lands and left her to freeze in Ithaca. To avoid embarrassment, she thought, he should at least inform her of his whereabouts. Helen knew that falling into "the language of reason and critical judgment" simply fueled the fires, but how could she content herself with feminine sighs of affection when everyone she knew commented on their "domestic felicity" and criticized *her* for letting an old man go off without his wife? Andrew deserved someone like feminist Harriet Stanton Blatch, she thought, someone who saw her husband at her convenience: a "steady-going domestically inclined, but independent minded one like me is just thrown away on you."[42]

Alongside embarrassment was her foreboding of being left alone. Helen's social position, in Ithaca as well as Berlin, derived in large measure from her husband. As a widow, she might be ignored or, worse yet, pitied; and she might be left without sufficient resources to provide for her unmarried daughter or to entertain or travel in the manner to which she had become accustomed. In an ordinary month, the White family spent $1,500–2,000, well within Andrew's income. But a divided estate, with a fraction for Fred's widow and three sets of grandchildren, might be too small. Andrew's will remained a constant source of tension despite revisions in Helen's favor after the deaths of Clara and Fred. As Andrew grew more feeble, especially after 1910, she pleaded with him not to leave her quarter of the estate in trust with one of his nephews as executor. Although she had no business experience, she thought her economic and legal judgment at least the equal of his and hoped to improve it with a little training. Her "feminine" preference for real estate over the more speculative stocks and bonds was actually a sound business practice, but her efforts to place financial affairs within the woman's sphere foundered because Andrew had "so little confidence in a woman's sense and ability to manage affairs" and in her understanding that there was a time to spend and a time to save ("I shall know the other when it comes"). Although she shrank from the prospect of contesting his will, she would do so "at the very worst." Her life—and that of her daughter—depended upon it.[43]

Helen knew that Andrew's death would end her quest for fulfillment in marriage. Although in a moment of fury he might say that he had "made her," she had not married for money or position—though perhaps that, and Karin, was all she had gotten. To the end, she hoped to receive what she "truly gave, devoted affection." Her "perfect frankness," though painful at times, was testimony to her belief that her marriage must work. She measured her own worth by the depth of the love she received; and without a husband, she would be robbed even of the ability to be noble in defeat.[44]

As Andrew's strength waned, he became ill tempered. His behavior required forbearance, Karin thought, but instead Helen was "restless and rebellious." The Whites opened a veritable second front in 1917 and 1918, battling furiously over the choice of a dessert or the quality of the handwriting of Andrew's daughter-in-law. When Andrew "worried himself into a rage," Helen relentlessly pursued him and her point, keeping at it until both were "white-hot with unnecessary fury." When Karin separated the combatants, Helen snuck back into her husband's room "and the storm broke afresh," raging until morning. At least once, the old man struck his wife "in a flinch of fury." As he tossed and turned to avoid death's stare, he offered Helen no last-minute reconciliation, no words of thanks or praise.[45]

In late October 1918, Andrew White suffered an attack, probably a stroke. Although not paralyzed, he lay helpless for a week. He died on November 4, an event Helen noted in her diary without betraying her feelings. It was as if her capacity for self-expression, her need for perfect frankness, had expired with him: "A. died after an unconscious night, without much struggle. . . . callers and telegrams all day." She was now a widow.[46]

As her husband was laid to rest beside his first wife, Helen's estrangement from Karin deepened. Unable to understand how her mother could have substituted contentiousness for compassion during her father's final illness, Karin vowed not to forget or forgive. Before 1918, she recalled much later, she had viewed her mother as "fundamentally fine, if superficially a nuisance." But for years she would remember Helen's resentment at the attention lavished on Andrew, her willingness to seize a pretext for a fight, however trivial, and to ignore his pathetic pleas that she not scold. Even in the greatest crisis of the family, Helen could not forget her own "wretched ego." After the "episode" of October and November 1918, Karin felt toward her mother "something very near loathing." Before her father died, she refused to enter his room when Helen was there. After he was gone, she thought her mother a "worthless human being" whose only interest was having people carry out her orders. Nothing Helen could do, "short of murder or grand larceny," would shock Karin, once she had seen the petty selfishness of which she thought Helen was capable.[47]

As Karin mourned her father, she also cried for herself. She was enough her mother's daughter to see that she must live at home and abandon what career and marital aspirations remained to her, but she resented the sacrifices she was about to make. As she saw it, she had lost her champion, the broadminded old man who was willing to let her strike out on her own. Now in her mid-twenties, Karin was yoked to her demanding mother forever.

NOTES

1. HMW to ADW, Sept. 28, 1900; HMW to Beatrice Magill, May 18, 1900; HMW to Family, Jan. 26, 1900, Jan. 19, 1902, May 18, 1904; ADW to Charlemagne Tower, Sept. 26, 1902, ADW Papers. For the reference to Ambassador White's "brilliant social establishment," see *New York Herald,* Aug. 9, 1902.

2. HMW to Family, Jan. 21–23, 1901; HMW to Beatrice Magill, Aug. 17, 1899; HMW to Family, Feb. 20, 1900.

3. HMW to Family, Feb. 28, 1900. Helen was flattered when the kaiser sought her out to offer condolences, even though he thought her sister had died. See Rowena Morse Langer to author, Nov. 17, 1986, author's files. For mention of Helen's frustration that she was too nearsighted to see royalty in resplendent detail, see Margaret Trevor Ford to author, Sept. 21, 1986, Sept. 30, 1986, author's files. On occasion, Helen went overboard as a self-proclaimed arbiter of taste. A silver piece made in honor of Andrew White was "an everlasting disgrace to your firm and your country," she told the manufacturers. "If I were in your place I would *entreat* to be allowed to replace it with one worthy of your name and worth the price paid." Though the ambassador did not disagree with his wife's aesthetic judgment, he was embarrassed by her harsh tone and apologized to the company for her letter, which had been written without his knowledge. See HMW to Messrs. Sharpe, Nov. 26, 1899; ADW to Hugo Sharpe, Dec. 10, 1899, both in ADW Papers.

4. George L. Burr to HMW, Aug. 20, 1898, Aug. 25, 1898, Sept. 14, 1898.

5. HMW to Family, June 22, 1900, Jan. 29, 1907, Sept. 17, 1900. For a discussion of White's views on politics and imperialism in the late nineteenth Century, see Glenn C. Altschuler, *Andrew D. White: Educator, Historian, Diplomat* (Ithaca, N.Y., 1979), chaps. 13, 14.

6. HMW to Papa and Sisters, Oct. 19, 1899.

7. HMW to Family, Sept. 17, 1900. Edward Magill's vote was a protest against American imperialism.

8. HMW to ADW, Mar. 28, 1911, ADW Papers. For an account of the debate over woman suffrage, see Aileen S. Kraditor, *The Ideas of the Woman Suffrage Movement, 1890–1920* (New York, 1965). Opponents of suffrage for women exploited xenophobia; this issue helped delay passage of a constitutional amendment guaranteeing women the right to vote.

9. HMW to Family, Apr. 24, 1900. See also ADW to HMW, Aug. 15, 1900, Aug. 21, 1900; HMW to ADW, Aug. 30, 1900, ADW Papers.

10. Fred White to ADW, Nov. 11, 1900, ADW Papers; HMW to Family, Mar. 25, 1901, May 30, 1901. For a discussion of developments in the White family, see Altschuler, pp. 261–67. With Ruth's marriage, Fred's suicide, and Clara's death in 1907, Andrew did change his will, providing for his grandchildren but leaving a larger proportion of his estate to Helen and Karin.

11. ADW to HMW, Oct. 25, 1902. See also HMW to ADW, June 22, 1900.

12. HMW, diary notes, Sept. 19, 1900.

13. HMW to Family, Mar. 31, 1901; KW to Little Beatrice, Mar. 8, 1904; HMW to Family, Mar. 7, 1904. See also HMW to Family, Mar. 25, 1901, Oct. 15, 1903; ADW to HMW, Aug. 30, 1900; ADW to Willard Fiske, Dec. 11, 1902, ADW Papers; ADW to D. C. Gilman, June 30, 1903, ADW Papers; "Address to Saturday Circle," undated ms., "Address on Fohr Region," undated ms. Ominously, Helen and Andrew fought just before the family returned to the United States. Although "deeply wounded" that he left first and failed to write for weeks, Helen

hoped for a "restoration of kindly relations," turning aside Andrew's suggestion that she tarry awhile in Alassio. "My wildest hope is that you will receive us with a certain degree of outward propriety at first. But *come* I must...." HMW to ADW, June 11, 1904.

14. Beatrice Magill to Family, Apr. 21, 1904. For an intriguing analysis of the increasing value of children at this time, see Viviana Zelizer, *Pricing the Priceless Child* (New York, 1985).

15. HMW to KW, Jan. 23, 1916; HMW to ADW, ca. Mar. 20, 1906; HMW to Family, Jan. 26, 1900; Margaret Trevor Ford to author, Sept. 21, 1986, author's files.

16. HMW to Family, Jan. 26, 1900, Jan. 2, 1902.

17. HMW to Family, Oct. 15, 1903, Aug. 23, 1905; HMW to ADW, Apr. 30, 1913, ADW Papers.

18. HMW to Family, Jan. 6, 1904. See also KW, *Diary,* May 1, 1907, KW Papers (all such references are to this source).

19. HMW to KW, Mar. 2, 1910.

20. KW, *Diary,* May 6, 1911, Mar. 6–8, 1906, Dec. 29, 1910, Feb. 24, 1906.

21. KW, *Diary,* Feb. 5, 1911, June 9, 1907, Aug. 21, 1909. See also KW, *Diary,* Feb. 19, 1906, June 4, 1907, Dec. 29, 1910. For a discussion of the Victorian preoccupation with privacy, see Peter Gay, *The Bourgeois Experience: Victoria to Freud,* vol. 1: *Education of the Senses* (New York, 1984), pp. 445–60.

22. KW, *Diary,* Feb. 14, 1909, Aug. 3, 1909, Dec. 26, 1910, May 21, 1911, Sept. 1, 1906.

23. HMW to ADW, Sept. 14, 1908, Aug. 13, 1908; KW, *Diary,* June 20, 1909.

24. ADW to HMW, Oct. 22, 1907. See also HMW to ADW, Aug. 13, 1903. Andrew's invidious comparisons between Ruth's musical talent and Karin's must surely have stung Helen. Actually, Karin had perfect pitch but was too impatient to master a musical instrument. After unsuccessful bouts with the piano and violin, she settled for a guitar. Margaret Trevor Ford to author, Sept. 30, 1986, author's files.

25. HMW to KW, Feb. 1, 1909; Mrs. Lanier to HMW, Dec. 2, 1910, Nov. 22, 1910. See also HMW to KW, Mar. 25, 1909, May 8, 1909, July 7, 1910; Beatrice Magill to HMW, ca. Dec. 1910 (fragment); KW to HMW, Mar. 21, 1909. Karin felt unequal to "filling a daughter's place" in such an exacting home, Mrs. Lanier believed, and was therefore unwilling to try. See Mrs. Lanier to HMW, Dec. 9, 1910. A friend of Helen's put it a bit differently: Karin "sees your force of mind, your physical strength and your capability of taking care of others so clearly, but she *does not,* indeed, I believe, cannot, realize that you have *need* of her." Lucy Cantley to HM, dated "Wednesday morning." Karin was glad to see her, Helen lamented, until she was denied "the *least thing* that *she wishes*—not a second longer. These are the terms on which what she calls affection is *peddled* out." HMW to ADW, Mar. 16, 1910, ADW Papers. See also HMW to ADW, Apr. 24, 1910, ADW Papers, for Helen's desire to tour Rome and Athens with Karin.

26. HMW to ADW, Feb. 8, 1911, ADW Papers; ADW to HM, Mar. 4, 1907, ADW Papers; KW, *Diary,* May 6, 1911, May 24, 1911; HMW to ADW, June 28, 1910, ADW Papers. See also HMW to ADW, ca. Mar. 1910, Apr. 24, 1910, Feb. 8, 1911, June 6, 1912, Aug. 11, 1912, May 29, 1915, ADW Papers. When Mrs. Lanier suggested that Karin might be interested in *Seven Great Statesmen,* Andrew replied: "I sometimes think that she has read so much imaginative literature that she has been spoiled for everything else, especially everything that may require thought.... least of all do I think that she would care for anything regarding myself." ADW to Mrs. Lanier, Oct. 11, 1910, ADW Papers.

27. HMW to Family, Jan. 1, 1905; HMW to KW, ca. Spring 1911 (fragment); HMW to ADW, Sept. 22, 1911, Jan. 17, 1914, ADW Papers.

28. KW, *Diary,* Feb. 17, 1914, Aug. 10, 1912, Aug. 22, 1913; KW to HMW, "Thursday Night" (ca. 1915); KW, *Diary,* Apr. 1, 1915. See also KW, *Diary,* May 21, 1911, July 31, 1912, Mar. 30, 1915; Mrs. R. B. Cary to HMW, Dec. 12, 1912, Dec. 27, 1912; KW to HMW, ca. Apr. 28, 1915; Joan Jacobs Brumberg, *Fasting Girls: The Emergence of Anorexia Nervosa as a Modern Disease* (Cambridge, Mass., 1988), p. 137. See also Michael Brooks, "Love and Possession in a Victorian Household: The Example of the Ruskins," in *The Victorian Family: Structure and Stresses,* ed. Anthony S. Wohl (London, 1978), pp. 82–100. Only when Helen bought gifts for Karin did the latter think lovingly of her mother. When Karin was twenty-one, Helen stole into her room and dropped a white velvet box, with a moonstone bracelet set in platinum, on her bed. "She loves to do that kind of thing for me," Karin acknowledged, "to get me the *things* I like—and it's so dear of her." KW, *Diary,* July 9, 1914.

29. KW, *Diary,* Apr. 1, 1915, Nov. 20, 1915, Nov. 21, 1916. See also KW to HMW, "Thursday Night" (ca. 1915).

30. HMW to KW, June 4, 1915, May 1, 1915, Apr. 9, 1915. See also Susan Reverby, *Ordered To Care: The Dilemma of American Nursing, 1850–1945* (Cambridge, U.K., 1987), pp. 77–94. In suggesting that Karin serve as secretary to her father, Helen ignored the advice of her sister Beatrice, who doubted, given the dispositions of both, that the plan would work on either side: "One gains nothing by shutting one's eyes to facts. . . . " Beatrice Magill to HMW, May 19, 1915.

31. HMW to KW, May 24, 1915, July 2, 1915. See also HMW to KW, May 1, 1915.

32. KW, *Diary,* June 9, 1915. See also KW, *Diary,* May 15, 1915, June 7, 1915.

33. KW, *Diary,* Nov. 20, 1915; HMW to KW, Nov. 13–15, 1915.

34. For a treatment sensitive to class differences in parental expectations for daughters, see Deborah Gorham, *The Victorian Girl and the Feminine Ideal* (Bloomington, Ind., 1982). For a discussion of the "explosive intensity" of the social ambitions of Victorian families, see Stephen Kern, "The Psychodynamics of the Victorian Family," *History of Childhood Quarterly,* 1, no. 3 (Winter 1974): 437–61.

35. KW, *Diary,* Nov. 21, 1916. See also KW, *Diary,* May 20, 1917, June 19, 1918, June 10, 1950; Margaret Trevor Ford to author, Sept. 30, 1986, author's files. For a discussion of the often "arbitrary control" exercised by head nurses, see

Reverby, pp. 65–76. Lengthened residence in the home of parents, Steven Mintz argues, could as easily be a source of strain as an opportunity for emotional intimacy. *A Prison of Expectations: The Family in Victorian Culture* (New York, 1985), p. 18. Unfortunately, Mintz does not give sufficient attention to mother-daughter relationships.

36. HMW to Family, Oct. 11–13, 1906.

37. HMW to Family, Apr. 16, 1914.

38. HMW to Family, Apr. 16, 1914; HMW to ADW, May 30, 1906. See also ADW to William Stoddard, Jan. 25, 1911, ADW Papers. In the paintings of the late nineteenth century, Bram Dijkstra argues, "it was virtually impossible for a 'pure' woman to stir without finding herself up to her neck in flowers." Passive, imitative, submissive, she shared the features "characteristic of the domestic garden." Most males "would have liked their women to take a few pointers from the flowers and learn to be silent too." *Idols of Perversity: Fantasies of Feminine Evil in Fin-de Siecle Culture* (New York and Oxford, 1986), pp. 13–16.

39. HMW to ADW, June 2, 1904; HMW to Family, Apr. 12–13, 1906.

40. HMW to Family, Feb. 25, 1905, Oct. 27, 1904; HMW to ADW, Jan. 15, 1914, ADW Papers. See also HMW to Family, Nov. 21, 1904; HMW to ADW, Aug. 16, 1908, Sept. 20, 1908, Sept. 28, 1914; HMW to EHM, Aug. 15, 1906; HMW to ADW, Dec. 7, 1904, Feb. 28, 1907, Mar. 2, 1907, Mar. 21, 1910, Feb. 2, 1911, Mar. 8, 1911, Apr. 11, 1911, Jan. 15, 1914, Jan. 17, 1914, ADW Papers. Andrew did not hear Helen's praise of his work, but his ears rang at the first sign of her "wet blankets." Nonetheless, he always asked her to read and evaluate. See, e.g., ADW to HMW, Mar. 1, 1907.

41. HMW to ADW, May 15, 1910, ADW Papers. See also HMW to Family, Dec. 30, 1906, Jan. 29, 1907; HMW to ADW, Apr. 18, 1910, Jan. 12, 1914, ADW Papers; L. Severance to HMW, Mar. 30, 1913, ADW Papers.

42. HMW to ADW, Dec. 8, 1904, Apr. 15, 1907, Apr. 5, 1910, ADW Papers. See also HMW to ADW, Feb. 27, 1910, May 19, 1910, Feb. 14, 1911, Aug. 13, 1912, ADW Papers; HMW to Family, Mar. 13, 1907, Jan. 21, 1908; ADW to HMW, Mar. 4, 1907, Jan. 21, 1908. Andrew saw his wife as anything but reasonable. He could not abide Helen's "dawdling" over things she should dispose of quickly. But most of all, her presence meant arguments: "It is like my asking you and Karin to close the doors after you as I am sensitive to currents of air. My request only led you to argue that there was no use in shutting doors— that people brought up in properly built houses never shut doors." That the couple could not travel together, Andrew regretted; but, evidently, Helen was "too old and *set*" to change. He knew "these causes of offense are contemptibly small," but his wife's shrill voice and scowl irritated him "like gravel in a shoe or a grain of sand in my eye," and he acted in ways that later made him sorry. See ADW to HMW, Mar. 2, 1904, Mar. 9, 1904, June 9, 1904.

43. HMW to ADW, Aug. 15, 1911, ADW Papers. See also HMW to KW, Aug. 24, 1911; HMW to ADW, Feb. 26, 1907, June 9, 1911, Jan. 31, 1913, ADW Papers; ADW to Horace White, ca. 1911, ADW Papers. When Andrew felt death imminent in 1910, he asked Helen not to go into any business as a

widow, including establishing a school for young women, because the initial outlay of money was too great. See ADW to HMW, "Wishes as to Funeral and Monument etc.," Feb. 8, 1910.

44. HMW to ADW, Aug. 6, 1915.

45. KW, *Diary,* June 19, 1918. See also HMW to ADW, Aug. 6, 1915.

46. HMW, *Diary,* Nov. 4, 1918. See also KW, *Diary,* Oct. 27, 1918. Andrew left his real estate in trust to Cornell, with the net income from the property divided among Helen (14/20), Karin (3/20), and Ruth (3/20). When Helen died, he stipulated, the money would be used to set up the Mary White Fund for the care of sick and injured professors, a President's House Fund, and the President White School of History and Political Science. Trust funds were also set up for all the grandchildren, out of White's personal estate, and Helen received a $60,000 bequest as well as the remainder of the estate. Last Will and Testament of Andrew D. White, June 11, 1918.

47. KW, *Diary,* Feb. 16, 1926, Feb. 18, 1926.

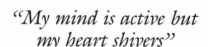

CHAPTER SEVEN

"My mind is active but my heart shivers"

It did not take long for Helen to recognize how vulnerable she had become as a widow. Andrew White left his house to Cornell University, to be used as the president's residence, and within days of the funeral, Jacob Gould Schurman let it be known that he was ready to move in. That Schurman was "insensitively precipitous" did not surprise Helen. The success of Sage College, she had told her husband, meant nothing to Schurman: "Only the better sort of men are ever in sympathy with the advancement of women. The spiritually dead are *always against it.*" She had no doubt shared her views with many members of the Cornell community, and now Schurman exacted his revenge. As she sorted through her belongings, surrounded by crates, paintings, and tapestries, with the furniture pushed to the side, she felt the burden of personal possessions and of relationships, past and present: "I wish I were an anchorite, living in a cave, drinking out of a gourd."[1]

As Helen would discover, she could not return to Quaker simplicity, nor did she wish to become a Hawthornian Woman of Adamant, choosing a solipsistic existence. Instead, she swallowed her pride and agreed to live with the family of Professor Morse, a Cornellian who was appalled by Schurman's discourtesy. It must have been difficult for her, sans servants, to accept hospitality without being able to reciprocate, to request and not command, to live in exile, albeit in elegance. She was almost seventy now, overweight, and more than occasionally tired, an old woman whose "constitutional slowness and ingrained inefficiency" complicated the task of reconstructing "livable conditions." Somehow she pushed herself out in search of a new home for herself and her daughter, and within a couple of months she purchased a lovely house on Eddy Street, on the east side of Ithaca. In gratitude, and perhaps also to help put humiliation behind her, she insisted that the Morses have a beautiful old English grandfather clock with Westminster chimes, a five-foot-tall Italian carved chest dating from the Renaissance, and a large ceramic Italian plate depicting Moses in the bulrushes.[2]

Unfortunately, finding and furnishing a house did not provide a permanent purpose for Helen's life. More and more she remembered Andrew as her anchor: she had edited and proofread his manuscripts, when she did not have the energy or discipline to do scholarship on her own; and the "pretty teas and nice dinners," the forays into Berlin society, the welcome by intellectuals on two continents, had come because she was the wife of an important man. When she traveled through Homer, New York, Andrew's birthplace, she imagined him as a little boy there; and then, with a sudden recognition that she did not "know where he is in the universe," she felt "that strangeness . . . that unreality" she had experienced ever since his death. Hadn't she assured Andrew that he would be reunited with Mary? Should Helen, then, expect to be eternally alone? As she gazed at his portrait, she resolved to honor his memory by taking care of his family and using his money to do good works. As a widow, she became a model wife, remembering only Andrew's accomplishments and the full life they had shared, fiercely protecting his reputation at Cornell. Was there a chance that she might yet earn a place at his side?[3]

Not certain what form good works should take, Helen sought to increase her resources by organizing "a simple and dignified mode of living." After all, she had managed quite nicely on a small income before her marriage. But, as Andrew had prophesied, extravagant habits were hard to shake. Helen could not manage without a retinue of butlers, cooks, chauffeurs, cleaners, and companions. Help was not cheap, especially for a lady with exacting standards, and few servants lasted more than a year; each newcomer also charged more than his or her predecessor. Whenever Helen sat down with the account books, her clear and keen mind entered a maze, with an impasse at every turn. How could she avoid spending more on her beloved garden? Did it make sense to curtail dinner parties or readings with the women from Sage, her principal links with the outside world? Could she deny Karin's requests for money? Resolve soon turned to resignation: "I don't know how it is—my large income just slips through my fingers."[4]

By the 1920s, Helen spent most of the day in her garden or else reading or listening to the radio. To some people, Karin remembered, she remained "immensely entertaining" and "incredibly generous":

> What she enjoyed—and she enjoyed a lot of things—she enjoyed like a child at the circus. She could suddenly come out with a half dozen words, exactly the right ones . . . that got it so neatly in the solar plexus, once and for all, that those who'd been bored, or angry or embarrassed, collapsed in shouts of laughter. She could puncture a certain type of insolent rudeness . . . with a tongue like a rapier in a master fencer's hand, and hold him up spitted and squirming. . . . She could, and did, talk about anything and everything.

To those who did not relish combat, Helen seemed formidable, an opinionated, truculent, perhaps mad woman who tried to dominate every situation "to the last and minutest detail." She provoked conflict, Karin thought, with more and more people "to fill up the void there's no doubt she felt when she was no longer 'Mrs. Andrew D. White.'" For a time Helen attended Greek classes at Cornell, but her frequent interruptions to correct the professor led to a request and then an order that she stay at home. Andrew's memory was best honored, she apparently concluded, when she remained in the private sphere, helping her family and not calling attention to herself. Even her activity in Albany ceased, in part because of her age but perhaps as well because lobbying was less legitimate when she no longer spoke for her husband.[5]

Family crises continued to command Helen's attention. Her sister Gertrude had been a source of concern to the Magill and White families since 1890, when she left the Society of Friends and Swarthmore to live with B. M. Kinney, a married man. For more than a decade, Gertrude traveled with her lover, first to the Midwest and then to England. Helen was convinced that Kinney had taken Gertrude to Boise, Idaho, to wreck her career as a minister, at which she had made a good beginning, to "ruin her and so have her in his power." The idea of a college-educated woman living in sin, "working on a miserable little one-horse or one-donkey newspaper in a little town in the wilds of the West," repulsed Helen, who vowed never to tell Karin that she had an Aunt Gertrude. When Gertrude's name came up by accident, Helen identified her as someone who lived with the Magill family when she was a little girl. Pity for her sister coexisted with dreadful embarrassment, and for her husband's sake Helen tried to keep her situation from public notice. As the years passed, the Magills made an uneasy peace with Gertrude, and though Helen refused to join in the family "circular letter" as long as her sister insisted that she be addressed as "Mrs. B. M. Kinney," she frequently sent money, taking care to remind Gertrude that marriage gave her the freedom to do so.[6]

By the turn of the century, Gertrude had developed an acute nervous condition, which Helen attributed to "the unnatural life that she must be forced to lead, to avoid having children." Sometime during the next decade, the relationship between Kinney and Gertrude ended and her mental condition deteriorated. Obsessed about her mind being read, and on the verge of violence, she agreed to return to the United States. Helen brought her to Ithaca and pooh-poohed her fears that she would be murdered, ignored her declarations of love for Kinney, and talked and read to her. Compassion was not a cure, however; nor would Andrew tolerate a disgraced and disruptive woman in his house. When several doctors pronounced Gertrude "crazy as a loon," Helen tried several institutions in New York and Pennsylvania before committing her sister to the Wiswall Sanitorium in Wellesley, Massachusetts.[7]

After Andrew's death, Gertrude remained the responsibility of Beatrice, who lived nearby in Kittery Point, Maine. To be sure, Helen paid the medical bills and sent expensive watches and silk dresses, but Beatrice bore the brunt of Gertrude's wrath, as well as expenses that strained the limited resources of a widow. Reports from the Magill sisters must have seemed like an indictment to Helen, who knew that she had once shunned Gertrude. Now that she was "so free to go and come," couldn't Helen visit Wellesley more often and buy some clothes? Marian wrote from faraway Chicago, enclosing a letter from Gertrude railing against "Beatrice's awful domination." Although she did not acknowledge that she was the object of Gertrude's wrath, Beatrice felt compelled to report that her troubled sister, who constantly broke watches and eyeglasses and soiled dresses, was "quite an expense to keep supplied." Helen sent money and no doubt felt that she should have done more.[8]

Mental problems also afflicted the White family. As Andrew entered his final illness, Ruth's marriage with Erwin Ferry deteriorated. Ferry claimed that Ruth's behavior was erratic: she spent vast sums of money and indicated she did not love him anymore. When Helen countered that he had married Ruth for her money, he became enraged and accused his stepmother-in-law of poisoning his daughter Priscilla (known to the family as Helen) against him. Helen tried to defend and conciliate at the same time. She dreaded a divorce, not least of all for the sake of the child, but knew that Ferry's charges were not without foundation. In fact, by the early 1920s Ruth was running up enormous bills, insisting on a divorce so that she could marry an actor, then pleading for reconciliation, or blaming Helen for her troubles, then begging for her help. On November 13, 1922, the court granted Ferry's request that his wife be declared "an improvident person" and placed in the care of one Harry Yundt. Ruth lingered until 1936, but there was little Helen could do for her.[9]

Karin, of course, remained Helen's most important responsibility—and her most conspicuous failure. When Karin returned home for her father's final illness, Helen hoped again for a companion and friend. They had so much in common, she thought: probing intellects, sharp tongues, Republican politics, a passion for music, gardening, and Europe. Helen claimed to know what interested her daughter, what gifts she cherished, what "irresistibly" hit her funny bone. As Karin shunned society even more than her mother, one might have expected the two to make peace out of shared loneliness. And in a sense they did, living together, attending concerts, traveling abroad. In fact, they often liked one another—when love didn't get in the way.

According to Karin, nothing had changed. Her mother's love made her impossible to live with for "anyone short of a saint or a doormat—and I was neither." It was the kind of love that was always "angrily, jealously counting returns, and finding them not up to its deserts." Karin's faults—self-indulgence and insolence—widened when placed above the earthquake that was Helen's temper. When they shared the same house, they "fought like two cats tied up in one sack."[10]

Years after Helen's death, Karin still bristled at efforts to control her through appeals to duty. Because she was unmarried, her mother treated her as "daughter, and not a person at all," insisting that she give up pleasures, plans, and possessions "for any reason or *for no reason.*" Parental prerogative did have its comical side: Helen forbade Karin to lock the bathroom door and often pounded on it while she was inside. In the name of economy, Helen denounced hot water baths as the "dreaded extravagance" of women. So Karin would sit by the heater (located in another room) until the tub was full, lest her mother turn the temperature down. On one occasion Helen rushed into the bathroom, "locking herself in, running the tub I'd heated, and *taking it herself!*" When pressed to explain, Helen reminded her daughter that "it was *her* house— . . . hers to decide about everything and anything in it!"[11]

Sometime after 1927, Karin moved out of the house. As always, a little incident with large implications was the precipitating cause. Helen believed that books were family possessions, not personal belongings, and as head of the household she claimed every case her "exclusive domain," every volume hers to read, lend out, "jumble in the attic, put on any shelf she pleased. . . ." Frequently, Helen gave Karin's books to departing guests with the breezy assurance that, since her daughter had already read them, they need not be returned. When Karin witnessed her mother's generosity, she locked up her "considerably depleted bookcase," only to have Helen destroy a book she inadvertently left out. An ugly confrontation ensued, with Helen icily announcing that Karin had no right to the books: "*Thy* books, as thee insists on calling them, in *my* house, are at *my* disposal; *any court* would know thee was quite insane not to realize that thee *own* only what I *permit* thee to own." Karin confided to her diary: "I've no respect for her, and a painfully inadequate supply of affection." If her mother would not allow even a book to be locked in her bedroom, she would find a place of her own, "quite amiably." If invited, she promised to visit, but if Helen tried to prevent her from taking anything out of the house, mother and daughter would not see each other again. Karin's sizable income, not subject to her mother's control, afforded her the upper hand, and she moved out, with her books and furniture in tow, leaving only the servants for Helen to dominate. Still, she did not go very far and continued to enjoy her mother "between fights," though the "cataclysmic uproar(s)" were too frequent for them to live under the same roof.[12]

Helen did not leave an account of the separation. No doubt she would have pleaded guilty to the charge that she was demanding, but she would have stressed a daughter's duty and her own responsibility for Karin's welfare. Even at thirty, Karin acted like a child, all take and no give, quick with a threat when she failed to get her way. In her lonely old age, it seemed, Helen was punished for having been an indulgent parent. From her perspective, it was she—not Karin—who was patient, passive, and put-upon. When she sought to clean the guest room, her daughter pounded her and pulled her hair. "I made no resistance and only asked her very gently, tho' urgently, [to stop]." Doors slammed and Karin spent the night with a friend. When Helen planned a trip to New York City, Karin refused to go and threatened to take an apartment alone. Everything "I do or wish is wrong," she sighed. "It seems no use to try to keep her"—but of course she did. Karin's departure was devastating: "I thought we should have so much together. But now it is the same with her and I must go on alone."[13]

Helen's search for companionship led inexorably to her sisters. She was never an "insider" in the group, Karin thought, because she "wanted to be *the* one in it." Nonetheless, she had been a benefactor to each of them, helping them find jobs early in their careers and providing financial assistance in times of crisis. As the eldest, she expected solicitude and devotion, not as a quid pro quo, but "from those whose Duty it is to give it to me." She excused Marian, ensconced in Chicago with a husband and four children, from all responsibilities save those of correspondent. Unmarried and teaching high school mathematics, Dora was often available, but Helen found her, in turn, "tactless" and so "perfectly defenseless" that she invited contempt. That left Beatrice, to whom she had always been close. Helen had brought her to Europe to study art and help raise Karin, who came to love her aunt as a mother. A lecturer in the history of art at Swarthmore from 1892 to 1902, Beatrice married John Campbell Robinson in Ithaca in 1904 but was widowed shortly thereafter. A volunteer nurse (one reason, no doubt, that Karin chose the profession) with the American Fund for French Wounded during World War I, she was in Paris when the Germans bombarded the city. Back home in Kittery Point, Maine, Beatrice often entertained the family.[14]

Like Helen, Beatrice believed that "all adult living is *duty*. If there's no obvious one at the moment, *you find one.*" Capable of resenting Helen's frequent reminders of how much she had done for her younger sister (who had, after all, more than earned her keep in Germany as "full-time companion, personal and social secretary, assistant baby-nurse and governess, part-time seamstress and lady's maid"), Beatrice nonetheless liked and loved Helen. Soon after Andrew's death, Helen began to spend every summer at Kittery Point and to entertain Beatrice in Ithaca and travel with her.[15]

The relationship endured for the rest of Helen's life but it, too, had its close calls. Unlike Dora, Beatrice was no pushover; "Beatrice never argues, *and never gives in,*" Sarah Magill had often observed. Helen respected a fixity of purpose that could be called stubbornness, even if she disagreed with it. More than once she was told she could not descend on Kittery Point with her ménage because other members of the family could not then visit; but neither could she come up alone, since Beatrice was not able or inclined to wait on her. Helen did not understand why her sister could not "easily manage . . . if Karin won't, . . . " adding: "I should think thee'd feel it thy pleasure, as well as thy duty." Yet on each occasion Helen backed down, and even Karin admitted that her mother, although "stubborn as a mule," could be reasonable.[16]

A trip to Europe in 1925–26 provided an "eye-opening shock" to Karin that contributed to her departure a year later and brought relations between Helen and Beatrice to the breaking point. Although Helen enjoyed sight-seeing (and could "still put in a day *and a series of days* that'd have knocked the spots out of most women 15–20 years younger"), she worried about her health and preferred to stay in her room. Karin, Beatrice, and Dora should stay with her, she thought, but Beatrice's intercession allowed Karin to go out on her own, without a chaperon. The crisis came when an exhausted Beatrice, in need of a break, embarked on a Roman excursion. Faced with the prospect of a duet with "poor, muddleheaded, obstinate, irritable Aunt Dora," Helen made "a hell of a row." A doctor, she reminded her sister, had pronounced her a sick woman, probably diabetic and in need of constant loving care from her family. The frustration of her wishes, "both great and small," might well affect her health. But Beatrice had made up her mind.[17]

Within a day or two Helen asked Dora and the recently returned Karin to telegraph Beatrice that she was dying. When the two refused to join in the deception, Helen erupted: "It *isn't* a lie! I *am* dying! My sister who has deserted me, she's left me alone here, alone, alo-o-one, when I'm *dying*. . . . It's her duty to stop amusing herself and come back and give me loving service *when I am dying*. . . . And it is thy duty to tell her so!" Either Dora buckled or Helen sent the message herself, for Beatrice came tearing back to Paris only to find her sister scurrying across the city buying clothes. Helen remained unrepentant: "Why, but I was dying. Of course I was!! Dressmakers? But I needed clothes. I'm in rags. We might meet people we know. . . . "[18]

When Helen grasped at illness and incapacity, her selfishness came from an unquiet desperation. She equated love with sacrifice; her life was to be measured by her devotion to her family. So willing to give, she needed "tangible proofs" of gratitude and affection. Thus, each test was the ultimate test; part of her wanted her family to falter, so she could drape herself in the mantle of martyrdom. But mostly she was discouraged and afraid, without the courage to "jump off" or go on alone:

> Probably many people have no idea what this means to me—to have no *close* companionship. My mind is active but my heart shivers—sisters are not to me what I am to them or would be, and friends are many and kind—but I want *closer* companionship, both giving and taking. . . . If I did not give out a good deal I should freeze to death inwardly. But I find comfort in thinking all I can about anyone whom I can help. . . . giving *things* is not the best of life—but it is better than nothing—if that is all that is wanted.

And so she pushed on, through the 1920s and into the early 1930s. Eventually she built her own home in Kittery Point, next to Beatrice, surrounded by a large and lovely garden.[19]

In 1936 Helen became incapacitated. Unable to leave the house, she required constant attention. Karin, who had been working in a hospital for three years, quit her job to rejoin her mother. For eight years the two women lived together, with Beatrice a few steps away, this time apparently in relative harmony. Since flowers brought a smile to Helen's face, Karin toiled in the garden, growing the huge dahlias—in golds and reds and maroons—that her mother loved, decorating the house with delphiniums and annuals—sweet pea, salpiglossis. Characteristically, the flowers Helen liked most were the hardest to grow, especially in years of drought, with "late, cold sunless springs." There was, Karin knew, "nothing better" that she could do for her mother than surprise her with a roomful of roses. Perhaps, finally, Helen could be sure she was loved.[20]

On October 28, 1944, a month before her ninety-first birthday, Helen Magill White died. In accordance with her wishes, her body was taken to Ithaca and buried in the antechamber of Sage Chapel at Cornell University. Once again, she could not secure what she coveted most, and so she rests, perhaps uneasily, near, but not next to, her husband.

NOTES

1. Rowena Morse Langer, "Memories of Helen Magill White," Nov. 17, 1986, author's files; HMW to ADW, Sept. 20, 1908.

2. HMW, *Diary*, Nov. 7, 1919. See also Langer, "Memories of Helen Magill White."

3. HMW, *Diary,* Nov. 1922–Jan. 1923, Oct. 13, 1920.

4. HMW, *Diary,* Nov. 19, 1922, Dec. 11, 1922.

5. KW, *Diary,* Feb. 16, 1954, July 25, 1956, KW Papers (all such references are to this source). See also Robert Preswick to author, Oct. 21, 1981, author's files. Dr. Preswick thought Helen "looked mad enough to bite a ten penny nail in half." Andrew White's taste in women must have been at "its lowest notch" when he married for a second time, Preswick told his friends in 1932, and everyone lamented the "rough life" Andrew had with Helen.

6. HMW to SWM, Oct. 29, 1893. See also HMW to EHM and Family, Dec. 15, 1899, June 11, 1901, May 29, 1907. Marriage, Helen believed, was a "modification, more or less satisfactory, of the old relation of captor and captive, which will prevail, in one form or another, whenever the relation of the weaker to the stronger sex is left quite unregulated by the general sense of the community." She thought it ironic that Gertrude allowed her to ask her husband for money when "she so cheerfully absolves the *not married man.*" A married woman was hardly a slave: she could leave her husband, no doubt injuring herself and her children, but could this be compared to the harm done to the offspring of not legalized unions? "That objection would seem to me enough to condemn all such license in sexual arrangements. A succession of cohabitations, for the pleasure of the individuals, cannot constitute a *home.* . . . " See HMW to Family, Nov. 7, 1906.

7. HMW to EHM and Sisters, July 29, 1899; HMW to Beatrice Magill Robinson, Sept. 17, 1913; HMW to ADW, Sept. 15, 1913, ADW Papers. See also HMW to ADW, July 27, 1913, Apr. 16, 1913, July 24, 1913, ADW Papers; KW, *Diary,* Aug. 2, 1913, May 4, 1914. Andrew refused to visit Helen's sister Beatrice when Gertrude was in the house. See Beatrice Magill Robinson to HMW, Sept. 29, 1915.

8. Marian Magill Jenkins to HMW, July 21, 1921; Beatrice Magill Robinson to HMW, July 1, 1923. Not surprisingly, Gertrude confided in Marian, who was too far away to threaten or constrain. She viewed Beatrice's visits with "terror," refused to go to Kittery Point, and discussed her plan to become a musical proofreader and songwriter. Gertrude Magill to Marian Magill Jenkins, July 9, 1921.

9. HMW to Erwin Ferry, Jan. 22, 1918, Jan. 29, 1918; Stuart, Simms, and Stuart to Frank Irvine, May 16, 1923.

10. KW, *Diary,* Feb. 16, 1954.

11. KW, *Diary,* July 24, 1950, Aug. 26, 1953. See also KW, *Diary,* Feb. 16, 1954.

12. KW, *Diary,* Feb. 16, 1954, July 25, 1956.

13. HMW, *Diary,* June 27, 1922, June 29, 1922. See also HMW, *Diary,* Sept. 14, 1923, and undated entry.

14. KW, *Diary,* Feb. 16, 1954.

15. KW, *Diary,* Aug. 21, 1948, July 24, 1950. Karin's conclusion that the Magill sisters "hung on rather grimly to as much family affection for [Helen] as they could possibly salvage," is, I think, unfair. See KW, *Diary,* Feb. 16, 1954.

16. Quoted in KW, *Diary,* July 24, 1950, Feb. 16, 1954.

17. KW, *Diary,* Oct. 16, 1925, July 24, 1950, Sept. 4, 1956.

18. KW, *Diary,* July 24, 1950. In Rome, Helen thought Beatrice "rude and unkind" and slapped her. HMW, *Diary,* Feb. 4, 1926. Karin's perhaps melodramatically staged scene did not record Beatrice's reaction or response.

19. HMW, *Diary,* undated entry. See also KW, *Diary,* Aug. 21, 1948. Helen also expressed the desire to "jump off" in a diary entry dated Nov. 1922–Jan. 1923.

20. KW, *Diary,* Aug. 6, 1948, Aug. 21, 1948, Feb. 16, 1954. Gardening became Karin's passion, practiced expertly at Kittery Point until her death in 1971. She had not gardened to please her mother, she insisted. KW, *Diary,* Aug. 21, 1948.

Index